Migration, Religious Experience, and Globalization

D1088691

2003
Center for Migration Studies
New York

Migration,
Religious Experience,
and Globalization

Center for Migration Studies
209 Flagg Place
Staten Island, New York 10304-1122

Library of Congress Cataloging-in-Publication Data

Conference on Migration and Theology (1st : 2002 : Tijuana, Baja
California, Mexico)
  Migration, religious experience, and globalization / edited by
Gioacchino Campese & Pietro Ciallella.
    p. cm.
English and Spanish.
Includes bibliographical references.
  ISBN 1-57703-029-X (alk. paper)
  1. Emigration and immigration–Religious aspects–Catholic
Church–Congresses. 2. Church work with immigrants–Catholic
Church–Congresses. I. Campese, Gioacchino, 1967 - II. Ciallella,
Pietro, 1971- III. Title.
  BX1795.E44C66 2003
  261.8'3682–dc21   2003053856

Table of Contents

Contributors

María Pilar Aquino   is professor of Theology and Religious Studies at the University of San Diego, California, USA.

Graziano Battistella, c.s.   is the director of the Scalabrini International Migration Institute (SIMI) in Rome, Italy.

Dianne Bergant, CSA   is professor of Old Testament Studies at Catholic Theological Union in Chicago, Illinois, USA.

Isaia Birollo, c.s.   is the General Superior of the Missionaries of St. Charles (Scalabrinians).

Michael A. Blume, SVD   is the Under Secretary of the Pontifical Council for the Pastoral Care of Migrants and Itinerant People in the Vatican.

Gioacchino Campese, c.s.   is a Ph.D. candidate in Systematic Theology at the Lutheran School of Theology at Chicago, Illinois, USA.

Pietro Ciallella, c.s.   is the Associate Director of CMS.

Raúl Fornet-Betancourt   is professor of Intercultural Philosophy and the director of the Latin American Department of the Institute of Missiology, Aachen, Germany.

Peter C. Phan   is the Warren-Blanding professor of Religion and Culture at the Catholic University of America in Washington, D.C., USA.

Flor Maria Rigoni, c.s.   is the director of Casa del Migrante / Albergue Belén in Tapachula, Chiapas, Mexico.

Olivia Ruiz Marrujo   is research professor of Anthropology at the Colegio de la Frontera Norte, Tijuana, Mexico.

Robert J. Schreiter, CSSP is the Bernardin Center professor of Vatican II Theology at Catholic Theological Union in Chicago, Illinois, USA, and professor of Intercultural Theology at the University of Nijmegen, the Netherlands.

Introduction

The present volume is a collection of some of the main talks and workshops presented during the First Conference on Migration and Theology entitled *Migration and Religious Experience in the Context of Globalization,* which took place in Tijuana (Mexico) from January 24–27, 2002. The two North American Provinces of the Scalabrinian Missionaries collaborated with the Transborder Institute of the University of San Diego (CA) to organize this event with the objective of celebrating the 100th anniversary of Bishop Giovanni Battista Scalabrini's visit to the Italian immigrants and his newly founded missionaries in the United States. In 1887, Scalabrini, Bishop of Piacenza in Northern Italy, a churchman of great pastoral sensibility and extraordinary faith, founded the Congregation of the Missionaries of St. Charles (also known as Scalabrinian Missionaries) to respond to the needs of the Italian emigrants who were leaving their country by the thousands in order to find a better life in the Americas. His intervention on behalf of the migrants continued with the foundation in 1892 of a lay association, the St. Raphael's Society for the Protection of the Emigrants, and in 1895 of the Missionary Sisters of St. Charles, also known as Scalabrinian Sisters.

The objective of this conference was to give a well-deserved tribute to this great man of faith and missionary action, and do so with an event that would reflect and further his pastoral vision and concrete involvement in the complex social issue that was and is, today more than ever, migration.

The main objectives of the Conference were basically two: first, to promote theological reflection on the social issue and concrete experience of migration. We gladly acknowledge that the theological literature related to migration is growing, a sign that more consideration is being given to this crucial theme by scholars.[1] Official statements by different Christian denominations are bringing to the attention of local communities the importance of the involvement in this matter of believers and the pastoral care of migrants

---

[1]For an updated bibliography of philosophical and theological literature on human mobility *see* the whole issue of *Studi Emigrazione* 34:128 (1997); Giovanni Graziano Tassello, Luisa Deponti and Christiane Lubos, "Filosofia e Teologia in Contesto Migratorio. Un aggiornamento Bibliografico," *Studi Emigrazione* 38:143 (2001) 655–739.

today.[2] At the same time, we have to recognize that relatively little has been done to incorporate the phenomenon of migration into the field of systematic theology. Second, this conference was intended to provide a forum and an opportunity for an encounter and a sharing of ideas, experiences and concerns about migration among people who often do not dialogue with one another: academic theologians, social scientists and pastoral agents. The purpose of that dialogue was to facilitate an interdisciplinary approach to the phenomenon of migration, and, particularly in our case, to develop a theology that takes into consideration the multiple dimensions of the complex and controversial issue of migration. Once again, even in this area, Bishop Scalabrini is a great example and an inspiration because he knew how to combine in the pastoral ministry effective and punctual action, an attitude of attentive listening to the experiences of the migrants, and serious study of the social phenomenon.[3]

The choice of Tijuana as the location for the conference was made purposefully. This blooming and now famous (or for some, "infamous") border city has been transformed in one powerful symbol of the profound changes caused by migration in North America. French philosopher Paul Ricoeur affirms that symbols are an invitation to think, and Tijuana is certainly one of those symbols that challenge and question, sometimes even beyond the limits of our ability to understand, our thought, and also our humanness. Tijuana is a symbol of the struggles and hopes of thousands of migrants, especially the most vulnerable among them, namely, the undocumented; a symbol of the success and failure of men, women and children who are betting their very lives in order to make their dreams of a "promised land" come true; a symbol, with its walls, of a certain "global" vision of the world that makes borders disappear for goods so that the "free market" can function without any obstacle, but builds bigger and more sophisticated barriers that become mortal obstacles, the "new Berlin wall," where the dreams of people who have been excluded from the "global village" are shattered.

---

[2]The most recent is the joint pastoral statement on migration entitled *Strangers No Longer: Together on the Journey of Hope* released by the Catholic Bishops of Mexico and the USA on January 22, 2003.
[3]Bishop Scalabrini's writings on migration have been recently translated in English and published by the Center for Migration Studies. *See* Silvano M. Tomasi, c.s. (ed.), *For the Love of Immigrants. Migration Writings and Letters of Bishop John Baptist Scalabrini 1839–1905.* New York: Center for Migration Studies, 2000.

Participation in the conference went beyond our expectations (more than 230 people), and the presence among the participants of immigrants, pastoral agents, social activists, church leaders and scholars of different Christian denominations shows that migration is undeniably an issue of great concern in our societies and churches. We want to take this opportunity to thank all of them, as well as the speakers who offered their reflections, and also those whose contributions are not included in this volume. In particular, we need to mention the invaluable contributions made by two co-organizers of the theological conference: Orlando Espín and Vincenzo Ronchi, c.s.

It was our decision to maintain some of the presentations in the original language in which they were delivered at the conference, which was bilingual (Spanish and English). For this reason three of the essays included in this volume are published in Spanish.

We want to express our gratitude to the Provincial Administrations of the Scalabrinian Missionaries in North America for their unwavering support to this whole project.

We would like to thank the Center for Migration Studies of New York, in the person of its Director, Joseph Fugolo, c.s., for enthusiastically agreeing to publish this volume. For the editorial work we are indebted to the staff of the Center for Migration Studies, especially Thomas Sullivan and Ramona Hesterhagen, and Armando Gomez, c.s., and Ramiro Chan, c.s. from the Scalabrini House of Theology in Chicago, IL.

Finally, our hope is that the conference, and this volume that represents its dynamism and wealth of contributions and experience, be not just a celebratory event, but also a point of departure for a new or renewed journey, and a challenge, for all those people of faith who are concerned with the well-being of migrants. May this serve to put migration, this "sign of our times," at the center of our theological reflection, and especially to give to the voices of the women, children and men who are risking everything to fulfill their dreams an authoritative place in our reflection and pastoral ministry.

Gioacchino Campese, c.s.
Pietro Ciallella, c.s.
January 28, 2003
Memorial of St. Thomas Aquinas

The Legacy of Blessed John Baptist Scalabrini

Very Rev. Isaia Birollo, c.s.
Superior General
Missionaries of St. Charles/Scalabrinians

We are here for the opening session of a theological conference on migration, organized on the occasion of the 100th anniversary of the visit of Bishop John Baptist Scalabrini, by the two North American Provinces of the Missionaries of St. Charles, the religious Congregation founded by Bishop Scalabrini to respond to the special needs of the emigrants.

I wish to briefly share with you, this evening, what we Scalabrinians value as our Founder's legacy in the pastoral work for migrants

SCALABRINI'S APPROACH TO THE PHENOMENON OF EMIGRATION

For Scalabrini, emigration is one of the aspects of the "social question," a term that in Scalabrini's time, in the last decades of the nineteenth century, was used to refer to the conditions of the workers and of the poor. One of the characteristics of Scalabrini is the scientific approach toward the social phenomena and he combines it with the search for practical answers, structured and institutionalized, according to the needs identified in his research.

Scalabrini recognizes that "social facts usually are not either good or evil, but can be either one or the other, depending on the circumstances." Emigration is a natural right. An individual can seek one's well being anywhere in the world. In reality, when emigration is abandoned to itself without advice and without guidance, or when it is induced by unscrupulous agents, it is like a fever that slowly consumes the social organism.

The practical conclusion drawn by Scalabrini is that there must be "freedom to emigrate but not coercion to force or to induce people to emigrate." "Emigration in almost all cases is not a pleasure but a necessity that cannot be avoided.... The immense majority is not fleeing from Italy because of unwillingness to work, but because there is no work. People are faced with a painful dilemma: either to steal or to emigrate. For the poor, the fatherland is the country that provides bread, especially when the land of their birth is known only through two hateful forms: taxation and military conscription."

Even though Scalabrini does not possess the technical terminology of sociology and anthropology he describes the phenomenon that has brought the formation of today's multiethnic and multicultural societies. In his study of the phenomenon of migration he is fascinated by the results produced by emigration into the Americas. He points out that a process of fusions and adaptations takes place in which the various nationalities meet, intermingle, forge themselves anew and give origin to other peoples.

Scalabrini is a man of faith and a bishop. Without confusing the levels of analysis, he confronts the socioeconomic and political vision of emigration with the values and convictions that come from his faith and his pastoral concerns.

SCALABRINI'S THEOLOGICAL VISION

Scalabrini's vision of emigration is enlightened by his faith in the Lord who guides history as divine Providence: "Emigration is a law of nature. The physical and the human world depend on this mysterious force, which stirs and mixes the elements of life without destroying them, which carries living organisms born in one place and scatters them throughout space, transforming and bringing them to perfection, thus renewing the miracle of creation at every moment." This description widens in the prophetic vision of the humanity which is guided by the Spirit: "While races intermingle, through the noise of our machines, on top of all this restless work, of all these gigantic activities, and not without them, a much more ample, noble and sublime enterprise is in the making here on earth: the union in God through Jesus Christ of all the people of good will" (New York Catholic Club, 1901).

Scalabrini looks at emigration as a shepherd who wants to be faithful to the mission that has been entrusted to him. In Scalabrini the concept of mission is all embracing and derives directly from the concept of Incarnation: in the Son, made man, the Father loves the whole person, even the "body, the flesh, the human soul. Now we are that flesh, those bones, we are that nature, we are a body with Christ and in Him and through Him we are made children of God, even more the same Son of God that prolongs God's presence in us" (Pastoral letter, Lent 1878).

PASTORAL RESPONSE

From this theological perspective some important consequences are derived, both in the pastoral and also in the ecclesial field. Scalabrini's project of intervention in favor of the emigrants is global and complex. Scalabrini is concerned about the welfare of the poor and the workers and wants to intervene both where they come from (the causes that provoke emigration) and where they are going.

He insists that it is necessary to give advice and guidance to those who are about to make the decision to emigrate, to accompany them to the ports of embarkation, assist them during the trip, and to help them in the time of insertion in the new environment. It is also necessary to declare an all-out war on the so-called "emigration agents." Scalabrini called them "merchants of human flesh"; he also referred to them as "those who smell the corpses."

His intervention has two characteristic elements: first of all the effort to create an awareness of the problem and to gather the most ample consensus around this issue, calling on the clergy, the laity and all the people of good will because Charity knows no partisanship. The second element is the will to take into consideration all the aspects of the problem, as a whole, because, "when we are dealing with emigration, religious, civil and national, public and private, cannot be separated without harm."

In regard to the laws to regulate emigration, Scalabrini is contrary to generalized restrictions that he considers useless, unjust and harmful: useless because they would never be able to eliminate emigration; unjust because they would impede the free exercise of a human right and harmful because emigration would take other ways, falling more easily in the hands of unscrupulous persons. He therefore concludes: "The important thing for a law is not to be liberal but to be good, and for me a good law is not one that is wider, but one that, based on justice, better provides for those needs for which it has been made."

Scalabrini often repeated what an emigrant wrote to him from Brazil: "Here we are like animals; we live and die without priests, teachers and doctors." Scalabrini added: "these, the three forms under which civil society presents itself to the mind of the poor."

In order to respond to the needs of the emigrants, Scalabrini, with the support of Pope Leo XIII, founded the Congregation of the Missionary priests and brothers. He also promoted the involvement of lay people. In 1891, in his first Conference on Italian Emigration he stated: "I founded two societies, one made up of priests, the other of lay people; one religious, the other lay; two societies to help and complement each other. The first is the Congregation of the Missionaries aiming especially at the spiritual welfare of our emigrants, the latter at their material welfare. The first attains its purpose by setting up churches, schools, orphanages, and hospitals, through priests united family-like by the religious vows of chastity, obedience and poverty, ready and willing to rush wherever they are needed, as apostles, teachers, doctors, nurses, according to the needs. The second society carries out its task by discouraging emigration when it is unwise, keeping an eye on the work of emigration agents, seeing to it that they do not violate the law, and, if everything else fails, counseling the emigrants and channeling them toward good destinations." In 1895 Scalabrini founded also a Religious Congregation of Sisters dedicated to service of the emigrants.

SPECIAL CHARACTERISTICS OF SCALABRINI'S APPROACH TO THE PASTORAL WORK FOR EMIGRANTS

The objective of the pastoral work of Scalabrini is the "evangelization of the poor and of the workers." He is concerned about the emigration of the poor classes: the farmers and laborers, the factory workers, the small craftsmen and merchants.

Scalabrini, with the support of the Pope, addresses himself to his brother bishops, those from the country of origin of the emigrants, Italy, and those from the countries of destination, in the Americas.

In the ecclesial prospective Scalabrini often compares the missionary work in the frontiers of Asia and Africa, where the Church invests its resources and people for the "expansion of the faith," with the extreme necessity of the "conservation of the faith" of the millions of poor Catholics "dispersed in the vast regions of the New World." It seems that Scalabrini is more inclined to think that the expansion of the Church will depend more on the human mobility rather than on the "*missio ad gentes*."

To the bishops of the countries of destination of the emigrants he communicates his profound conviction that the goal of their pastoral attention to them should "bring together the dispersed children of God into one family" and therefore the perfect communion and participation in the local Church, that would see itself enriched with a new life and new forms of Christian piety.

This objective could be reached if the process of integration of the emigrants was encouraged but not forced. The pastoral care of the diocesan bishop for the emigrants is manifested when he establishes a pastoral relationship with these children of God who have arrived in his diocese by assigning to their care missionaries who are familiar with their language and their traditions.

The missionaries would recreate that environment that the emigrants had left in their own countries and that would sustain them in their first impact with a world that was completely different.

Scalabrini here combines the insights of someone who has a prolonged experience of care of souls among the poor. We recognize here Scalabrini the catechist and his exhortations to the Catholic mothers. For Scalabrini, faith is transmitted mostly through the parents, especially through the mothers, and is inseparably joined with the mother tongue, especially in the poor person who has not been able to obtain a formal education. "A very apt element in the preservation of the faith is exactly the preservation of the language of origin. This is not the place to investigate what may be its mysterious reason, but daily experience tells us that as long as an individual, a family, or a whole community preserves its own language, it will not likely lose its own faith" (Memorial p. 224).

Scalabrini does not utilize the terms of the social sciences, as personal or ethnic identity, but he describes their content and role as an attentive observer.

"The affectionate care of the apostle" of the emigrants consists therefore in a delicate work of transplanting, where a motherly sensitivity is needed in order that the roots of the transplanted may not dry up and, maintaining their strength, they may, little by little, reach out in the unfamiliar soil.

We can therefore summarize the following intuitions of Scalabrini's pastoral heart:

- **Attention to migrants' culture:** in its evangelizing attention toward the children of poverty and labor, the Church must respect the particular ethnic and linguistic cultures of migrants, precisely because culture is the "normal" way of living and conserving the faith, especially for people (such as migrants) who are culturally less sophisticated.

- **The "providential" view of the phenomenon of migration:** Scalabrini realized that the children of poverty and labor, who in human and sociological terms seemed to be a mass of exploited people and failures, were in fact the builders of a new society and were the special place and instrument for the building up of the Kingdom – "the union of Christian peoples," as he called it. This is a prophetic view, which reads history not with the key of efficiency, appearance and the dominant economy, but with that of the wisdom of God, who uses what is not in order to put to shame what is. This "wisdom reading" of migration is the treasure that Scalabrini left to the Church.

- **The "pentecostal communion" among cultures, ethnic groups, languages and religions:** Scalabrini wrote about this intuition to Pope Pius X one month before his death in 1905. After pastoral visits to the United States and Brazil, he realized that migration (including Italian migration) was entering a new phase; thus, the Church had the task of "smoothing" or "softening" cultures, helping them to enter into communion with one another. This is Scalabrini's spiritual testament, which he entrusted to his children and to the Church.

Immigrants at Risk, Immigrants as Risk: Two Paragdims of Globalization

Olivia Ruiz Marrujo
El Colegio de la Frontera Norte, Tijuana

Drawing largely on research on Mexican and Central American immigration to the United States, this article explores the relationship of risk to international undocumented migration, an association found with increasing regularity in public policy discussions, academic forums and the mass media. On the one hand, immigrants are seen as a population at risk, vulnerable to abuse by authorities and private citizens and to the possibility of death and injury by accidents. On the other hand, immigrants are presented as a risk to the economy, social integrity and cultural identity of society. It is argued that the complex and contradictory terms of the association, subsumed in these two positions, reflect contemporary debates about national and personal identity as well as inquiries into human nature intrinsic to this period of globalization.

To say that international migration, especially undocumented immigration, the focus of this article, involves risk is to state the obvious. The connection between the two is evident in the death of almost 2,000 migrants along the Mexico-United States border since October 1994 and underlies the statement that Operation Gatekeeper "maximizes the risk to life."[1] The relationship, however, also belies claims that Mexican immigration to the United States is "a threat to national security" or, in the words of Samuel Huntington, "a unique, disturbing, and looming challenge to our cultural integrity, our national identity, and potentially to our future as a country" (2000:5).

Complex and contradictory, the association colors most treatment of the immigration issue in the mass media, public opinion polls, academic forums and public policy debates at all levels of government as well as by religious congregations and nongovernmental organizations. To be sure, the Janus-headed character of the relationship seems at times both to subvert all efforts

---

[1]Personal communication of Claudia Smith at the California Rural Legal Assistance Foundation. Operation Gatekeeper, initiated in 1994, is a strategy devised by the INS to block the flow of undocumented immigrants across the San Diego-Tijuana border.

to sort out the reality of immigration and to circumvent any possibility for the peoples, social groups and institutions struggling with the issue to reach any kind of consensus. At the same time, I propose that those concerned with the well-being of migrants, that is, as I will argue later on, concerned with the well-being of our human species, must make an effort to clarify the terms of the association. As people and groups dedicated to understanding the movement of women, men and children in the world today, we have much to gain by such a reflection. To be sure, in deconstructing the relationship we approach one of the ontological crossroads of our contemporary human condition as citizens of an increasingly interconnected or, to use the term in vogue today, global world.

What does it mean to call something a risk? Far from an academic exercise, it engages us to think critically about the language and actions that shape our everyday lives. Indeed, the term is one of the most ubiquitous in use today, especially in developed industrial societies. This is due, according to Beck and Giddens, to the underlying notions of insecurity, danger and uncertainty, "induced and introduced by modernity," which the notion subsumes (Beck, 1992:21; Giddens, 1990, 1998). Elsewhere, Lash and Wynne propose that the concept lies at the center of all reflection on the crisis of the modern world, where everyday threats to a person's well-being give rise to a general sentiment of living at risk and feed a parallel sensation of defenselessness in the face of it (1992:3). To be sure, insofar as risk is an integral part of discussions about public security, national sovereignty, the environment, sex, food, health and immigration, it has become deeply embedded in the collective imagination of contemporary societies.

As is evident from the many and often contradictory ways in which the term is associated with immigration, the identification reflects differing perceptions and interests; it is socially construed. Of course, deaths and assaults occur, the results of migrants' encounters with potential dangers – a freight train, a thief. Yet, upon transcribing these events to another order, beyond that of a series of tragic occurrences (be they deaths or assaults), in exploring how they become engaged (or are made to participate) in an ongoing debate on (undocumented) immigration, they contribute to the ways in which we make normative sense and establish truth not only about immigration but also about society, daily life, the nation and the wider world around us. As such, risk events and the discourses about them must be situated within the power struggles taking place in our society, in its institutions, organizations and social groups (Beck, 1992:4), that is, in the brew of shifting group alliances and disputes for power particular to this stage of late capitalism. The association between immigration and risk locates the movement of people in the maelstrom of the contradictions and complexities inherent to this phase of globalization. As such, immigration, insofar as it is tied to risk, incorporates characteristics of global capitalism. Or, I would propose, immigration has become a metaphor for risk.

As a metaphor it embodies the opposition of the immigrant *at* risk and the immigrant *as* risk – two perspectives appearing frequently in discussions of international migration today. On the one hand, it is argued that immigrants present a threat to society, which is falling victim to the dangers (crime, disease, for example) these displaced (or out of place) people present. By implication, immigrants are responsible for their own misfortunes, be they deaths, the loss of limbs, or operations such as Gatekeeper. Inevitably, this approach drives all discussion of immigration into the bunkers of national interests, security and sovereignty. The alternative view, on the other hand, argues that immigrants live at risk, victims of dangers created, accepted and ignored by the countries of origin, transit and destination, thus situating the movement of people around the globe within the framework of national and international human rights. From this perspective the responsibility for these migrants and for their misfortunes, is ours.

The idea of the immigrant *as* risk, as its embodiment, is familiar to most in the developed industrial world. The challenge is to understand why it brings such epistemological comfort. I suggest that inasmuch as this point of view presents immigration as a risk to the fabric and integrity of modern industrial nations, its roots lie in the founding of nations and the construction of their identities and in the traditions and myths that have defined, consolidated and justified these national ways of being.

Historically, the process of building and confirming the identities of modern industrial nations has drawn on dualities opposing civilization and barbarism, development and underdevelopment, north and south, dichotomies which today arise repeatedly in discourses that present the immigrant as a risk. These binarisms underlie Huntington's comparison of Mexican migration to the United States to an invasion and his proclamations this Mexican presence threatens the security of North American society (Huntington,

2000:5). They also ring in the words of Regis Debray when he opposes the "nuclear and rational north" to the "conventional and mystical south" (Debray cited in Bigo,1997:94) and reappear in the affirmations of Patrick Buchanan (his *The Death of the West* . . .) and the rantings of LePen in France. To be sure, as human beings we often model and defend our identities, as well as the loyalties they command, through opposition to someone or something else, be it a person or a country, construed and imbibed as the embodiment of an opposing (and often degraded or inferior) idea of self. One of the most efficient ways of unifying a people, as is well known, is to create a common enemy. Dualisms of the sort employed by Huntington, Debray, Buchanan and LePen, however, have played a singular and formative role throughout the history of European and North American capitalism.

As reflected in literature and oral tradition, the social imagination of nineteenth century Europe often labeled those en route or on the road "nomads" or "strangers" or "foreigners," that is people different from and potentially, if not intrinsically, subversive to the domestic order, a threat to everything considered civilized (Stallybrass and White, 1986:128). This was the heyday of imperial capitalism, of rapid and often chaotic destabilizations of societies and consequent human uprootings and displacements; of colonial acquisitions without parallel of territories in Africa and Asia and often violent encounters between Europeans and non-Europeans. Still in the throes of nation-building, the continent struggled with new ideas of sovereignty and citizenship, political and legal maxims central to modern nations. While both notions referred to the enclosing of territories and juridically bound people to specific lands, they also set up and enforced elaborate means to exclude those who fell outside the legal perimeters of nation-states. As such, they lay the groundwork for one of the principle contradictions of modern nations, that is the tension between an administrative management, or societas, of different ethnic groups and a national communitas based on a shared sense of self, history and destiny (Joppke, 1999:5; Guidieri and Pellizzi, 1988:11–12).

Not surprisingly, the nineteenth century, the birthplace of nationalism, witnessed strenuous, if not turbulent, efforts to implant a national identity or ideal (Anderson, 1991:4). It was a period obsessively concerned with race and racial mixture. Gobineau in France and Chamberlain in Germany wrote on the risks of miscegenation, the racial foundations of national greatness, and the role of race in creating, in Chamberlain's words, "a firm national union . . . [a]

common memory, common hope, common intellectual nourishment" (Chamberlain, 1912(1):297). This was to be the imagined community, the national fraternity of "deep, horizontal comradeship" which, in Anderson's words, would make it "possible for so many millions of people, not so much as to kill, as willingly to die for such limited imaginings" (1991:7).

Across the Atlantic, hostility towards the uprooted and displaced, the forbears of modern immigrants, also thrived, stoking North American nativism. Ranging from "a mild suspicion of foreigners to virulent bigotry and hatred, from concealed thought to violent action," it gave birth to anti-foreign political parties in the first half of the century, fueled by the "know-nothing" revolts of the 1850s and led to demands for restricting naturalization in the 1880s and 1890s (Fehrenbacher, 1969:101, Higham, 1965:4, 97). As in Europe, anti-foreign sentiments went hand in hand with racism, to which the eugenics of Nott and Gliddon and the lynchings of the Chinese in the 1870s and their mass expulsion in the 1880s crudely testified (1855; Higham, 1965:25). In short, in the world of nineteenth century capitalism, the stranger and foreigner were often viewed as a risk, a threat to things "native." In this light, the rejection of the immigrant today draws on taxonomies and rankings of peoples that have deep roots in an historically specific cultural inheritance.[2]

Today, by way of this manicheism, the notion of the immigrant at risk reduces the options of the national "body" to dichotomies of insider and outsider, purity and pollution, integrity and dismemberment in the face of possible, real, imagined or feared arrivals of people from afar or simply not of one's place or home. Immigrants, in this sense, not only present one more risk; rather, in personifying the stranger and foreigner, they embody risk. Visible, tangible, they put a face to an abstraction, rendering concrete the losses, doubts and fears unleashed by events, seemingly external in origin – among them crime, disease, public insecurity, unemployment – which threaten "native" epistemological and physical security. It is worth asking to what point does this particular association of the migrant with risk supply an instrument to symbolically control or bind the contours of daily life, to purify it? In materializing so many dangers to "our way of being," to what extent does this displaced "other" provide a way to purge daily life of what "we"

[2]Developed industrial nations, of course, do not have a monopoly on anti-immigrant sentiments, as the treatment of immigrants in countries of Latin America, the Middle East and Asia shows.

fear may threaten it and to reconstruct the borders – both geographical and normative – of the national body, which seem increasingly permeable and frail in the face of globalization?

In this sense, the idea of the immigrant as risk is enmeshed in the permanent construction and reconstruction of contemporary identities, of ways of living, both personal and national. It lies at the heart of communities' searches for meaning as they confront the accelerated movement of capital and people due to globalization and the consequent social, cultural and economic upheavals of our times.

From this perspective, the idea of the immigrant as a risk lies at the center of the struggle to define the national (and, consequently, the personal). It alludes to the constant reshaping and reaffirmation of nations and states and to efforts to impose a pedagogical project, which is always the outcome of political and social struggles in which specific groups come to power and impose norms, laws and a common sense among the residents of a country (Bhabha, 1994:149). To imagine immigrants as a threat to the integrity of a nation places them at the epicenter of all strivings to control the State and establish an ideal national identity to which all residents of a nation should or must conform (Pohlenz, 1997:77).

The immigrants' presence is a permanent fixture in this struggle inasmuch as they draw attention to the marginal and the uncertain in society – that which is not hegemonic (indeed, deemed non-national or even anti-national) and often distrusted or feared; challenge the idea of a homogeneous and cohesive national ideal, bearing witness, instead, to the cultural, social, economic, legal and political fissures and ruptures of daily life; diversify daily life by working, playing and forming families according to customs and habits sometimes, perhaps often, at odds with local ways of doing things. The immigrants' presence can be seismic, even if they are mostly unseen and unheard, for their existence questions, if not defies, many of the precepts of the nation-state and the ideals it represents and defends. Among the issues the immigrants' presence raises are: what is national (what is North American?); who has a right to citizenship (who qualifies for United States citizenship?); and who has and should have access to a country's resources – both material and symbolic. The immigrants' presence may question the fixity and legitimacy of cultural traits judged natural or native to a place – speaking English, for example. As such they may voice the concerns and demands of minority peoples in a country.

Faced with the challenge of the foreign and distinct, deemed potentially destabilizing, the state and the coalitions it represents mobilize to defend existing laws and norms or erect new ones intended to uphold the national ideal, the cornerstone of the social order. Two recent examples in the United States are the wave of English-only propositions that swept through the country in the late 1980s and early 1990s and the recent Supreme Court decision outlawing the ability of undocumented workers to sue for back pay. The greater the sense of danger, the greater the force summoned to close-off the nation to any "threat" from inside or out (Bigo, 1997). Bigo refers to these calls to arms as "identity controls" which the nation-state activates in the face of any perceived challenge to its hegemony.

Risk, at the same time, shapes immigration due to the many dangers immigrants face and the frequent and often devastating consequences of those encounters. Along the Mexico-United States border it includes, for example, drownings in the Rio Bravo and the All American Canal in the Imperial Valley and death due to hypothermia in the mountains to the east of San Diego and dehydration in the Sonoran desert on both sides of the international line. It also entails the possibility of robbery, assault, rape, extortion and loss of limbs due to falls from trains and trucks. Those who leave home without documents live uprooted, invisible lives under constant fear of discovery and expulsion from the United States.

To propose that immigrants live *at* risk encourages us to look at human mobility from the point of view of the person who migrates, from his or her aspirations, dreams and suffering, as a reflection of our universal drama as women and men. It takes us beyond the narrow boundaries of a country, or a national body, to a consideration of the human species, of the rights that arise "because one belongs to the human species." These are *natural rights* which each of us "possesses because one is a person," "rights which are due to a man [sic] not in virtue of human institution but in virtue of his [sic] essential nature," that is, "independently of their recognition by the State" (Barba, 1997:16; Olimon Nolasco *et al.*, 1993:57–58; Welty, 1960:209–210). Far from emphasizing our differences and summoning us to their defense, this vision underscores our common humanity and encourages and enables us to recognize it in the lives of each individual of our species, not only in those who belong to our tribe, be it the family or nation. Just as Simone Weil argues that a "geometrician looks at a particular figure to deduce the universal properties of a triangle," this way of thinking urges us to see in each human being "each component of the human species" (1996:125). It takes us beyond communities based on the narrow supremacy of national and ethnocentric interests and asks us to measure our actions in light of the effect they have on the well-being and integrity of others (Barba, 1997:20). In protecting the lives of migrants, our fellow beings, we protect all that is elemental to our survival as a whole. I refer here, for example, to the basic necessities that women, men and children have for food, shelter, education, heath care, work and play, the cornerstones of individual human dignity and societal well-being.

Looking at immigration through the lens of human rights we face one of our greatest challenges – to make palpable our common reality, that is to assume the plight of others (that of immigrants in this case) as ours and to assume it with the commitments and responsibilities which that identification entails. As such, the debate between immigrants *as* risk and immigrants *at* risk lies at the core of all inquiries into our human nature, that is, what we are and want to make of ourselves and what we would like to cultivate in our communities to respond to the options and limitations of this specific period of global capitalism. The debate forces us to recognize that while we spend much time protecting our tribal differences and distances, our social nature as a species, that inborn safeguard against our self-absorption and self-destruction, demands that we live in solidarity with each other. Indeed, our survival depends upon it. As prisoners secluded in solitary confinement understand all too well, isolation, literally, can kill, or at least drive a person mad, in itself a kind of death. But once we recognize the contradictory impulses of our nature what options do we have?

We can, on the one hand, withdraw to our Hobbesian lairs, cultivating a hostile, segregated world of centers and peripheries, ins and outs, a world distinguished and defined, in the best of terms, by distrust and distance, and in the worst, by the possibility of annihilation. This is not the community of our species but the groupings of our interests, greeds, fears and hatreds – in short, of our dismemberment, the abandonment of our selves and retreat from our planetary human condition.

The alternative lies in the recognition of our universal humanity. Rooted in human rights, it leads us towards the preservation, if not resuscitation, of the moral fabric of our species, towards a basic and inalienable respect for the dignity of each person and compels us to define the terms of that respect, that is, the concrete rights it embodies. It requires, for example, that we "develop credible standards and legal precedents to establish the rights [of migrants] – standards that oblige governments to make them a priority" (Press, 2000:14). It means we must pressure not only governments to assume responsibility for human rights violations but also private citizens and demand respect for law protecting immigrants' rights, some of them laid down in the Universal Declaration of Human Rights. It insists that we make a commitment to the economic and social development of the places of origin to fight the poverty that lies at the root of so much human displacement.

At the same time, this alternative point of view encourages us, in the words of Gramsci, to cultivate "a consciousness of who we really are . . . as a product of an historical process which until today has deposited . . . an infinity of traits," even if it has not left "an inventory" (Gramsci cited in Said, 1980:73). We can begin with the way we think about and narrate our history as a species. To write it through the lens of human mobility implies parting from the fact that migration, along with births and deaths, is one of the basic building blocks of all communities and nations. It means recognizing, also, that there is no place on earth that has not either received or expelled people and that throughout history migration has been one of the fundamental survival strategies of all human beings, indeed, of all living things. As a result, we are all the children of migrants and the products of migrations, however recent or distant that migratory past.

In the end, the opposition of these two views – of the immigrant at risk and the immigrant as risk – takes us back to the ancient struggle between Eros and Thanatos, between the impulses of solidarity and life – which Freud defined as "that which holds all living things together" – and dismemberment and death (Freud, 1961:44). We know we can destroy ourselves and too often put into practice the instruments of death – among them Operation Gatekeeper. At the same time, throughout human history the spirit of Eros has remained within reach, stubbornly resisting attempts by the world's powers to dismember the planet, to paraphrase Bauman (1991:13). Without falling into illusions of a rosy and lineal march towards the future, it behooves us to defend the life impulse, which is to imagine and work for alternative ideals for the future. This may seem illusory, deceptive, utopic. In response to these charges we should recall Marcuse who warned us that the system wins and guarantees its success to the extent that we can not imagine anything else. At least the spirit of Eros should encourage us to seek the truth of our human condition, which is the wellspring of our humanization. As Bishop Juán Gerardi of Guatemala exhorted upon presenting *Guatemala Nunca Más*, the truth report that bore witness to over three decades of ethnocidal violence and forced migration in that country, "The root of human degradation comes from the deliberate opposition to truth which is the radical reality of . . . human beings. To open ourselves to the truth and to come face to face with our personal and collective reality is not an option that can be accepted or rejected. It is an undeniable necessity for all those people and each society that desires to be human and free" (2000).

REFERENCES

Anderson, B.
1983   *Imagined Communities. Reflections on the Origin and Spread of Nationalism*. London-New York: Verso.

Barba, J. B.
1997   *Educaciòn para los Derechos Humanos*. México: Fondo de Cultural Económica.

Bauman, Z.
1991   *Modernity and Ambivalence*. Cambridge: UK Polity Press.

Bhabha, H. K.
1994   *The Location of Culture*. London: Routledge.

Beck, U.
1992   *Risk Society*. London: Sage Publications.

Bigo, D.
1997   "Security, Borders, and the State," *Borders and Border Regions in Europe and North America*. Ed. P. Ganster *et al*. San Diego: San Diego State University Press/Institute for Regional Studies of the Californias.

Buchanan, P.
2002   *The Death of the West: How Dying Populations and Immigrant Invasions Imperil our Country and Civilization*. New York: Thomas Dunne Books.

Chamberlain, H. S.
1912 orig.
1899   *Foundations of the Nineteenth Century*. J. Lees trans. London: John Lamp, Ltd.

Fehrenbacher, D. E.
1969   *The Era of Expansion: 1800–1848*. New York, London, Sydney, Toronto: John Wiley & Sons, Inc.

Freud, S.
1961   *Beyond the Pleasure Principle*. New York/London: W.W. Norton & Company.

Giddens, A.
1998   "Sociedad de Riesgo: El Contexto de la Política Británica," *Estudios Demográficos y Urbanos*. Mexico: El Colegio de México, Vol. 13, Núm. 3(39).

_____
1990   *The Consequences of Modernity*. Cambridge: Polity Press.

Gobineau, J. A.
1915
[1853–1855]
The Inequality of Human Races. 4 Vol. Collins trans. New York: Putnam.

Guidieri, R. and F. Pellizzi
1988   "Introduction: 'Smoking Mirrors' – Modern Polity and Ethnicity," *Ethnicities and Nations, Processes of Interethnic Relations in Latin America, Southeast Asia, and the Pacific*. Houston, TX: The Rothko Chapel.

Higham, J.
1965   *Strangers in the Land. Patterns of American Nativism 1860–1925*. New York: Atheneum.

Huntington, P. S.
2000   "Reconsidering Immigration. Is Mexico a Special Case?," *Backgrounder*, November. Washington, DC: Center for Immigration Studies.

Joppke, C.
1999   *Immigration and the Nation-State. The United States, Germany and Great Britain*. Oxford: Oxford University Press.

Lash, S. and B. Wynne
1992   "Introduction," *Risk Society*, U. Beck. London: Sage Publications.

Nott, J. C. and G. R. Gliddon
1855   *Types of Mankind; or, Ethnological Researches, Based Upon the Ancient Monuments, Paintings, Sculptures, and Crania of Races, and Upon Their Natural, Geographical, Philological and Biblical History*. Philadelphia: Lippincott.

Olimon Nolasco, M., E. B. Barcelo and J. R. Vera
1993   *Los Derechos Humanos*. México, México: Instituto Mexicano de Doctrina Social Cristiana.

Pohlenz Cordova, J.
1997   "Formación Histórica de la Frontera México-Guatemala," *Las Fronteras del Istmo*. P. Bovin (coord.). México: Centro de Investigaciones y Estudios Superiores en Antropología Social/Centro Francés de Estudios Mexicanos y Centroamericanos.

Press, E.
2000   "Human Rights: The Next Step," *The Nation*, Vol. 271, No. 21, December 25.

Said, E. W.
1980   *The Question of Palestine*. New York: Vintage Books.

Stallybrass, P. and W. Allon
1986   *The Politics and Poetics of Transgression*. New York: Cornell University Press.

Weil, S.
1996   *A la Espera de Dios*. Madrid: Editorial Trotta.

Welty, E.
1960   *A Handbook of Christian Social Ethics. Vol. I, Man in Society.* West Germany: Herder and Herder.

La inmigración en contexto de globalización como diálogo intercultural

Raul Fornet-Betancourt
Institute of Missiology, Aachen

1. OBSERVACIONES PRELIMINARES

Me parece innegable el hecho de que los que trabajamos en el campo intelectual y nos entendemos o se nos entiende como "profesionales del saber," asistimos desde hace ya varias décadas a un fuerte movimiento de redefinición de las fronteras disciplinarias establecidas por la hegemonía de la división occidental del saber y de su ordenamiento académico.

De manera que podemos constatar hoy un aumento importante de planteamientos interdisciplinarios e incluso transdisciplinarios que, con su nuevo espíritu, van logrando que el discurso de los llamados "profesionales del saber" vaya adquiriendo una nueva calidad, al articularse como un discurso más integral que sabe superar la fragmentaria visión de las cosas que nos suelen ofrecer los discursos de las disciplinas aisladas.

Hay que reconocer, sin embargo, que es verdad también que todavía estamos muy lejos de haber superado el hábito de pensar desde el horizonte epistemológico y metodológico con el que nos equipa nuestra formación académica dentro de la "disciplina" de una área de estudio determinada.

Por eso, además, continuamos todavía, a pesar de nuestros ejercicios o entrenamientos en interdisciplinariedad, viendo nuestra propia disciplina como la primera referencia para enfocar los temas que estudiamos o los problemas con que nos vemos confrontados. Y seguimos también definiendo nuestra propia "profesionalidad" o competencia frente a lo real fundamentalmente desde el horizonte de la disciplina que representamos.

Como no me considero una excepción, pienso que es conveniente por eso, antes de entrar en materia, hacer algunas observaciones previas en relación con el punto de vista disciplinario desde el que voy a tratar el tema. Empiezo entonces por aclarar que hablaré de la inmigración desde la perspectiva de la filosofía.

Mi enfoque no será, por tanto, ni sociológico ni político ni económico ni teológico, etc. Es cierto que mis reflexiones procurarán tener, en la medida de mis posibilidades, como transfondo mayor los conocimientos de dichos enfoques,[1] pero no asumen ninguna de sus perspectivas disciplinares como eje para centrar su discurso sobre la inmigración. Ese eje para nuestra reflexión se lo pedimos justamente a la filosofía. Mi enfoque es, pues, un enfoque filosófico. Pero ¿qué es un enfoque filosófico?

Estoy conciente de que con esta pregunta planteo en realidad un problema de fondo que no puede ser tratado en el marco de una nota preliminar. Se ve, en efecto, que estamos ante la compleja cuestión de la definición de eso que llamamos filosofía o de su misma autocomprensión. Y ésta es una cuestión cuyo tratamiento llevaría a tener que revisar la historia del origen y desarrollo de las tradiciones de ese saber que, con el nombre explícito de filosofía o no, se va articulando como filosófico en las distintas culturas de la humanidad. Consciente, por tanto, de que el transfondo histórico-sistemático al que nos remite la pregunta acerca de qué es un enfoque filosófico, no puede ser tratado aquí, me limito en esta primera observación preliminar a explicar brevemente la tradición filosófica que facilita mi horizonte de comprensión y que me sirve para calificar de filosófico el enfoque del tema cuyo estudio nos convoca hoy.

---

[1] De la inmensa bibliografía sobre la inmigración destaco aquí las obras siguientes: Abad, L. A. Cucó, A. Izquierdo, A., *Inmigración, pluralismo y tolerancia*, Madrid 1993; Balibar, E., Wallerstein, I., *Race, nation, class: ambiguous identities*, London/New York 1991; Barwig, K./Mieth, D. (eds.), *Migration und Menschenwürde. Fakten, Analycen und ethische Kriterien*, Mainz 1987; Bouhdiba, A., *La migration arabe*, Paris 1978; Brisson, M., *Migraciones... ¿Migraciones alternativa insólita?*, San José 1997; Brubaker, R. (ed.), *Immigration and the politics of citizenship in Europe and North America*, Boston 1989; Contreras, J., *Los retos de la inmigración: racismo y pluriculturalidad*, Madrid 1994; Dietz, G., *El desafío de la interculturalidad. El voluntariado y las ONG ante el reto de la inmigración*, Granada 2000; George, P., *Les migrations internationales*, Paris 1976; y *Etude sur les migrations de population*, Paris 1977; Hoffmann-Novotny, H.J., "Migração," en: Enderle, G./Homann (eds), *Dicionário de ética econômica*, São Leopoldo 1997, pp. 402–407; Hollifield, J.F., *Immigrants, markets and states*, Cambridge (USA) 1992; Izquierdo, A., *La inmigración inesperada*, Madrid 1996; Lapeyronnie, D.D., *Immigrés en Europe*, Paris 1992; Lucas, J.D., *El desafío de las fronteras: derechos humanos y xenofobia frente a una sociedad plural*, Madrid 1994; Noiriel, G., *The French Melting Pot: Immigration, citizenship, and national identity*, Minneapolis 1996; Pajares, M., *La inmigración en España: retos y propuestas*, Barcelona 1998; Sayad, A., *L'inmigration ou les paradoxes de l'altérité*, Bruxelles 1991; Siebert, H. (ed.), *Migration: a challenge for Europe*, Tübingen 1994; Suarez-Orozco, M.M. (ed.) *Crossings: Mexican Immigration in Interdisciplinary Perspective*, Cambridge (USA), 1998; Touraine, A., *Pouvrons-nous vivre ensemble?*, Paris 1997; Treibel, A., *Migration in modernen Gesselschaften*, Weinheim/München 1990; y la bibliografia que citaremos más específicamente en las notas que siguen.

Como se sabe, al menos en Occidente, el debate sobre la naturaleza y el sentido del saber filosófico ha transcurrido en gran parte como una confrontación entre dos perspectivas fundamentales que se han presentado muchas veces como dos formas alternativas para la articulación de la filosofía como tal. Son éstas, por una parte, la tradición que consolida e impone Immanuel Kant al elevar la ciencia moderna occidental a un único paradigma válido para hacer filosofía en sentido estricto; y, por otra parte, la tradición socrática – no ajena a otras tradiciones no occidentales como la del confucionismo en China o la de los profetas de Israel – que entiende la filosofía en términos de saber práctico sapiencial, esto es, como *sabiduría* que, sin cerrarse al saber "científico," nos abre a las fuentes de sentido de la vida, nos enseña a leer nuestros mundos de vida y a interpretar sus signos, pero sobre todo a tomar una postura ética en nuestras vidas.

Pues bien; sirva esta indicación esquemática como marco de referencia para explicar que mis reflexiones aquí se encuadran en el horizonte de esa tradición de la filosofía como *sabiduría* para la vida y para el mundo, como saber con voluntad de servir de orientación práctica en la vida de los seres humanos. En mi percepción esta tradición hace hoy su camino en forma de una filosofía contextual e intercultural; ya que ésta es una filosofía que no está interesada en saber "ideas," en producir "pensamientos," sino que su interés es más bien el aprender sobre el mundo y a vida compartiendo los saberes prácticos encarnados en los contextos o mundos de vida concretos en los que la gente *lleva su vida*, y fomentado el diálogo entre las prácticas culturales que se configuran desde esos saberes o tradiciones de hacer y de pensar.

Por esta vía de la afirmación de la contextualidad de nuestros saberes y del diálogo entre las tradiciones culturales que encarnan, aspira además la filosofía contextual e intercultural a contribuir a la creación de las condiciones que nos permitan discernir hoy *qué* es lo que realmente debemos saber y *para qué* debemos saberlo.[2] Dicho en otros términos: desde la perspectiva de fondo de la tradición en que me ubico, un enfoque filosófico se distingue por su pretensión de ser un saber que conoce con sabor de realidad (gustando realidades y sus interpretaciones) y que comprende por eso de una cuestión fundamental, a saber, la pregunta por la calidad real de nuestra vida y de sus condiciones.

---

[2] Cf. Fornet-Betancourt, R., *Transformación intercultural de la filosofia*, Bilbao 2001.

Debido a esta contextualidad e interculturalidad inherentes – dicho sea de paso que contextualidad implica ya siempre culturalidad, ya que contexto no es un simple espacio geográfico sino también un horizonte hermenéutico, un mundo de vida – el saber filosófico puede y debe plantear preguntas tales como estas: ¿Nos gusta la vida que llevamos? ¿Podemos realmente disfrutar la vida que llevamos o el llevar la vida nos cuesta tanto que nos impide disfrutar el buen sabor de vivir? ¿Qué conocimiento necesitamos para saber disfrutar la vida y dejar que otros disfruten la vida también?

Pero el saber filosófico tiene además que atreverse a orientar a la gente en el tratamiento de estas cuestiones.

La segunda observación, que complementa la anterior, es la siguiente. Es evidente que por su carácter contextual e intercultural la posición filosófica de la que parto aquí, tiene que relativizar fuertemente las fronteras establecidas por el orden del saber académico dominante entre las distintas disciplinas como fronteras entre campos de competencia y de responsabilidad frente a la realidad y a la vida. Pensemos, por poner ahora este caso concreto, en las divisiones disciplinares entre teología, filosofía o religión.

En Occidente esta división disciplinaria, que refleja a su vez una fragmentación de la realidad y de la vida, responde en gran parte a las necesidades específicas de un proceso de modernización que – para ir al punto que aquí nos interesa – tenía como uno de sus pilares la búsqueda de recetas científico-técnicas para todos los problemas de la humanidad en todo el planeta. Por eso en el transfondo de nuestra división disciplinaria del saber se encuentra un espíritu de racionalización y de secularización del quehacer intelectual que ha impuesto como norma de buena ley que ciertas disciplinas, como la filosofía por ejemplo, deban desarrollar su reflexión no solamente acentuando su autonomía y diferencia frente a la teología y/o religión sino evitando incluso todo lo que pueda indicar un recurso a tradiciones de saber sapiencial religioso.

Por esta razón quiero aclarar que relativizo también el peso del secularismo latente en nuestra división del saber heredada y que parto de una concepción de la filosofía que, superando el miedo moderno al "contagio" teológico o religioso, considera – por interés de la calidad humana integral de su reflexión – importante también asumir en su proceso de pensamiento la sabiduría que se nos trasmite en tradiciones que el espíritu reinante en nuestra división del saber margina como tradiciones religiosas, no científicas. Dicho positivamente: mi enfoque filosófico se alimenta también de experiencias sapienciales que, como la herencia bíblica cristiana, nos abren e impulsan a la práctica de un universalismo concreto centrado en el valor de la hospitalidad y de la justicia.

¿Cómo podría, sin caer en la mala fe, una reflexión filosófica sobre la inmigración excluir de su "démarche" las pistas de acción ética que nos trasmiten tantos pasajes bíblicos?[3] ¿Cómo cerrarse a la posibilidad de pensar y "verificar" hoy la parábola del buen samaritano como un paradigma de vida, de conocimiento y de acción en nuestro mundo?[4]

Porque quiere aprender a saber también desde y con tradiciones semejantes, la posición filosófica que inspira mi enfoque – esta es mi tercera observación – considera que para pensar *bien* tan importante es cuidar la *coherencia lógica* de nuestra argumentación como su autenticidad y *verificación amorosa*, es decir, velar tanto por no cometer "errores lógicos" como por no cometer "faltas de amor" en nuestra forma de pensar.[5] En este sentido nuestro enfoque filosófico tratará de distinguirse por ensayar una reflexión filosófica en la que la dimensión del *logos* se ve enriquecida no sólo por la del *ethos* sino también por la del *pathos*.[6] Se trata, dicho en otros términos, de intentar un ejercicio de pensamiento que, consciente de que arranca siempre de lo que debe a otros – la familia, los amigos, las tradiciones compartidas, etc. – fomenta el *agradecimiento* como su talante de fondo y se desarrolla desde él como un pensamiento que no objetiva cuando piensa porque crea comunidad, y la confiesa articulándose como pensamiento que raciocina con *simpatía* y *compasión*.[7] Este pensar *agradecido*, que nos salva de caer en el error destructor de la ingratitud,[8] es, además, un pensar *gratificante*; un pensar que intenta contrarrestar las situaciones de *des-gracia* y que, por ello, piensa para contribuir a *agraciar* su tiempo, su realidad, su cultura, en fin, al ser humano y su mundo todo.

---

[3]Ver por ejemplo: Exodo 22, 20; Levítico 19, 33–34; Deuteronomio 10, 19; 27, 19; o Mateo 25, 35.

[4]Cf. Ricoeur, P., *Histoire et vérité*, Paris 1964, págs. 99 y sgs.

[5]Recordemos la exigencia radical que planteaba ya en este sentido el viejo principio de filosofia cristiana, subrayado en la modernidad por Goethe, que asentaba que sólo se puede conocer bien lo que se ama. Ver también: Scheler, M., *Liebe und Erkenntnis*, Bern 1955; y más recientemente: Panikkar, R., "La dialéctica de la razón armada," en: *Concordia* 9 (1986) 68–89; y "La mística del diálogo," en: *Jahrbuch für Kontextuelle Theologien* 1 (1993) 19–37.

[6]Cf. Raúl Fornet-Betancourt, *Interculturalidad y globalización*, Frankfurt 2000, págs. 79 y sgs; y la bibliografía ahí indicada.

[7]Cf. Heidegger, M., *Qué significa pensar?*, Buenos Aires 1964; especialmente págs. 134 y sgs. Ver también su *Carta sobre el humanismo*, Buenos Aires 1963; así como *Vorträge und Aufsätze*, en: *Gesamtausgabe*, tomo 7, Frankfurt/M 2000.

[8]Cf. Ortega y Gasset, J., *Ideas y creencias*, en: *Obras completas*, tomo 5, Madrid 1983, especialmente págs. 398 y sgs.

De donde se sigue, esta es mi cuarta y última observación preliminar, que en la perspectiva de la tradición filosófica con la que trabaja mi enfoque, el pensar filosófico es un raciocinio para el que la dimensión de la "praxis" no es una esfera que viene después de la "teoría y en la que ésta buscaría su "aplicación." No, se trata más bien de una forma de pensar que, cuando piensa, está ya *en plan de hacer*; un pensamiento que piensa como arte de saber hacer realidad.

Valgan, por tanto, estas breves indicaciones como explicación del punto de vista (filosófico) desde el que articularé mis reflexiones sobre el tema de esta conferencia. Pero antes de pasar a ellas, debo hacer de nuevo otras observaciones, aunque en realidad tienen que ver directamente con el tema; pues se trata de aclarar brevemente en qué sentido tomaré los conceptos centrales que definen mi tema. De manera que estas observaciones sirven para enmarcar temáticamente mis reflexiones sobre la inmigración.

2. EXPLICANDO LOS TÉRMINOS

2.1 Inmigración

Basta con repasar la historia de la humanidad para comprender que la inmigración es un fenómeno tan antiguo como la humanidad misma y que constituye además un hecho que ilustra como pocos que la historia de la humanidad es una historia marcada por el dolor. Y basta leer los informes de la ONU para darse cuenta que la inmigración es hoy uno de los grandes desafíos con los que se ven enfrentados nuestras sociedades actuales.[9]

Con razón, pues, habla Étienne Balibar de la inmigración como de un hecho político mayor[10] que pone al desnudo los límites de nuestro orden social, económico, político, jurídico y cultural, en una palabra, las fronteras de exclusión de la democracia liberal imperante.

---

[9]Ver los distintos informes del Alto Comisionado de las Naciones Unidas para los Refugiados, en especial los de 1995–1998 y de 2000/2001: UNHCR, *Zur Lage der Flücht-linge in der Welt. UNHCR-Report 1995/96. Die Suche nach Lösungen*, Bonn 1995; UNHCR, *Zur Lage der Flüchtlinge in der Welt. UNHCR-Report 1997/98. Erzwungene Migration: Eine humanitäre Herausforderung*, Bonn 1997; y UNHCR, *Zur Lage der Flüchtlinge in der Welt. UNHCR-Report 2000/2001. 50 Jahre humanitärer Einsatz*, Bonn 2000. Y para el caso de América Latina: Díaz Luz, M., A. Gómez, *Las migraciones laborales de Colombia a Venezuela durante las últimas décadas*, Caracas 1991; Escobar, R., *La iglesia católica y las nuevas migraciones en América Latina y en el mundo*, Ciudad del Vaticano 1991; CELAM (ed.), *Migraciones: Actualidad y pastoral*, Bogotá 1989; *La migración. Aspectos bíblicos, teológicos y pastorales*, Bogotá 1992; y *Derechos humanos y migraciones en América Latina*, Bogotá 1994.
[10]Cf. Balibar, E., *Les frontiéres de la démocratie*, Paris 1992, p. 51.

Y si la inmigración nos revela esta otra cara de la historia de la humanidad es, fundamentalmente, porque es inmigración de gente pobre. Sobre este transfondo indico, por tanto, que asumo este término de inmigración no para designar la movilidad de los ejecutivos, de las personas de negocios, de las grandes estrellas del deporte o de la "cultura" y ni siquiera de los estudiantes que se van de su país asegurados con una beca de estudios, sino para reservarlo como denominación de esos pobres de este mundo que – sean refugiados, desplazados, exiliados o "trabajadores extranjeros" – se ven obligados a emigrar para tratar de *ganarse la vida* o de asegurar sus vidas y las de sus familias *en otro lugar* (extraño). En breve: inmigración indica para mí la condición del pobre extranjero.[11]

Por otra parte debo notar que, si bien la inmigración así entendida nos confronta, como se insinuaba antes, con un desafío político, social y económico de primer orden, no será desde esa óptica desde la que reflexione sobre ella. Es decir que veré en la inmigración (como condición del pobre extranjero) ante todo una *situación antropológica*.

Sin menospreciar la importancia de analizar la inmigración como "problema" social, político o económico, la enfocaré aquí como una manera de vivir la y de estar en la *conditio humana*. Quien dice "soy emigrante" confiesa una manera específica de *llevar la vida* y, con ello, de vivir su *conditio humana*. De ahí, pues, que centre mi atención ahora en este nivel de *situación antropológica* que implica la inmigración.

Puesto que se trata de la inmigración de la gente pobre, la inmigración, en el rostro sufrido y temeroso del pobre extranjero, nos indica además que la *situación antropológica* que en ella se contextualiza es una situación que nos confronta con un modo de estar en lo humano que es difícil y precario. En el inmigrante como pobre extranjero *vemos* que la inmigración es, en efecto, una situación en la que *cuesta más* llevar la vida.[12] La inmigración nos abre los ojos, nos quiebra el espejismo de la realidad irreal de un mundo donde todos tienen

---

[11]Cf. Freijó, A. "El inmigrante y su realidad social. Quién es inmigrante?, en: *Misiones extranjeras*, 181 (2001) 26–35.

[12]Nos inspiramos en Jon Sobrino quien ha escrito: "Vivir en este país es siempre una carga muy dura de llevar. Oficialmente, la mitad de la población vive en pobreza, grave o extrema. De la otra mitad, otra buena mayoría vive con serios agobios y dificultades, todo lo cual se agrava con las catástrofes . . . Vivir es, pues, una pesada carga, pero no lo es para todos por igual. Como siempre, lo es muchísimo más para las mayorías pobres." "Reflexiones a propósito del terremoto," en: *Misiones extranjeras* 181 (2001) p. 88.

las mismas posibilidades para llevar su vida y nos hace "tropezar" con la cruel realidad real del mundo de los pobres extranjeros en nuestras fortalezas del "bienestar."

Sobre las implicaciones de esta visión de la inmigración volveré luego. Pero quiero ahora adelantar mi tesis: Esta visión de la inmigración defiende, en lo esencial, que la inmigración, y los inmigrantes no son un "problema." Si hay un "problema" en la inmigración como dimensión de nuestra realidad humana, ese problema estaría más bien en la manera cómo respondemos o nos comportamos ante ella los que formamos parte de las sociedades "receptoras" y, con nosotros, nuestras instituciones.

El problema que veo, es por tanto, el problema de la respuesta ante las necesidades legítimas (económicas, culturales, religiosas, etc.) de los inmigrantes. ¿Qué vida dejamos que lleven? ¿Le aligeramos la carga del llevar la vida o se la hacemos más pesada? La respuesta a esta pregunta es el verdadero problema de la inmigración, y no el fenómeno como tal.

2.2 Globalización

Aunque es una palabra de moda de la que hacemos un uso casi inflacionario en los más diversos campos, el término "globalización" sigue siendo un concepto ambivalente e incluso confuso. Sin entrar aquí en una aclaración conceptual, que implicaría necesariamente revisar la enorme bibliografía existente,[13] me limito a señalar que distingo tres niveles:

El nivel, digamos, real que estaría conformado por los "hechos fuertes" de la globalización de los mercados, de las finanzas, de la información, de una

---

[13]A título de ilustración citemos: Altvater, E./Mahnkopf, B., *Grenzen der Globalisierung*, Münster 1997; Apel, K.-O., V. Hösle, R. Simon-Schäfer, *Globalisierung. Herausforderung für die Philosophie*, Bamberg 1998; Araújo de Oliveira, M., *Desafios éticos da Globalização*, São Paulo 2001; Beck, U., *Was ist Globalisierung?*, Frankfurt/M 1997; Chomsky, N., H. Dieterich, *Globalisierung im Cyperspace*, Bad Honnef 1996; Dierckxsens, W., *Los límites de un capitalismo sin ciudadanía*, San José 1997; Fornet-Betancourt, R. (ed.), *Kapitalistische Globalisierung und Befreiung*, Frankfurt 2000; García Canclini, N., *Consumidores y ciudadanos. Conflictos multiculturales de la globalización*, Mexico 1995; Giddens, A., *The Consequences of Modernity*, Oxford 1990; Girardi, G., "Globalización cultural y su alternativa cultural," en: *Exoco* 39 (1997) 26–34; Hinkelammert, F. (ed.), *El huracán de la globalización*, San José 1999; Robertson, R., *Globalization: Social Theory and Global Culture*, London 1992; a sí como los numerosos monográficos de las siguientes revistas: *Das Argument* (Neoliberalismus als Globalisierung) 217 (1996); *Cristianismo y Sociedad* (Globalización, ecumenismo y responsabilidad cristiana) 129–130 (1996); *Deutsche Zeitschrift für Philosophie* (Globalisierung, Medien und Demokratie) 6 (1997); *Novos Estudos* (Visões da globalização) 49 (1997); y *Widerspruch* (Globalisierung) 31 (1997).

estrategia militar, de una forma de administración de la vida pública, de los problemas ecológicos, etc.

El nivel ideológico sería el uso que se hace de esos "hechos," especialmente por el neoliberalismo. Es decir la instrumentalización de los procesos "reales" de globalización para imponer el diseño político del capitalismo neoliberal a todo el mundo. Este uso ideológico pretende crear el espejismo de una humanidad entrelazada e interdependiente para ocultar que la globalización actual significa, en sus consecuencias reales, el fortalecimiento de la hegemonía del Imperio en un mundo de mundos que se empobrecen. Por eso, a pesar de su novedad histórica indiscutible, la globalización (neoliberal) debe verse en línea de continuidad con la historia del colonialismo y del imperialismo. Y de aquí justamente la urgencia de saber distinguir en este proceso entre "realidad" e "ideología."

El nivel de lo que llamo el "espíritu" de la globalización que sería algo así como la "filosofía" que se quiere propagar como postura fundamental para llevar la vida en nuestro mundo actual.[14]

A la luz de esta distinción es preciso entonces, entender por "globalización" o "contexto de globalización" el proceso complejo y multidimensional de expansión de un "espíritu" como principio generador de una determinada manera de vivir y como tendencia general para configurar el mundo. Este "espíritu," que se manifiesta y encarna en principios muy concretos como la primacía de lo económico-rentable o de la consiguiente centralidad del mercado o de la necesidad de la competitividad entre individuos, cambia la sustancia misma de lo humano y el horizonte referencial para saber qué es lo que realmente debemos ser y cómo deberíamos convivir en nuestro mundo. Por este "espíritu" la globalización (neoliberal), como bien ha subrayado Orlando O. Espín, "... is *not* something that occurs *outside* of us, somehow alienating us from our *true* religious, cultural, national, or personal *essence*. Globalization occurs within and among all of us, and beyond us. And in this sense one could say that globalization is always experienced *locally*. Globalization has impacted and continues to impact cultures and epistemologies: our ways of being, of thinking, of knowing, of acting and of believing."[15]

---

[14]Cf. Fornet-Betancourt, R., "Aproximaciones a la globalización como universalización de políticas neoliberales: Desde una perspectiva filosófica," en: *Pasos* 83 (1999) 9–21.

[15]Espín, O.O., "Inmigration, Territory, and Globalization: Theological Reflections," en: *Journal of Hispanic/Latino Theology*, 3 (2000) p. 50.

Por eso también hay que ver la globalización, o, el "espíritu" de la misma no tanto como un *contexto* de nuestras vidas y de nuestros mundos de vida, es decir, no como un contexto de contextos, sino más bien como un *estado* de vida y de mundo que nos impulsa a ser de una manera determinada. Dicho en otras palabras: el "espíritu" de la globalización promueve un nuevo *tipo* de ser humano: el ser humano sistemático que cambia la memoria por la fragmentaria funcionalidad en una "sociedad" sin proximidad ni vecindad y que, sin historia, es decir, sin comunidad, queda en el fondo desconectado del ritmo de la vida pero instalado por hipnosis en un mundo de realidades sin peso de vida, artificiales y de imágenes.

Este cambio en la sustancia misma de la humanidad del ser humano es lo que más me interesa sobre lo que llamamos globalización. Pues entiendo que ese giro antropológico que está fomentando el "espíritu" de la globalización (neoliberal), es precisamente lo que explica que hablar de la inmigración en contexto de globalización signifique hablar no de la libre y solidaria acogida de los inmigrantes como seres humanos, como hermanos y hermanas, sino de un proceso de exclusión en el que el inmigrante, como el forastero o extranjero en *El Castillo* de Franz Kafka,[16] se encuentra a cada paso con la incomprensión, la desconfianza, la sospecha y el rechazo de los señores y habitantes del "Castillo," ya que éstos representan un *tipo* de ser (humano) deshumanizado que desconoce el valor de la hospitalidad y de la convivencia. Y esto quiere decir para mí que no sólo fallan las instituciones y las leyes y ordenanzas del "Castillo." Falla también la humanidad de sus habitantes, fallamos, en última instancia, nosotros mismos. La interiorización del "espíritu" de la globalización (neoliberal) quiebra la relacionalidad y la comunión en nuestra sustancia humana y con ello motiva esa conducta hostil ante el inmigrante. O sea que en el contexto de globalización hay que tener en cuenta que la pregunta por el cómo respondemos ante la situación antropológica de la inmigración debe ser vista en su nivel institucional o estructural, pero sin olvidar el nivel personal que tiene que ver precisamente con la interiorización del "espíritu" de la globalización (neoliberal) por cada uno de nosotros. Pero será en el tercer apartado donde ilustraremos más en concreto esas consecuencias institucionales y/o personales del "espíritu" de la globalización (neoliberal) para el trato con los inmigrantes.

---

[16]Cf. Kafka, F., *Das Schloß*, Frankfort/M 1983.

2.3 Diálogo intercultural

Como actitud y práctica que se afinca en la experiencia de que la "identidad" que llamamos nuestra – tanto a nivel personal como cultural o religioso – se la debemos a otros y, por cierto, también a esos otros que consideramos extranjeros, ya que nos hacemos lo que somos sobre la base de tradiciones permeadas por el trato con otras tradiciones y en continua cooperación práctico-vital con los "otros;" como tal actitud y práctica, repito, el diálogo intercultural simboliza para mí en este contexto un "espíritu" alternativo que busca la corrección de la tendencia antropológica que quiere cimentar el "espíritu" de la globalización (neoliberal). Su objetivo es, por eso, más importante que su concepto.[17] O, si se prefiere, su concepto se va verificando en la práctica de esa *postura* que se opone y *contradice* al "espíritu" de la globalización (neoliberal) con la hospitalidad y la convivencia como orientaciones fundamentales para la buena y lograda realización de la humanidad en todos los seres humanos. Lo importante es, pues, esa práctica de acogida grata que invierte la óptica que ve al inmigrante desde los intereses del orden institucional establecido por la sociedad mayoritaria, para proponer la perspectiva relacional de la *postura conviviente* desde la que no se ve al inmigrante como un ser extraño a quien hay que preguntarle si se parece o puede parecerse a los miembros de la sociedad mayoritaria, es decir, qué sabe de y sobre "nosotros," sino que se le ve como un ser humano (con su dignidad, cultura, historia, religión) al que ya le debemos parte de lo que somos y que puede seguir enriqueciéndonos. De aquí que desde esta óptica de la convivencia la pregunta al inmigrante es la pregunta dialógica – y no la inquisitorial y burocrática pregunta por los "papeles" – que le cuestiona sobre lo que sabe de sí mismo y lo que se puede aprender de su mundo y sus tradiciones.

En este sentido la inmigración, vista – insisto en ello – desde la perspectiva de la interculturalidad, es un lugar privilegiado para la práctica y la vivencia del diálogo intercultural. Más aun: la inmigración es el rostro en el que podemos leer hoy acaso con más claridad la vocación intercultural del ser humano y recuperar así nuestra memoria de peregrinos de la humanidad. Pero para que la inmigración sea realmente esa escuela de interculturalidad, tenemos que oponer con firmeza la lógica amorosa de la convivencia a la lógica de la exclusión de la globalización en curso que hace de los inmigrantes un simple "factor" económico o un problema de integración social, cuando no los desprecia como indeseables. También sobre esto volveré en el próximo apartado.

---

[17]Lucas, J.D., "Ciudadanía y Unión Europea intercultural," en: *Anthropos* 191 (2001) p. 97.

Por otra parte deseo advertir todavía que el objetivo del diálogo intercultural de hacer de la inmigración un lugar privilegiado de práctica de la interculturalidad, esto es, el trabajar – como dice el título de la ponencia – por que la inmigración en el contexto de la globalización sea realmente un proceso de diálogo intercultural, es algo que implica una revalorización de las tradiciones de identidad de las diferentes culturas de la humanidad. Esta revalorización no significa evidentemente ninguna defensa de las identidades heredadas como realidades ontologicamente fijas, pero sí el reconocimiento de que son *historia* que nos condiciona en nuestros modos de ser, que nos ayuda a comprendernos a nosotros mismos y a los demás y que, por tanto, también necesitamos como memoria que nos ayuda a discernir qué es lo que podemos dejar sin perdernos totalmente.

Por esta revalorización de las tradiciones de identidad como puntos históricos de la luz que nos alumbra en la peregrinación hacia la humanidad, el diálogo intercultural es un ejercicio de acompañamiento mutuo entre miembros de diferentes culturas por el que se aprende justamente a vivir la identidad propia compartiéndola y transformándola por la mutualidad y la convivencia. Esto supone, naturalmente, aprender a compartir el mundo con justicia, a eliminar las fronteras de la asimetría de poder en todas sus formas, desde la social hasta la genérica.[18]

Por último quiero observar que el diálogo intercultural en el marco concreto de la inmigración significa para mí la exigencia ética de redimensionar no sólo nuestras tradiciones de origen sino también los fines mismos a los que ellas apuntan; es decir, no sólo redimensionar nuestro pasado sino también nuestro futuro con la visualización de fines más universales y ecuménicos.

3. LA INMIGRACIÓN EN EL CONTEXTO DE LA GLOBALIZACIÓN Y EL DIÁLOGO INTERCULTURAL

3.1 La realidad verdadera de los inmigrantes en el contexto de la globalización del neoliberalismo

Lo primero que llama la atención cuando se reflexiona sobre la realidad ver-

[18]Cf. Aquino, M. P., *Our Cry for Life: Feminist Theology from Latin America,* New York 1993; "Directions and Foundations of Hispanic/Latino Theology," en: Bañuelas, A. J. (ed.), *Metizo Christianity. Theology from the Latino Perspective,* New York 1995, pp. 192–208; y "Theological Method in U.S. Latino/a Theology. Toward an Intercultural Theology for the Third Millennium," en: Espín, O. O., M. Díaz, (eds.), *From the Heart of our People,* New York 1999, pp. 6–48.

dadera, vale decir, sobre la situación antropológica en que se encuentran los inmigrantes en el contexto de la globalización (neoliberal), es la contradicción manifiesta que se da entre el discurso de la ideología dominante sobre la globalización de la humanidad en un mundo que supuestamente derriba las fronteras al configurarse como una "aldea global" y el trato real (político, social, económico, cultural, etc.) que se les da a los inmigrantes; un trato prescrito desde un marco de legislación y de legalidad *nacionales* que, de entrada, le regatea e incluso niega a los inmigrantes derechos fundamentales, violando con ello su dignidad humana.

En su realidad verdadera, pues, los inmigrantes se ven afectados "por una contradicción diaria al constatar que no tienen los mismos derechos que los ciudadanos"[19] de la nación receptora. De modo que forma parte de la vida diaria de los inmigrantes tener que llevar su vida en un contexto donde su exclusión social y política es una práctica institucionalizada. Dicho de otro modo: en el contexto de la globalización (neoliberal) tenemos un orden político que no sólo es "compatible con la exclusión, sino que *institucionaliza la exclusión.*"[20]

Y es que la globalización (neoliberal) no se orienta en los principios de la justicia y la igualdad (desde los que hay que reclamar los mismos derechos para todos los seres humanos sin discriminación de ningún tipo), sino en una lógica de mercado capitalista que se concreta en la expansión de los intereses del capital de las empresas y grupos hegemónicos de los países ricos, así como en la consolidación de sociedades escandalosamente asimétricas y excluyentes. La globalización (neoliberal) no globaliza el mundo; globaliza *sus* intereses; y es por eso que en su figura neoliberal la globalización es incompatible con un proceso de universalización de la justicia y la igualdad. Globalizar los intereses y el espíritu del neoliberalismo significa ciertamente crear una red de complejas actividades, conexiones y procesos en todo el mundo. Y en este sentido se puede hablar de una globalidad del neoliberalismo en la superficie del planeta. Pero esto no significa necesariamente un aumento de comunicación y universalidad en el mundo. Todo lo contrario: la globalidad de la lógica del mercado es sinónimo de empobrecimiento porque degrada las relaciones humanas como estrategias de cálculo económico y convierte al

---

[19]Zapata-Barbero, R. "Dilemas de los Estados democrático-liberales para acomodar políticamente a la inmigración," en: *Anthropos* 191 (2001) p. 59.
[20]Lucas, J. D., *op. cit.*; p. 106. (subrayado en el original).

mundo en un simple campo de acción económica y financiera. Para vidas y formas de vida que no parezcan rentables o no puedan rentabilizarse, no hay lugar en ese mundo globalizado. Éste es un mundo donde, aunque pueda parecer paradójico, hay cada vez menos vida y menos mundo porque cada vez son más las y los que no pueden llevar *bien* su vida ni cultivar sus mundos.

Esta ley de la exclusión rige tanto en las sociedades motoras de la globalización (neoliberal) como en las sociedades periféricas que sufren los efectos de su expansión. Pero, para volver al punto que aquí es relevante – la exclusión de los inmigrantes –, señalaré ahora sólo el aspecto de que, argumentando la supuesta defensa del bienestar de los miembros de las "sociedades ricas," el estado liberal se ampara en el concepto de ciudadanía (¡nacional!) para justificar legalmente la marginalización de los inmigrantes. La ciudadanía se levanta entonces como una frontera que hace de las "sociedades ricas" algo muy parecido al "Castillo" de Kafka, que resulta prácticamente inaccesible para los extranjeros.

De aquí precisamente las tragedias diarias, que todos conocemos, de esas mujeres y esos hombres que arriesgan su vida, y muchas veces la pierden, tratando de llegar al "Castillo," como es el caso de las "pateras" con africanos en las costas de España.

Pero la frontera de la ciudadanía no sirve sólo para controlar la entrada de inmigrantes. Pues es una frontera que golpea con fuerza destructora la vida de los inmigrantes que han logrado entrar en el territorio del "Castillo." Para estos inmigrantes (que, repito, designan la realidad humana de los hombres y mujeres pobres que llegan a las "sociedades ricas" huyendo de la pobreza, de la guerra, de la persecución o violencia en sus países de origen),[21] sean o no reconocidos y tratados como "legales," la ciudadanía, en su concepción actual desde el horizonte de los estados liberales (nacionales), representa la frontera entre la exclusión y la inclusión en importantes esferas de la vida pública, convirtiéndose así en una auténtica barrera que impide a los inmigrantes desempeñar su "oficio" de seres humanos con plenitud de derechos y poderes.

Desde la barrera de la ciudadanía se legaliza e institucionaliza – como se decía antes – la exclusión de los inmigrantes porque con la ciudadanía se invierte o, mejor, se pervierte el orden ético condensado en el principio de la igual dignidad de los seres humanos al hacer del reconocimiento como ciu-

---

[21]Cf. Freijó, A., *op.cit.*; págs. 26 y sgs.

dadano por parte del estado la condición indispensable para tener acceso y poder disfrutar de los derechos de ser humano. No el ciudadano, el ser humano es, en verdad, el sujeto de derecho; el que realmente tiene derecho a tener derechos.[22] Pues, como ya apuntó José Martí, "... dígase hombre, y ya se dicen todos los derechos."[23]

De esta suerte los derechos *debidos* al ser humano se convierten en limosnas[24] que se tienen que mendigar y que se dan según las reglas y los intereses de los señores del "Castillo." Esta ciudadanía excluyente es un poderoso instrumento de selección y de control de los inmigrantes. Es el parámetro desde el que se toma la medida y se vigila a los inmigrantes. Es el marco que determina el carácter de lo público y que decide sobre el orden en el que los inmigrantes deben integrarse y cómo deben hacerlo.

Por eso la ciudadanía también está en el trasfondo de otro de los fenómenos que más llaman la atención en la situación de los inmigrantes en el llamado mundo globalizado. Me refiero al intento de las sociedades "receptoras" por asimilar y/o integrar a los inmigrantes, pero en condiciones que no pongan en peligro el orden público establecido y respetado por sus ciudadanos. La definición de lo público desde una ciudadanía entendida como culturalmente homogénea hace así que a los inmigrantes se les vea y trate como "invasores" que hay que neutralizar precisamente por medio de la asimilación y la integración en el orden establecido, esto es, *concediéndoles* una "participación" en lo público controlada por los ciudadanos y obligándoles a privatizar todo aquello que no esté a tono con el orden de la ciudadanía.[25]

Por esta razón no me parece exagerado constatar que el espacio público de muchas sociedades que se autodenominan multiculturales y que se felicitan por sus políticas de integración, es hoy para los emigrantes un espacio de observación y de control donde sienten a diario el "ojo vigilante" de los "ciudadanos" y sus instituciones que, como la mirada del otro en el mundo de la mala fe descrito por Sartre,[26] los objetiva y aliena, además de presionarlos para que rompan con su historia, sus tradiciones y costumbres, en una palabra, con su propia cultura.

[22]Cf. Lucas, J. D., *op.cit.*; págs. 107 y sgs.
[23]Martí, J., "Mi raza," en: *Obras Completas*, tomo 2, La Habana 1975, pág. 298.
[24]Cf. Moscoso, A.C., "Inmigrantes y desplazados," en: *Presencia Ecuménica* 52 (1999) pág. 9.
[25]Cf. Zapata-Barrero, R., *op.cit.*, págs. 61 y sgs.
[26]Cf. Sartre, J. P., *L'être et le néant*, Paris 1943, especialmente págs. 310 y sgs.

A la luz de lo dicho anteriormente el diagnóstico es claro: la realidad verdadera de los inmigrantes en el contexto de la globalización del neoliberalismo es una situación caracterizada por el escándalo de relaciones tremendamente asimétricas que "justifican" el maltrato de su dignidad humana. La condición humana de los inmigrantes está realmente en una situación de *malestar* y de *desgracia* porque no se les deja ser, porque no se les alivia la carga del llevar la vida.

Desde la perspectiva de este diagnóstico sería, por tanto, testimonio del cinismo más descarado pretender presentar la inmigración hoy como una realidad de diálogo intercultural. El maltrato diario de la dignidad humana en las mujeres y hombres que llamamos inmigrantes, el desprecio y la marginalización de sus culturas y tradiciones, en una palabra, la práctica legal de la exclusión institucionalizada evidencia que nos encontramos más bien ante la negación radical del diálogo intercultural.

Y por lo expuesto se comprende que negación de diálogo intercultural no se refiere aquí a la ausencia de un abstracto diálogo de culturas, sino que nombra una realidad concreta de trato injusto. Por eso decía arriba que, desde mi punto de vista, la inmigración no es el problema; el problema es nuestra respuesta: nuestra respuesta ante el trato que están sufriendo hoy en el contexto de la globalización (neoliberal) los emigrantes. Mencionaba también que el diálogo intercultural representa para mi una respuesta alternativa a la que da el "espíritu" del neoliberalismo, porque intenta poner en marcha una práctica de solidaridad radical que se haga cargo de la situación antropológica de los inmigrantes para compartir mundo y vida con ellos, y hacer factible un proyecto de humanidad universal mediante el acompañamiento mutuo. A continuación trataré de ilustrar algunos rasgos de esta alternativa, que será al mismo tiempo una propuesta de cómo hacer para que la inmigración sea verdaderamente una experiencia concreta de diálogo intercultural.

3.2 El diálogo intercultural como respuesta justa ante la situación de los inmigrantes

Consciente de que se plantea en un contexto que, como se ha visto, se caracteriza por la asimetría de poder, por la negación de derechos fundamentales, por la marginalización cultural e incluso la humillación personal de las mujeres y hombres que calificamos de inmigrantes, el "espíritu" del diálogo intercultural empieza por *contradecir* la concepción de una ciudadanía excluyente afirmando la fundamentalidad prepolítica de la dignidad del ser humano.

Al ser humano no lo acredita un pasaporte ni un número de seguro social ni mucho menos una tarjeta de crédito. Su credencial más digna de crédito (y la que, por tanto, lo convierte en un ser con derecho a tener derechos) es su corporal realidad humana.

De ahí que, desde la perspectiva intercultural, es inmoral, y debería ser por los mismo también ilegal, hablar de ilegales o indocumentados.[27] Por eso, en este contexto, el diálogo intercultural con los inmigrantes empieza por pedir la eliminación de una legalidad que sanciona la asimetría entre ciudadanos y extranjeros. Sin simetría en los derechos no puede haber en realidad un verdadero diálogo entre representantes de culturas y mundos de vida diferentes.

Pero la interculturalidad pide más de nosotros. Pues es una práctica de vida y de reflexión que entiende que no basta con solucionar el status jurídico de los inmigrantes, sea ya por la vía de la "legalización" como extranjeros residentes o sea por la aparentemente generosa vía de la naturalización. Pues los inmigrantes, sean legales o nacionalizados, siguen siendo objeto de exclusión sistemática. Para la interculturalidad hay que ir más a fondo, es decir, dar una respuesta antropológica, y ver además que la solución jurídica debería ser un resultado de la primera.

Antes de seguir con una breve explicación de la respuesta antropológica me permito aclarar, para evitar cualquier malentendido, que la prioridad que le doy a la necesidad de promover una respuesta antropológica ante las necesidades y la situación de la condición humana de los inmigrantes, no implica en mi punto de vista una desvalorización de la alternativa jurídica, sobre todo evidentemente cuando ésta se formula como una demanda intercultural de transformación radical del concepto de ciudadanía en el sentido de una ciudadanía cosmopolita, pero que no olvida el momento contextual del arraigo.[28]

---

[27]Cf. Freijó, A., op.cit., pág. 32.
[28]Ver sobre esto: Balibar, E., op.cit.; Lucas, J.D. (ed.), Los derechos de las minorías en una sociedad multicultural, Madrid 1999; Kaufmann, M. (ed.), Integration oder Toleranz? Minderheiten als philosophisches Problem, Freiburg 2001; Kymlicka, W., Multicultural Citizenship. A liberal theory of minority rights, Oxford 1995; Muguerza, J., Ética, disenso y derechos humanos, Madrid 1998; Villoro, L., Estado plural. Diversidad de culturas, México 1998; Zapata-Barrero, R., Ciudadanía, democracia y pluralismo cultural: hacia un nuevo contrato social, Barcelona, 2001; así como los números monográficos de las revistas: Anthropos (Ciudadanía e interculturalidad) 191 (2001); y Contrastes (La democracia de los ciudadanos) 1 (1996).

Para que los inmigrantes puedan llevar bien su vida y desarrollarse como personas es absolutamente necesario resolver el status jurídico rompiendo, justamente con un derecho intercultural, el marco de la legalidad de los estados (nacionales) liberales. Esto es indiscutible.

Mi prioridad de promover la respuesta antropológica no debe entenderse, por tanto, como un relegar a segundo plano la lucha jurídica por universalizar los derechos del ciudadano a todo ser humano, sino que atiende sobre todo a la convicción personal de que el "espíritu" del neoliberalismo produce hoy un determinado tipo de ser humano (tipo humano en el que se agudizan las consecuencias de la revolución antropológica promovida por el capitalismo[29]), cuyo desafío reclama no solamente un reordenamiento jurídico de las bases de nuestras sociedades sino, y sobre todo, la articulación de una antropología alternativa. Paso, pues, a explicar brevemente algunos de sus rasgos fundamentales.

La idea principal es aquí la de una antropología contextual,[30] es decir, la de una práctica de ser humano o de humanidad que, haciéndose cargo de la situación real de la condición humana en los inmigrantes como personas a las que les cuesta más llevar la vida, apunta al alivio de esa carga articulándose en el diario vivir como hospitalidad y convivencia, que va más allá de lo que se debe por el derecho.

Lo primero sería comprender la situación de los inmigrantes como personas que, con papeles o sin ellos, sienten "dolor de la tierra" porque han abandonado su patria, sus familias, sus amigos, sus lugares de recuerdos compartidos, etc., y sufren el rompimiento de las tradiciones que han alimentado su vida hasta el momento de emigrar. Pero los inmigrantes sufren también por las esperanzas frustradas en la "tierra prometida;" por los sueños que no pueden realizar o simplemente por el desengaño que implica la experiencia de no encontrar el trabajo deseado.

Partir de aquí para el diálogo intercultural con los inmigrantes o, dicho con más propiedad, para hacer de la inmigración un ejercicio vivo de diálogo

---

[29]Cf. Fornet-Betancourt, R., "Aproximaciones a la globalización como universalización de políticas neoliberales: Desde una perspectiva filosófica," loc.cit.; Kosik, K., "Die Lumpenbourgeoisie, die Demokratie und die geistige Wahrheit," en: *Concordia* 35 (1999) 3–14; y Hinkelammert, F., *El grito del sujeto*, San José 1998; sin olvidar naturalmente los análisis de Marx, Mounier, Heidegger, Fromm y Sartre, entre otros.

[30]Cf. Poché, F., *Sujet, parole et exclusión. Une philosophie du sujet parlant*, Paris 1996.

intercultural, supone una práctica de humanidad compasiva; apostar por un tipo humano que cultiva como elemento central de su realización la compasión ante el dolor del otro porque sabe sapiencialmente que sin enternecimiento no hay proximidad, y que sin proximidad no hay práctica de humanidad. A este nivel el "espíritu" alternativo del diálogo intercultural se concreta en una práctica de subjetividad afectiva que nos aproxima y nos mueve a responder con la apertura de nuestro mundo para que el otro entre con su mundo, con sus memorias y tradiciones, es más, para compartir su mundo y su cultura, de manera que su vínculo con las referencias de identidad propias no se conviertan para él en un simple recuerdo de lo pasado o perdido.

Partir de esta experiencia significa, en concreto, saber responder a la nostalgia de los inmigrantes o a sus miedos de perder la identidad con una práctica de convivencia que no sólo tolera sus mundos sino que los ve como fuente para redimensionar el mundo propio, el espacio de nuestra condición humana desde otras perspectivas y experiencias. Y significa también un proceso de acompañamiento para que los inmigrantes se orienten mejor en el mundo "receptor," sepan leer sus "códigos;" pero también – y con esto volvemos a subrayar la importancia de la esfera del derecho – para reclamar su derecho a la participación plena en la configuración pública – política, religiosa, cultural, etc. – de las sociedades "receptoras."

La antropología de la convivencia y de la hospitalidad, que supone y anima a la vez el diálogo intercultural, es, por tanto, práctica de acogida y de justicia al mismo tiempo. Acoge a los inmigrantes y los cuida y los protege en sus diferencias porque sabe del peso doloroso que significa llevar la vida en "tierra extraña," pero sin olvidar que cuidado y protección de los inmigrantes son actitudes que reclaman su articulación en instituciones justas que redimensionen los derechos de todos.

Por eso, en un segundo momento, la práctica de humanidad que emana del "espíritu" del diálogo intercultural subraya que la inmigración no será realmente un lugar de convivencia intercultural mientras no logremos suprimir la inmoralidad de las instituciones vigentes configurando un mundo de convivencia justa y solidaria cuyas instituciones sepan dar cabida a todas las diferencias y sancionen la exclusión como un crimen contra la humanidad, como un acto de terrorismo social.

De esta forma la inmigración será, de verdad, una escuela de diálogo intercultural donde todos y todas aprenderemos de los encantos de ser humano y haremos del mundo un hogar que celebra la vida buena y justa en todos y todas, con todos y todas; es decir, un mundo sin la asimetría entre los que viven y los condenados a ver el espectáculo de la vida que llevan unos pocos en sus reductos excluyentes de abundancia.

Ruth: The Migrant Who Saved the People

Dianne Bergant, CSA
Catholic Theological Union in Chicago

PRELIMINARY REMARKS

Before addressing the specific topic of this workshop, it is important that I make several points. First, one of the pivotal theological effects of Vatican II is the revitalization of biblical theology. While this turn to the Bible continues to manifest itself in many ways, one of the most significant has been the search for the biblical foundation or justification of current pastoral practice or spiritual trend. This search has resulted in the retrieval of much rich theological, pastoral, and spiritual tradition. It has also provided the church with an appreciation for the ongoing presence and direction of the Spirit of God and insight into the theological development that this presence and direction have brought forth.

Second, biblical language is basically metaphorical in character. Imaginative and paradoxical, it opens us to possibilities of expression and insight that precise philosophical or descriptive discourse cannot provide. It generates impressions rather than propositions. It seeks to capture the power and emotion of the event of God and to draw the hearer (only secondarily the reader) into an experience that transcends both the past and the present, and opens to the future. It is important to understand this dimension of religious language, not only for the sake of a method of interpretation that will reveal original meanings (theological reconstruction), but also for the sake of one that will provide new understandings (constructive theology).

Third, it is important to be aware of the limitations of any search for the biblical foundation of theological perspectives, pastoral practices, or spiritual trends. In some circles what is called biblical theology is really a use of biblical passages as proof-texts to legitimate some current reality. This technique does not read the biblical material within its own literary or historical contexts and, consequently, does not accurately deal with the theological meanings that the text itself might yield. In more critical circles, the approach most often used today is some form of historical-criticism.

This approach can be both enhancing and limiting. History is an important factor in our tradition and precedents can ground our perspectives, our practices, and our trends. However, precedents can too often be used in order to proscribe, while the ongoing presence of the Spirit of God frequently brings forth realities that are new. Therefore, care should be taken when we are comparing a feature from ancient society with something similar in the contemporary world. What appear to us to be obvious similarities may have quite different significance because of differing contexts.

Finally, we must be attentive to the specific method used to interpret the Bible. Contemporary communication theory has helped us to distinguish three different worlds in relation to the text: the historical world out of which the text grew; the literary world created by the text itself; and the present world of the reader. Each world is relatively independent of the others. However, the world of the text is indebted to the world out of which it grew for its literary structure and for the fundamental meaning which that structure expresses. This does not mean that the sense of the text is restricted to its original meaning and cannot generate a plurality of fresh legitimate meanings. It means instead that any proposed meaning is restricted by the literary structures and content of the original text. In other words, we cannot arbitrarily ascribe meaning to a text if that particular text does not contain words or images that can carry that meaning.

Following the insights of this theory of communication, we realize that interpretation is more than just the gathering of information about the text itself or its earliest settings (historical criticism in a narrow sense). Rather, interpretation can be defined as the meeting of the world of the reader with the world of the text in such a way that the message of the text takes hold of the reader and transforms the world of the reader. Interpretation is the unfolding of the message of the text in a new context. Aspects of this message may or may not be the same as was originally intended. All this suggests that the Bible's revelatory character is not limited to its normative content (*traditum*), but also includes its formative process (*traditio*).

THE BOOK OF RUTH

The theme of this conference is migration. While the Book of Ruth is a complex piece of literature containing many interrelated themes and motifs, its relevance for this conference is the role that migration plays in the story. (Examples of related themes include feminism, ethnocentrism, hospitality, monarchy, etc.) In order to discover the significance of this particular theme, we must first look at the basic structure of the book. All commentators recognize the subtle yet defining influence played by the Davidic monarchy. Though it is only referred to at the end of the story, and there only explicitly in a look to the future, the theme serves as a framework for the story and, therefore, sets the tone of the entire book. The book begins with an account of the family of Elimelech, whose name means 'God is my king,' and it ends with a genealogy of David. In fact, the last word of the book is the name of that great king – David. Most scholars today believe that the book was written in defense of the legitimacy of the Davidic dynasty.

The opening phrase of the book, "Once in the time of the judges," suggests that the events recounted occurred in a period of history before the time of the storyteller. The phrase itself has become a technical way of referring to a time, in Israel's early history, of great political and social disintegration. This was a time of violence and vengeance, a time when everyone did as they pleased (*see* Jgs 17:6; 21:25). Disintegration is emphasized by the writer in order to demonstrate the need for some form of strong central controlling power. Royal propagandizing is obvious. Without going into a debate over the dating of the book, one might suggest that it appeared at a time when David was accused of having Mobile ancestry, or perhaps later when Solomon's dalliance with foreign alliances led others to question his right to rule both the southern and the northern tribes. In either situation, the story could have demonstrated how God's plans for the monarchy were forwarded through the agency of a foreign woman.

Two Hebrew words are used by the biblical authors to distinguish those who belong to other nations. Though the words are sometimes used interchangeably, *nokrî* usually refers to transient foreigners and *ger* to sojourners or resident aliens. When Ruth introduces herself to Boaz, she identifies herself as a stranger (*nokrîyâ*) rather than a resident alien. There is no way of knowing whether this designation should be understood as Ruth acting out of self-effacement or the author underscoring the vulnerability of Ruth's social situation. Either way of understanding this self-identification fits the character of the story. *Nokrîyâ* (stranger) is the same word used by the author of Proverbs to designate women whose foreign practices might lead Israelite men astray (*see* Prv 2:16). By using it to identify herself, Ruth acknowledges that there could be reasons why people might not trust her. However, we will see that she proves herself to be more than trustworthy, for this stranger is the one through whom the remnant of Israel will be saved.

Although the book is named for Ruth, one wonders if Naomi might not be the real principal character of the story. After all, it is her family that migrates to Moab; she is the one who is left widowed and childless with no possibility of remarrying and thereby regaining some form of male protection; it is Naomi who directs Ruth to capture the interest and the commitment of Boaz in order to ensure his redemption of the property and protection of the family of Elimelech; finally, it is Naomi who is said to have gained an heir in the child Obed (Ru 4:17). Not only is the lineage of Elimelech restored, but his widow is no longer without support. In a very real sense Naomi represents the vulnerable remnant of Israel, and it is through Ruth that this remnant is restored. The strange and potentially dangerous woman has become the agent of God's salvation.

Various literary techniques develop the tensions that carry the dynamic of the story. In each of these tensions, the first element is one of destruction and hopelessness, while the second is one of prosperity and new life. The story opens with famine but it closes in Bethlehem, which means 'House of bread'; it begins with the death of Elimelech and the end of his lineage, and it ends with the birth of the child who will restore that lineage; the Israelites first migrate to a foreign land, but then return home; the Moabitess Ruth leaves her home and is finally incorporated into the Israelite family. In each of these tensions, God's plans for the family, and ultimately for the monarchy, were moved forward through the agency of a foreign woman. It is clear that the theme of salvation is the key that opens the meaning of the entire book.

Moab was located directly east of the land of Israel, on the opposite side of the Dead Sea, in what is today modern Jordan. In the eyes of the Israelites, it was not merely a foreign land, it was frequently despised. Several prophets hurled pronouncements of doom against that nation. Therefore, the famine suffered by Elimelech's family must have been severe for them to have migrated to this frequently hostile land. In addition to this, the marriages of the sons suggest that the family intended to remain in that foreign land. However, fate had other plans. All three men die, leaving the women bereft of the legal protection that women in patriarchal societies receive from men. Naomi means to send her Moabite daughters-in-law back to their families of origin, for it is impossible for her to supply them with another son to continue the name and lineage of her dead husband.

The story hinges on two of the major kinship practices of the ancient world, the law of levirate and the law of redemption. These laws were meant to safeguard both the integrity of the clan and its property. The law of levirate gets its name from the Latin *levir* meaning brother of the husband. This law states that, if a man dies without leaving an heir, one of his surviving brothers is required to take the widow as his own wife. The first-born of that union is considered the child and legal heir of the deceased man. This practice accomplished three goals: it guaranteed the survival of the deceased man's name; it assured that his property remained within his clan; and it made provision for the care of his widow.

The First Testament contains two examples of levirate marriage, the stories of Tamar (Gn 38) and of Ruth. Evidently, the earlier ancestral tradition, that of Tamar, was well known by the time of the writing of Ruth, for the author of that latter book makes reference to Tamar and then traces the descendants of her son Perez through Obed, the son of Ruth, to king David (Ru 4:12). Both Tamar and Ruth had to resort to some form of trickery in order to get the men in their lives to accept their levirate obligations. It seems that the biblical authors used this social custom to show that the promises of God, which were eventually fulfilled through David, would be thwarted neither by historical events (dying without issue) nor by human infidelity (reluctance to assume responsibilities).

According to the law of redemption, members of a clan had an obligation to help and to protect each other's person and interests. If, because of a temporary financial setback, an Israelite had to be sold into slavery in order to pay debts, a near relative had the duty to redeem that person. If it was the inheritance that had to be sold in order to pay a debt, the relative had priority over all other potential purchasers. In this way the family property would be kept within the family.

The story of Ruth combines the custom of levirate marriage with the duty of redemption. When Naomi tells Ruth that Boaz is "one of our next of kin" (2:20), she uses the word *go'el* (redeemer). However, Boaz was neither a brother of Ruth's deceased husband nor was he even the closest in kinship, and so strictly speaking the law of levirate did not apply in his case. If he was to act as *go'el*, the nearest of her deceased husband's kin would first have to relinquish his rights to the property about to be sold by Naomi. This is done in accordance with the laws of redemption (Lv 25:47–49). When this unnamed relative does relinquish his rights, the symbolic act of exchange which he performs (Ru 4:7–8) is suggestive of the ceremony associated with a man's refusal to comply to the obligations of levirate (Dt 25:9). In this one act the man disavows his levirate responsibility and he relinquishes property rights associated with it. Thus Boaz is permitted to step forward to claim the hand of Ruth, the widow of Mahlon, and to take charge of the inheritance of her deceased husband.

The interweaving of these two customs might reflect an actual historical development in Israel's law and practice. The fact that Elimelech's land did not revert to his closest male kin but was Naomi's to sell might show a development in property laws. On the other hand, the author of the Book of Ruth may have combined the levirate custom and the law of redemption for the purposes of this particular story. It becomes a way of incorporating the non-Israelite ancestress of David into the community. This book is an example of the concern, within some circles in Israel, for the questions of universality and inclusivity.

The radical character of the book is evident on various levels. First, it challenges certain forms of misogynism. It is the story about women, told from a woman's point of view. Though there is no concrete evidence to support or to challenge the claim, some have even argued that its author was a woman. All of this is remarkable for a piece of literature that supports a patriarchal social structure and its male-centered kinship customs. Second, its concern for social justice is obvious, for it demonstrates, beyond question, God's provident care for those who seem to slip through the cracks of society's social services. Finally, it unseats attitudes of ethnocentrism. In this obviously Israelite story the uncompromising loyalty of a member of an ethnic group that was considered suspect by the Israelites reveals itself again and again. Perhaps the best known passage of the book is Ruth's impassioned avowal of commitment to Naomi herself and all that is part of Naomi:

> But Ruth said, "Do not press me to leave you or to turn back from following you! Where you go, I will go; where you lodge, I will lodge; your people shall be my people, and your God my God. Where you die, I will die – there will I be buried. May the Lord do thus and so to me, and more as well, if even death parts me from you!" (Ru 1:16–17)

Where you go, I will go implies that Naomi will never have to be alone. She may not have a husband or sons, but she has a faithful daughter-in-law companion. In fact, at the end of the book the women tell Naomi that she is worth more to you than seven sons (4:15). Although Orpah, the other daughter-in-law, returns to her people of origin, Ruth rejects the possible security of a household of her own. With the words "where you lodge, I will lodge" she promises to establish her home with the solitary Naomi. Though a stranger in the eyes of the Israelites, she decides that "your people will be my people." Perhaps the most radical transformation of which she speaks is the religious one: "Your God will be my God." With these words, Ruth accepts all of the responsibilities associated with the covenant, realizing that she may have to struggle to realize all of its privileges. Her final words bind her to these promises for life: "Where you die, I will die – there will I be buried." She calls down the wrath of God upon herself should she ever be disloyal to these promises. Before she could become the agent of redemption for Naomi, Ruth stripped herself of any semblance of security, identifying totally with Naomi's vulnerability.

THE MIGRATIONS OF ISRAEL

The story of Israel's salvation begins with the account of God's election of the family of Abraham and the promise of land (see Gn 12:7; 26:3–4; 28:13). This tradition provides a kind of religious explanation for the migrations of this particular people. One of Israel's important creedal statements begins with a characterization of its ancestor (Jacob/Israel) as a wanderer who was called by God and told to migrate through several foreign lands before entering into and occupying land that had been promised to him and to his descendants. The general contours of this account probably originated with actual events in Israel's history. However, their theological importance rests in the way they were remembered and how that remembrance enhanced and continues to enhance the faith of the community.

Two other themes, ownership of the land and good will toward the sojourner or alien, help us to understand how Israel viewed migration. First, the land itself is consistently referred to as a gift (see Dt 1:8) or as an inheritance that Israel merely held in trust (see Nm 35:2). If the land is God's, then God can freely bestow it on whomever God chooses, and God can take it back if and when the gift is defiled. This is precisely what Israel believed (see Lv

18:26–19). Even if, in obedience to God, Israel seized control of the land from its previous inhabitants, there was no guarantee that it would hold this control permanently. That depended upon their faithfulness to the covenant. Ultimate control was always in God's hands.

A second theme that is pertinent to the topic of migration is good will toward the sojourner. Unfortunately, too many people think that ancient Israelite law was severe and unbending. This is an inaccurate characterization of a legal tradition that made explicit provisions for the most vulnerable groups within the community, namely, the sojourners, the orphans and the widows (*see* Dt 14:28–29; 24:14, 19–22; 26:12–13; 27:19; *see also* Lv 19:9–10). These were the people who had no adult male Israelite protector (the manner through which, in a patriarchal society, individuals are able to participate). Therefore, by law they became the special concern of the entire community. The sojourners who lived with the Israelites enjoyed certain privileges. They were included in the covenant community (*see* Dt 9:9–12; 31:12) and the celebrations that surrounded it (*see* Dt 16:11, 14; 26:11; Jos 8:30–35). Their presence was valued because it was a constant reminder that Israel too had been a sojourner (*see* Dt 10:19; 23:8). As God had shown solicitous concern for Israel, so Israel was expected to treat other sojourners with comparable concern.

If we are to understand the religion of Israel, its fundamental self-identity, the laws that sprang from this identity, and the language used to describe it, we must realize the importance of a sense of vulnerability. This is the trait that best characterizes the faithful Israelite. Made from the very dust of the grave (*see* Gn 3:19), snatched by God from the hands of the Egyptians (*see* Ex 3:8), borne up as if on eagles wings and brought to the place of covenant (*see* Ex 19:4), considered least among the nations (*see* Dt 7:7), Israel had little in which to take pride. In fact, its greatest achievement was the realization that all people, young and old, rich and poor, Israelite and sojourner, are *anawim*, "little ones" whose greatest dignity is to stand needy before the prodigal God.

What better group of people to exemplify Israel's vulnerability than sojourners? They not only reminded the people of their past, but were a constant challenge to their present good will.

A MESSAGE FOR TODAY

The above explanation may illuminate some of Israel's attitudes toward its own experiences of migration as well as toward the presence of sojourners in its midst; but it does not directly address the difficulty that we have with some of the narratives, narratives that justify Israel's own migration at the expense of others and narratives that regard forced migration as divine punishment for sin. Still, the Bible does provide us with some clues as to how these passages might be understood today. As the ancient community carried the biblical message from one historical situation to the next, it allowed the needs of the moment to seize whatever in the message could speak meaningfully to a faithful people. This is precisely what we today must do. We must bring our religious tradition to bear on the needs of today.

Rereading the Bible in a new context requires that we first carefully uncover all of the issues present within the passage. Next, we must analyze the contemporary situation to discover whether the biblical message is intended to strengthen us in our faith or provide us with a prophetic challenge. It is not enough to see lines of correspondence between the ancient culture and a present day one. Frequently these lines serve as elements within the story rather than issues of theology. For example, contemporary migration, whether voluntary or forced, is a political reality rather than a religious one. Therefore, we today must explain it politically and look for political solutions to the problems that it engenders and not revert to an ancient religious worldview that is foreign to our contemporary way of thinking and that might view forced migration as a punishment for sin.

Without denying that anxiety and confusion, deprivation and rootlessness are ingredients of every life, we can safely say that the ruling group in society is seldom migrant. They are usually secure in their accomplishments, convinced of the soundness of their opinions, and far from the struggles of others. Any assurance that they are a people especially chosen by God to whom promises of future prosperity and peace have been made could very well instill in them the notion that what they have is theirs by right rather than in trust. Furthermore, if this ruling group places the blame for forced migration on the people who carry such a hardship, they might tend to exonerate themselves, the fortunate ones, from the responsibility of caring for and empowering the less fortunate in society.

Those in today's world who are enduring forced migration are undoubtedly disheartened and shattered, confused and in turmoil, not knowing what to believe or whom to trust. They need to be strengthened in their faith and assured of the abiding providence of God. However, this kind of assistance must be done by means of effective action and not merely through pious exhortation. The Bible maintains that the sojourners have a right to expect that their human dignity will be respected by their hosts and that they will enjoy protection under the law. On the other hand, they have a responsibility to comply with the law of the land within which they are sojourning. The Bible does promise that they will enjoy God's providence, but that they will experience it through collaboration with others.

It is clear that Israel's migrations played an important role in its understanding of God's loving concern. It is also clear that ancient Israel interpreted the migrations of other people in the manner in which they affected its own well-being, not the well-being of others. As heirs to the religious traditions of the Bible, we are challenged to embrace its values even though we do not fully share the worldview that engendered them. Therefore, whenever we consider the migration of any people for any reason, the Bible reminds us that: the land which we inhabit ultimately belongs to God; God's generous care is constant and universal; and we are called to extend genuine hospitality toward those who, like us, are sojourners in the land.

RUTH: A METAPHOR

Returning to the topic of this conference, we might ask: How then does the figure of Ruth serve as a contemporary metaphor of the migrant? Actually, Ruth is not a true metaphor of migration, so much as she is an example of it. The story itself is quite straightforward in this regard. In line with so much of the biblical tradition, it is clear that the migrant is a metaphor for the true Israelite, and the Book of Ruth shows that Ruth herself is a metaphor for the agent of salvation. The correspondences that can be drawn between Ruth and contemporary migrants are not in themselves issues of theology. They simply serve to outline the profile of the migrant. In other words, like Ruth, today's migrants cross racial, ethnic, cultural, political, or social boundaries. As is the case with many migrants, Ruth's legal status was ambiguous. Though she identified herself as a 'stranger' or transient foreigner, she is portrayed in the story as a 'resident alien.'

In the biblical tradition, the migrant status itself is not the issue. Rather, it is the vulnerability that this status engenders that holds theological possibility. When Israel proclaimed, "My father was a wandering Aramean" (Dt 26:5), it was acknowledging that rootlessness was at the heart of its identity, and any security that it might gain would be given by a provident God. Even when the nation was established in the land, its migrant origins served to remind them that true stability is found only in God. Thus, the migrant is a metaphor of the true Israelite. Totally dependent upon the hospitality and generosity of others, she reminds them of God's graciousness to them.

While Ruth certainly functions in this vulnerable way in the book that bears her name, she plays an even more specific role. She is a linchpin between Israel's past and its future. It is through her that the lineage of Elimelech is restored; it is from her that the Davidic line is established. As stated earlier, if Naomi represents the remnant of Israel, then Ruth is the agent of its salvation. The theological implications of this are striking. First, Israel, initially in the person of Naomi and then in Boaz, had to welcome Ruth and accept her into the family before God could work through her for its salvation. This dimension of the metaphor is consistent with God's mysterious manner of dealing with the people of Israel throughout the entire biblical story. The degree of Israel's blessing by God was frequently determined by the measure of its openness to the dispossessed. Second, Ruth would not have been an agent of restoration had she not first committed herself to Naomi and then boldly presented herself to Boaz. This shows that God may well accomplish salvation through the agency of others, but those others are usually active, not passive, agents.

Returning to the question posed earlier, we might ask: How does the figure of Ruth serve as a contemporary metaphor? Before we can address this question, we must look at the character and function of metaphor generally. Most metaphors compare two significantly different objects in order to uncover the presence of a particular characteristic which is obvious in one of them but not in the other. Every metaphor consists of three elements: the vehicle; the referent; and the tenor. The vehicle is the member of the comparison to which the characteristic naturally belongs. The referent is the other member, about which the comparison is made. The tenor is the analogue, the actual characteristic of comparison. A look at the statement, 'The migrant is a metaphor for the true Israelite,' will illustrate this. Here, the vulnerability (the tenor of the metaphor) of the migrant (the vehicle) is attributed to the Israelite (the referent). The vulnerability disposes the person to trust in God. It is really this disposition of heart that constitutes the true Israelite.

The story of Ruth demonstrates that openness to and incorporation of the vulnerable migrant is the way to restoration or salvation. As shocking as such a concept may be to ethnocentric purists, it should not surprise those acquainted with the biblical tradition. Time and again we read how God chooses the weak of the world to confound the strong; the stone that was rejected becomes the cornerstone. God used Deborah and Jael to outwit the Canaanite soldiers, the frightened Gideon to save the Israelites from the Midianites, and the young David to defeat the giant Goliath. That the vulnerable should be agents of salvation demonstrates that the glory of victory belongs to God alone. To say it another way, the blessing of salvation comes from without (God) not from within (ourselves). The migrant Ruth is a metaphor of this theological tenet.

This examination has been primarily concerned with the world of the story itself (the world within the text). In order to appreciate various elements of that story, historical information has been provided (the world behind the text). However, the real interest in this passage is its value for today (the world in front of the text). Once the story has been analyzed, the reader is challenged by the power of the metaphor(s). Questions can be posed:

1)   In what ways might the metaphor of the vulnerable migrant reveal to us today the character of the true believer? This question forces us to consider questions about our own security and the lengths to which we might go to ensure it, the depth of own trust in God, our willingness to relinquish our autonomy and allow ourselves to be dependent upon others. A second question is related to the first.

2)   In what ways might the migrant act as an agent of our own salvation. This second question forces us to consider the biases that still enslave our minds and hearts (gender, race, ethnic origin, class, physical ability, etc.), our own greed and selfishness, our arrogance in the face of the need of others, etc.

The story of Ruth will be alive and revelatory for us if we allow its message to transform our minds and hearts. This is the function of hermeneutics, and it can only be accomplished by the reader(s).

REFERENCES

Bronner, L.L
1994   *From Eve to Esther: Rabbinic Reconstructions of Biblical Women* Louisville: Westminster/John Knox.

Bush, F.
1996   *Ruth/Esther* (Word Biblical Commentary, no.9). Dallas, TX: Word Books.

Farmer, K., and A. Robertson
1998   "The Book of Ruth," in The New Interpreter's Bible (Vol II). Nashville: Abingdon.

Gadamer, H.-G.
1975   *Truth and Method.* New York: Seabury.

Gallares, J. A.
1992   *Images of Faith: Spirituality of Women in the Old Testament* Maryknoll: Orbis.

Hamlin, E. and J. Hamlin
1996   Ruth (International Theological Library). Grand Rapids: Eerdmans.

"Interpretation of the Bible on the Life of the Church," *The Interpretation of the Bible in the Church*
1994   Pontifical Biblical Commission.

LaCocque, A.
1990   *The Feminine Unconventional: Four Subversive Figures in Israel's Tradition.* Minneapolis: Fortress.

Levine, A. and J. Levine
1998   "Ruth," in *Women's Bible Commentary* (expanded edition). Louisville: Westminster/John Knox.

Linafeld, T.
1999   *Ruth* (Berit Olam: Studies in Hebrew Narrative & Poetry). Collegeville: Liturgical Press.

Nielsen, K.
1997   *Ruth* (The Old Testament Library). Louisville: Westminister/John Knox.

Nowell, I.
1997   *Women in the Old Testament.* Collegeville, MN: Liturgical Press.

Pressler, C.
2002   *Joshua, Judges, and Ruth* (Westminister Bible Companion). Louisville: Westminster/John Knox.

Ricoeur, P.
1976   *Interpretation Theory: Discourse and the Surplus of Meaning* (8th printing). Forth Worth: Texas Christian University Press.

Sakenfeld, K. D.
1999   Ruth (Interpretation: A Bible Commentary for Teaching and Preaching). Louisville: John Knox.

Weems, R. J.
1988   *Just a Sister Away: A Womanist Vision of Women's Relationships in the Bible.* San Diego: LuraMedia.

Migration and the Social Doctrine of the Church

Michael A. Blume, SVD
Pontifical Council for the Pastoral Care of Migrants and Itinerant People

If there is an issue today that affects the dignity of individual persons and society, which cries out for justice, requires solidarity, and calls for coordinated action that promotes the common good at the national and international levels, it is that complex of experiences that we call *migration*. Dignity, solidarity, common good – these are three of the pillars of the Social Doctrine of the Church (SDC), which has a contribution to make to a world where often dramatic movements of people are realities of every day.

Dignity, solidarity, common good: these are not humanitarian ideals or political slogans. They are a synthesis of what Jesus Christ proclaimed as Good News and lived out even to death on the cross. Jesus Christ, who came that all might have life and have it in abundance (*see* Jn 10:10), "reveals man to himself and brings to light his most high calling" (GS 22). This life is inseparably linked to a complex of relationships: to other people and groups (social, cultural, and national), the earth and creation, and ultimately the Holy Trinity.

These relationships determine whether individuals or groups have a land and home they call their own or whether they have to get uprooted in the search for a dignified life or even for escape from persecution and death. Unfortunately these relations, instead of reflecting the gospel and making migration a chance for enriching contacts among cultures and civilizations, are usually disrupted, making migration a problem. That is why there is a social teaching of the Church that, among other issues, also addresses migration.

SOME SPECIFIC QUESTIONS ABOUT MIGRATION IN THE SDC

The SDC has evolved in response to concrete questions. The first "social encyclical," Leo XIII's *Rerum Novarum* (1891), for example, was a response to the nineteenth century industrial revolution and its disastrous effects on the lives of millions of workers. The same Pope "not only upheld vigorously the dignity and rights of the working man but also defended strenuously those emigrants who sought to earn their living abroad."[1] The great movements of people, which Vatican II considers a sign of our times (*see* GS 4–6), is one of the concerns that helped expand the breadth and depth of the SDC. So what are some important issues in migration that the SDC addresses?

Right to Emigrate, Including the Right to Seek Asylum

The first is the right to emigrate. "Among man's personal rights we must include his right to enter a country in which he hopes to be able to provide more fittingly for himself and his dependants" (PT 106). The SDC has repeated this on many occasions and in many ways.

What is the basis of this right? It is the dignity of the human person, created in the image of God, the God of life. The human person has a right to live in a way befitting the image of God, fulfilling his/her vocation through the God-given duty of labor (*see* Gen 3:19). Work is rooted in the human person who participates in God's creative act of being fruitful, multiplying, filling the earth, and subduing it (*see* LE 3). Labor is not only about survival but also about developing one's personality, family, culture, social and political life.

So every human person has an inalienable right to life and the activities needed to sustain and develop it.[2] Obviously when these rights are continually impeded, people have a right to go where they hope to start again to live humanly.

The protection of human dignity and life itself becomes evident in the more dramatic forms of migration, especially in the case of refugees. While there may be justified limitations on immigration, respect for the fundamental right of asylum can never be denied when life is seriously threatened in one's homeland (RCS 6; *see also* Appendix One).[3]

---

[1]Pius XII, Apostolic Constitution *Exul Familia*, (1952), Title 1.

[2]Specifically, these are the right to have one's own country, to live freely in one's own country, to live together with one's family, to have access to the goods necessary for a dignified life, to preserve and develop one's ethnic, cultural and linguistic heritage, to publicly profess one's religion, to be recognized and treated in all circumstances according to one's dignity as a human being. These rights are concretely employed in the concept of universal common good, which includes the whole family of peoples, beyond every nationalistic egoism. The right to emigrate must be considered in this context. The Church recognizes this right in every human person, in its dual aspect of the possibility to leave one's country and the possibility to enter another country to look for better conditions of life (Message for the Day of Migrants and Refugees 2001, n. 3. Henceforth Message, followed by the date).

[3]This point is supported by Article 31(1) of the 1951 Geneva Convention on the Status of Refugees, the foundation of modern asylum law, which recognizes that entering a country, even illegally, for the purpose of seeking asylum is not a crime.

IS THE RIGHT TO EMIGRATION ABSOLUTE? CAN IT EVER BE LIMITED?

The SDC also recognizes the right of states to control entry of persons and their borders. They have a right and duty to protect their sovereignty as well as the internal order that guarantees security, basic human rights and freedoms. Thus states can make practical decisions that control immigration.[4] It is, however important to remember the principle that *immigrants must always be treated with the respect due to the dignity of every human person*. In the matter of controlling the influx of immigrants, the consideration which should rightly be given to the common good should not ignore this principle. The challenge is to combine the welcome due to every human being, especially when in need, with a reckoning of what is necessary for both the local inhabitants and the new arrivals to live a dignified and peaceful life.[5]

This position is quite different from sometimes bitter debates on migration controls or even "zero migration." To be morally justified, however, a decision to restrict immigration has to take into account several issues, such as:

First, there is an obligation to search for the truth about migration, its benefits in society, and critically examine the notions circulating in the media, on talk shows, and in bars. Decisions based on insufficient information harm not only migrants but also those who make them. Only the search for the truth brings freedom, peace, and justice.

Second, limiting migration cannot be based on egoistical motives, *e.g.*, the hope of preserving a certain lifestyle while the greater part of humanity lives below the poverty line.[6] The discussion of the rights of states and their citizens cannot be separated from *solidarity*, which is also basic to Catholic social teaching. Solidarity is based on our common human origin and equality and is manifest in the quest for a more just social order. "Socioeconomic problems

---

[4]Certainly, the exercise of such a right [to enter another country] is to be regulated, because practicing it indiscriminately may do harm and be detrimental to the common good of the community that receives the migrant. Before the manifold interests that are interwoven side by side with the laws of the individual countries, it is necessary to have international norms that are capable of regulating everyone's rights, so as to prevent unilateral decisions that are harmful to the weakest (Message 2001, n. 3).

[5]Pope John Paul II, Message for the Celebration of the World Day of Peace 2001 n. 13.

[6]In this regard, in the Message for Migrants' Day of 1993, I called to mind that although it is true that highly developed countries are not always able to assimilate all those who emigrate, nonetheless, it should be pointed out that the criterion for determining the level that can be sustained cannot be based solely on protecting their own prosperity, while failing to take into consideration the needs of persons who are tragically forced to ask for hospitality (Message 2001, n. 3).

can be resolved only with the help of all the forms of solidarity," including at an international level, on which world peace in part depends.[7] There needs to be a globalization of solidarity.

Third, another pillar of CSD, the *universal destination of goods*, needs to enter any discussion of restrictions, for "the goods of creation are destined for the whole human race" (CCC 2402). "Peace and prosperity . . . belong to the whole human race: It is not possible to enjoy them in a proper and lasting way if they are achieved and maintained at the cost of other peoples and nations by violating their rights or excluding them from the sources of well-being" (CA 27).

Thus we can understand the exhortation of *Ecclesia in America*: "The Church in America must be a vigilant advocate, defending against any unjust restriction the natural right of individual persons to move freely within their own nation and from one nation to another" (n. 65).

So can states limit or control migration? The answer is "Yes, but . . ." It can be done when accompanied by two actions.

The first is a severe examination of conscience based on the three principles mentioned above. Here the Church is called to be prophetic in forming society's conscience and helping in its examination. It has a right and duty to speak on this issue, being "an expert in humanity" (SRS 7 and 41) that keeps recalling the basics about human dignity and a more just and fraternal social order.

The second is the need to put this discussion into the context of another pillar of the SDC, namely just international cooperation[8] on migration that serves the common good of both the receiving and the sending countries. Support of this cooperation is evident in the presence of the Holy See as an observer in the International Organization for Migration, a forum for discussion of "ordered migration," in the United Nations High Commissioner for Refugees as a full member and in other U.N. discussions on the international economic order as an observer, in the Pope's appeal for reduction or cancellation of international debt, and in the Holy See's support for the 1990 Convention on the Rights of All Migrant Workers and Their Families.[9]

---

[7]CCC 1941. *See also* the whole context in CCC 1939–1941.

[8]*See* CA 57, LE 23, LG 66; Message 1991 n. 2; 1995 nn. 2 and 4

[9]*See* discourse of Pope John Paul II to the Fourth World Congress on Migration (*L'Osservatore Romano*, 10 October 1998, p. 8) and his earlier statement in the 1980 Message: This huge flux includes hundreds and thousands of emigrant husbands and wives who are obliged to submit to forced separation, even if one may note with relief that the reuniting of spouses and families is becoming an increasingly strong concern and interest in legislation and international agreements aimed at regulating or disciplining migratory policy (n. 1).

Regarding borders in this part of the world, Church teaching raises serious questions about the morality of tolerating crossings and barriers that cause death and injury. To this can be added the abuse of migrants in transit by police or vigilantes and the dubious practice of interdiction at sea, whether in the Gulf of Mexico or on the Pacific, with the real possibility of *refoulement*.[10]

Migrants, with few exceptions, are people looking for a decent life. The reaction of states and law-enforcement officials to them as they carry out their duties must be appropriate and proportionate and respectful of human dignity.[11]

Families in Migration

The family is one of the great themes in the SDC, for it is "the *original cell of social life* . . . the natural society in which husband and wife are called to give themselves in love and in the gift of life" (CCC 2207). This gift of God is also deeply affected by many factors today, including migration, as Pope Pius XII knew very well fifty years ago when he published the Apostolic Constitution on migration, *Exul Familia*, a title already reflecting concern for the family in migration.

The Right to Migrate with the Family. Among the rights of the family is "the right to emigrate as a family in search of a better life" (FC 46). They do this to fulfill duties for "the physical, spiritual and religious welfare of the family" (MM 45). The need to seek a worthy livelihood constitutes a right to migrate, and that is all the more so when migration is forced.

---

[10]The principle of *non-refoulement* is sacred in international refugee law and is violated by policies and actions that limit access to asylum procedures or return people to places where they face persecution or torture. *See* RCS n. 14; 1951 Geneva Convention, Article 33.

[11]Those responsible would do well to reflect on what the Pope recently said about legitimate defense against terrorism and realize that they are not dealing with terrorists:

There exists therefore a right to defend oneself against terrorism, a right which, as always, must be exercised with respect for moral and legal limits in the choice of ends and means. The guilty must be correctly identified, since criminal culpability is always personal and cannot be extended to the nation, ethnic group or religion to which the terrorists may belong. International cooperation in the fight against terrorist activities must also include a courageous and resolute political, diplomatic and economic commitment to relieving situations of oppression and marginalization which facilitate the designs of terrorists. The recruitment of terrorists in fact is easier in situations where rights are trampled upon and injustices tolerated over a long period of time. (Pope John Paul II, "Message for the World Day of Peace 2002," n. 5.)

If such precautions are to be exercised in dealing with terrorists, what should be done in the case of people who are looking for a job?

The right to migrate includes the right to be with one's family.[12] The human person in his/her primary relations takes precedence over political considerations as well as production and profit. That leads John Paul II to protest against "systems that perpetuate the forced separation of spouses"[13] or of parents from children:

> The Church repeats with insistence that . . . the protection of families, and particularly of those burdened by further difficulties of being migrants and refugees, constitutes an indispensable priority . . . 'What God has joined together, let no one separate' sounds like an implicit condemnation for a society that grants economic advantage to the detriment of moral values.[14]

These are quotations from sixteen years ago. They do not seem to have lost any of their urgency.

When we consider the normal obligations of society towards the family and its development as well as the rights of the family itself (*see* FC 46), it is reasonable to also draw the conclusion that there is a *right not to migrate* or, put positively, "the primary right of man to live in one's homeland."[15] Migration so often means this right is not respected, as individuals and families are unable to fulfill their basic obligations to themselves and their children in a particular society.

Rights of Immigrant Families in their Country of Arrival. The Church's pastoral outreach brings it face to face with the need to defend the value of the family, its freedom of movement and decision-making, its right to educate children and bring them up "in accordance with the family's own traditions and religious and cultural values" and the other rights of the Charter of Rights of the

---

[12]GS 66 has a clear statement on this that builds on earlier teachings of John XXIII and Pius XII: "All the people . . . must treat them [migrants] not as mere tools of production but as persons, and must help them to bring their families to live with them."

[13]"The Serious, Sorrowful and Complex Conditions of Families involved in the Difficult Situation of Emigration" (Message 1986). The 1993 Message, "Problems of the Migrant Family," takes similar positions as a contribution to the International Year of the Family. His 1980 Message also deals with migrant families, "An ever more Adequate and Enlightened Pastoral Care of Families in Emigration."

[14]Message 1986.

[15]Pope John Paul II, Message to the Fourth World Congress on the Pastoral Care of Migrants and Refugees, n. 2.

Family (*see* Appendix One). The SDC also insists that states have the obligation to assure to immigrant families what it guarantees to its own citizens.[16] Denouncing abuse of these rights, she asserts that the family has preference in cases of conflict between society and family. There should be no discrimination against migrant families.

The Christian communities in host countries are called to solidarity and burden sharing with migrant families. Papal documents appeal to them to accept immigrants so that no one is without a family in this world. The church should be that family, especially for the heavily burdened. In the Church no one is a stranger.

Migrants in their New Home

Respect for their Culture. This brief section briefly touches the complex area of families and individuals being inserted into a new society, new culture, and new experience of being Church. The issues are even more urgent since globalization includes strong tendencies towards the "homogenization" of cultures, "*the slavish conformity of cultures*, or at least of key aspects of them, to cultural models deriving from the Western world" and "*the aggressive claims of some cultures against others.*"[17] The SDC requires that the "cultural practices which immigrants bring with them should be respected and accepted, as long as they do not contravene either the universal ethical values inherent in the natural law or fundamental human rights."[18]

In this context it is not surprising to recall themes of earlier Messages for the Day of Migrants and Refugees. "Respect and Increase the Cultural Identity of Migrants" is the theme of the 1981 Message. Culture is closely linked with migrants' identity, both personal and spiritual, as well as with their faith. It also gives them something to fall back on as they meet a new and alien society, often dominated by very secularized attitudes and approaches.

---

[16] "Taking into account their particular needs, the state's task is to ensure that immigrant families do not lack what it ordinarily guarantees its own citizens. In particular, it is the state's duty to protect them from any attempt at marginalization or racism, promoting a culture of convinced and active solidarity. For this purpose it provides the most appropriate and concrete measures for their acceptance, together with those social services likely to foster for them too, a peaceful life and a development that respects their human dignity" (Message 1994).

[17] Pope John Paul II, Message for the Celebration of the World Day of Peace 2001 n. 10, 9, and n. 8.

[18] *ibid.* n. 13

The Church has a special role in this area. The experience is that assuring migrants feel at home in a local church[19] is the first step to "integration" into it. Feeling at home necessarily means being themselves in "language, liturgy, spirituality, particular traditions." That is the path to the kind of "ecclesial integration, which enriches the Church of God and which is the fruit of the dynamic realism of the Incarnation of the Son of God."[20] When not forced ahead nor held back, migrants make their own contribution to the catholicity of the church, *i.e.*, that "complete openness to the other, a readiness to share and to live in the same ecclesial communion."[21] The teaching and experience of the Church here can be a lesson to civil societies that struggle with their multi-cultural challenges.

Migrants and Human Labor. "Human work is a key, probably the essential key, to the whole social question,"[22] states John Paul II in the Encyclical *Laborem Exercens*. Since migration is so often in search of work, it is closely linked with labor as one of the first themes of the SDC, as I mentioned earlier.

The SDC has great concerns for migrant workers, particularly for the serious problems they face: discrimination and xenophobia,[23] deception regarding contracts or conditions of work, treatment as tools and not persons, dangerous occupations (the three D's: dirty, dangerous, demanding), long working hours, pay lower than that of citizens for the same job,[24] poor housing or none, and non-integration into social life.[25] The message of Church documents and teaching to governments and others responsible for such situations is clear: they must protect all workers from these evils, even if they are migrants and not citizens, and work together with all nations to deal with labor migration at its roots, which means seeking a just global economic

---

[19]The 1982 Message, "Specific Church Presence in the Structures and Organs for the Pastoral Care of Migration," concentrates on the specific purpose of ecclesial structures and organisms for the pastoral care of emigrants. Regarding the development of pastoral approaches that respect and promote the languages and cultures and ecclesial traditions of migrants, *see also* CCL 787 §1, 769, 518, and 214.

[20]"The Right of Believing Migrants to Free Integration into the Church," Message 1986. *See also* the 1981 Message, "Respect and Increase the Cultural Identity of Migrants."

[21]Message 1986.

[22]LE 3.

[23]"The Condition of Migrants as a Challenge to the Vocation of the Christian" (Message 1983).

[24]*See* CA 8, which refers immediately to the exploitation of women and children, some of whom are migrants.

[25]*See* GS 66 and PP 69.

order.[26] Local churches have a special call to solidarity with migrant workers and to formation of public opinion to promote justice for them.[27]

Since attitudes towards migrant workers often reveal a thinly veiled racism, this issue also needs to be faced. The Holy See has made its position on racism and xenophobia clear many times.[28] Its participation in the World Conference Against Racism (Durban, September 2001) also included consenting to the propositions in its Declaration and Program of Action, which has some forty points dealing with the issue. These merit our attention for developing our programs of education and pastoral care.

Legal or Illegal, Documented or Not

Undocumented or irregular migration is an issue that arouses many emotions. Without going into details of a complex question, I simply want to state the principles on which the SDC operates regarding this question.

But first a preliminary remark: there are *no illegal migrants*, for migrants are persons, and no person is illegal. Persons can engage in illegal movements but their Creator does not do illegal things. There is a need to change language that already carries with it a judgement. I believe Church documents are already correcting their previous language as we have in the Message of 2000, which speaks of "'clandestine,' men and women in illegal situations." *Ecclesia in America* n. 65 calls for attention "to the rights of migrants and their families and to respect for their human dignity, even in cases of non-legal immigration." This is only respect for the truth. Illegality is not necessarily a result of personal bad will. Judgement needs to be suspended when we speak about people, particularly at this moment when the tendency to judge is very strong. The dignity of a person in an irregular situation does not expire as a visa or a passport does.

Here are its most important points on this issue:[29]

1)   While illegal immigration has to be prevented, the criminal activities that exploit immigrants must also be combated. In the long term there

---

[26]*See* CA 52.

[27]"Specific Church Presence in the Structure and Organs for the Pastoral Care of Migrations" (Message 1982).

[28]*See* the Pontifical Council for Justice and Peace, *The Church and Racism: Towards a More Fraternal Society* (Vatican City 2001).

[29]This section is based on the 1995 Message.

has to be international cooperation which aims to foster political stability and to address the causes of irregular migration.

2) The Church respects civil law, including migration law, but also advocates that it be just.

3) Anti-immigrant propaganda can infect the Christian community, which has to be helped to understand why some migrants act illegally.

4) Migrants in such situations need to be helped to live and, when possible, to regularize their status. If a the community gives shelter to migrants in irregular situations, the aim is not "civil disobedience" but the defense of people who have not been properly treated before the law or whose cases merit review.

5) When no solution is foreseen, these migrants can sometimes be helped to be accepted in another country. If that fails, they need to be assisted to return in dignity and safety to their country of origin.

6) The Church is called to advocate with governments for more adequate legislation, in particular for the case of *de facto* refugees who cannot return home without risking their lives.

7) The Church is the place where these immigrants are "recognized and accepted as brothers and sisters. It is the task of the various dioceses actively to ensure that these people, who are obliged to live outside the safety net of civil society, may find a sense of brotherhood in the Christian community" (n. 5).

One final point is that there are situations where there is no legal way to be regularized or to return home. Solidarity calls for finding a way out of such situations. In 1998, as one example, Pope John Paul II, during the Fourth World Congress for Migration, spoke about his Jubilee year plea for condoning or reducing international debt. He then appealed for something analogous for migrants: a significant gesture "through which reconciliation, a dimension proper to the Jubilee, would find expression in the form of an amnesty [in Italian, *sanatoria*] for a wide range of those immigrants who, more than the others, suffer the drama of precariousness and uncertainty, that is, those who are illegal."[30] It is notable that some episcopal conferences have taken up that call in their respective countries.

[30]Pope John Paul II, Message to the Fourth World Congress on the Pastoral Care of Migrants and Refugees, n. 2.

Replacement Migration

In March 2000 the United Nations Population Division, Department of Economic and Social Affairs, published *Replacement Migration: Is it a Solution to Declining and Aging Populations?*[31] Its basic message is that the average age of the populations in developed countries will increase significantly in the next fifty years, and that the population of working age people will decline while those of retirement age will increase. In some countries the decrease of the population of its citizens is irreversible in the medium term. One solution is increasing migration to these countries so that industries, services, social welfare, etc. can continue. The report offers different hypotheses for how this might happen, but the increase in migration, even in countries where some politicians dream of "zero migration," is almost inevitable. In one hypothesis, just to give an example, the United States would need to accept more than eleven million a year as compared to the less than one million a year at present.

Last November, I attended a major meeting of the International Organization for Migration (IOM) in Geneva, at which this report was presented by its main author. Surprisingly, there was very little negative reaction. Even some European Union countries, which are most affected by this report, recognized its importance.

Of the many issues raised in the report, I want to focus on a migration issue, the so-called "brain drain." The fact is that developed countries are already recruiting talent outside their borders. The United States, for example, recently made an exception to its 1996 immigration law and authorized issuing 600,000 visas to information technology workers, most of whom come from India. The search for foreign talent sometimes even becomes a "hunt for brains," not a brain drain. That raises questions of justice: does anyone have the right to buy talent from developing countries simply on the basis of having money to do this? Is it right to attract people who have been educated and raised in their homelands at much cost to their own social and educational services to serve the interests of businesses in other countries?

This is a serious moral question that also affects the *personal capital* available in many countries. A recent statement of the U.S. Bishops Conference rais-

---

[31]Population Division, Department of Economic and Social Affairs, U.N. Secretariat, *Replacement Migration: Is it a Solution to Declining and Aging Populations?* (New York, 21 March 2000). Also available at www.un.org/esa/population/unpop.htm.

es the issue: "While we welcome all the new immigrants and recognize that our Church, like the United States as a whole, has come to depend upon the many talents and profound energy of newcomers, we must also remind our government that the emigration of talented and trained individuals from poorer countries represents a profound loss to those countries."[32]

In terms of SDC, the solution needs to be elaborated on the basis of solidarity, the universal destination of the goods of the earth, international common good, and the priority of persons over work and possessions. This needs to be proclaimed in its education and formation programs and advocacy in order to form the conscience of individuals and nations as a whole in facing this issue. During the IOM meeting of last November, it was heartening to hear many developed countries affirm the need for international agreements on migration to assure that both the countries of origin and those of destination share the benefits of migration. It is still to be seen how noble discourses of international conferences are translated into action over the next years. I believe that this is a point well worth monitoring.

SOME FINAL OBSERVATIONS ON THE SDC ON MIGRATION

It should not surprise us, then, that there is a broad convergence of the SDC on migration with many people of good will who are not particularly religious. That is the result of right reason about the human person and can lead to a rich dialogue between Christian and humanitarian thinkers. I would add, however, that Christian faith, among other things, protects the results of right reason and even goes beyond it. For example, to the right of leaving one's country, the SDC adds the "right to enter a country in which he hopes to be able to provide fittingly for himself and his dependents" (PT 106).

Faith, furthermore, protects justice, human dignity and solidarity from being hijacked by ideologies and politics that have their own agendas. Thus, the SDC considers human rights as rooted in the person. That is radically different from dominating currents of thought today, where rights are conceived more in terms of what public opinion believes or law recognizes than in reference to anything transcendent. The fact remains that when the Creator is

---

[32]U.S. Catholic Bishops, *Welcoming the Stranger Among Us: Unity in Diversity* (Washington DC, USCC, 2000) p. 8.

denied or ignored, the creature is also easily sacrificed. Migrants and refugees, for example, can be easily pushed aside by "policy decisions" and language that deprive them of their individual human dignity.

What all the discussion on the SDC and migration tries to do is put into action the consequences of our faith, based on the Word of God and proclaimed in the scriptures. "You shall not oppress a resident alien; you know the heart of an alien, for you were aliens in the land of Egypt" (Ex 23:9). Every generation had to learn this lesson, rooted in the collective history of God's people. And so, in consequence, "When an alien resides with you in your land, you shall not oppress the alien. The alien who resides with you shall be to you as the citizen among you; you shall love the alien as yourself, for you were aliens in the land of Egypt: I am the LORD your God" (Lev 19:33). This alien, loved by God, is a kind of "sacrament" of the Beloved Son: "I was a stranger, and you welcomed me" (Mt 25:35). Recalling God's love in Christ's sacrifice, St. John reminds us: "Beloved, since God loved us so much, we also ought to love one another" (1 John 4:11). Our situation of being aliens, estranged from God by our sin and separation from the Covenent is changed in the redeeming act of Jesus in His death and resurrection: "So then you are no longer strangers and aliens, but you are citizens with the saints and also members of the household of God" (Eph 4:19). The SDC helps us live out that reality as individuals and a community of believers in Christ in the world of human mobility.

ABBREVIATIONS

CA John Paul II, *Centesimus Annus*, the 100th Anniversary of *Rerum Novarum*, 1991

CCC *Catechism of the Catholic Church*

CCL Code of Canon Law

FC John Paul II, *Familiaris Consortio*, Apostolic Exhortation on the Role of the Family in the Modern World (1981)

GS Vatican Council II, *Gaudium et Spes*, Pastoral Constitution on the Church in the Modern World, 1965

LE John Paul II, *Laborem Exercens*, On Human Labor, 1981

LG Vatican Council II, *Lumen Gentium*, Dogmatic Constitution on the Church, 1964

MM John XXIII, *Mater et Magistra*, Mother and Teacher, 1961

PP Paul VI, *Populorum Progressio*, On the Progress of Peoples, 1967

PT John XXIII, *Pacem in Terris*, Peace on Earth, 1963

RCS Pontifical Council for the Pastoral Care of Migrants and Itinerant People and Pontifical Council "Cor Unum," *Refugees: A Challenge to Solidarity* (Vatican City 1992)

SRS John Paul II, *Sollicitudo Rei Socialis*, The Social Concern of the Church, 1987

APPENDIX
CHARTER OF THE RIGHTS OF THE FAMILY

Presented by the Holy See to all persons, institutions and authorities concerned with the mission of the family in today's world October 22, 1983

Article 12

The families of migrants have the right to the same protection as that accorded other families.

a) The families of immigrants have the right to respect for their own culture and to receive support and assistance towards their integration into the community to which they contribute.

b) Emigrant workers have the right to see their family united as soon as possible.

c) Refugees have the right to the assistance of public authorities and International Organizations in facilitating the reunion of their families.

The Human Rights of Migrants: A Pastoral Challenge

Graziano Battistella, c.s.
Scalabrini International Migration Institute

Human rights have acquired a prominent place in political parlance. They constitute a cornerstone of the activity of the United Nations, particularly through standard-setting and programs of action following the many international conferences; they are a mandatory reference in addresses by world leaders; they are included in the mission statements of countless NGOs; and no government can afford being accused of violating them. Eli Wiesel (1999) has summarized it well: "The defense of human rights has, in the last fifty years, become a kind of worldwide secular religion."

At the same time, an assessment of the progress achieved in the respect of human rights yields mixed results. Tragedies erupting with disheartening regularity around the world testify to unsettled problems and to violence still considered as a valued currency to face those problems. The attempt to insert human rights in a variety of international activities, such as peace, development, and the environment has largely remained an advancement in perspectives, but did not yield concrete results. The need for more achievements and more creativity has spurred the UN initiative to "mainstream human rights." This has led to cooperative efforts among UN agencies, such as the Office of the High Commissioner for Human Rights (OHCHR) and the United Nations Development Program (UNDP).

The link between human rights and development was articulated in the 1986 Declaration on the Right to Development ("The right to development is an inalienable human right"), and it was re-expressed at the 1993 Vienna Conference on human rights and in the mandate to the High Commissioner for Human Rights. UNDP then made the realization of human rights an integral part of its agenda on sustainable human development, including eradication of poverty. This led to the 1998 Oslo Symposium on Human Development and Human Rights and to the Human Development Report 2000, which "clearly underlines the fact that human rights are not, as has sometimes been argued, a reward of development. Rather, they are critical to achieving it" (UNDP,

2000:iii). The expression is not to be read with the traditional division between rights and the debate on which rights come first in mind, but as the subordination of economic structures to the rights of the person.

In the continuous refinement of concepts related to the advancement of recognition and protection of human rights – and inadequate results confirming that such recognition and protection have not been achieved – the situation of migrants stands out with a dissonant tone. The reluctance of countries to ratify international conventions related to migration speaks of resistance to approaching migration from a human rights perspective. This not only diminishes the level of protection accorded to migrants but also impoverishes the human dimension of migration. Consequently, initiatives in favor of the recognition and protection of the human rights of migrants need to be fostered.

From a Christian perspective, such initiatives occupy a central role in the pastoral care of migrants. However, how should such role be understood in reference to other aspects of the pastoral care of migrants? What is the approach of the Church to human rights in general? What is the situation of migration in reference to human rights?

To articulate the main argument and answer those questions, this paper will examine first the current situation in the formulation and support of the human rights of migrants; it will then look at the approach of the Church to human rights; and finally to the protection of the human rights of migrants as pastoral care.

THE LARGER CONTEXT

For a proper perspective on the issue under discussion it is necessary to insert migration within the larger context. Such context is characterized by uneven development among nations, which determines the macro conditions behind migration flows, the type and direction of flows, the vulnerability of migrants and the limited recognition of their human rights. The economic and social trends which have occurred in the past twenty years, conveniently summarized in the term 'globalization,' have exacerbated migrants' vulnerability, without providing effective protection.

International migration, in its various forms – migration for settlement, labor migration, migration of highly skilled workers, foreign students, refugees, asylum seekers and environmental migrants – almost doubled from

84 million in 1975 to the estimated 150 million in 2000 (IOM, 2000). Many more countries have become origins of migration flows, and movements in various directions have been added to the traditional south-north direction of flows, so that it can be said that migration is now a global phenomenon. Because of the role it plays in economies of countries of origin and destination and because of the dynamics which sustain migratory movements, migration has also become a structural component of societies, a variable in the development projects of governments, families and individuals. Results, however, do not necessarily correspond to projects.

The study of migration determinants has produced various competing theories. In addition to the motivation generated by wage differentials between countries of origin and countries of destination, researchers have analyzed the role of the family in its desire to minimize risks, the responses to relative deprivation, the attraction of secondary labor markets created by upward social mobility, the impact of linkages established through colonialism and investments, the exchanges resulting from a systemic approach, and the role of social networks. The results have been that no single theory is sufficient to explain the determinants of migration, which cannot be reduced to automatic movements as a result of push and pull factors (Massey *et al.*, 1998).

Migration theories, however, largely influenced by political economy, have dedicated little attention to human rights. Relegated to the concern of legal experts or activists, human rights have been examined in regard to the protection of migrants. However, echoing the human rights mainstreaming initiative at the United Nations, we suggest injecting a human rights approach in the analysis of the origin of migration. This can be done as a corollary of the linkage between human rights and development.

Such a link was established in the Declaration on the Right to Development, adopted by the General Assembly in 1986,[1] which calls the right to development an inalienable human right, and was reaffirmed in the 1993 Vienna Declaration and Program of Action, which makes it an integral part of fundamental human rights. The discussion at the Oslo Symposium concluded that "human development and human rights are directly related, consistent and mutually reinforcing approaches." Their relationship is circular, as "the achievement of each is linked to the achievement of the other." They differ in

---

[1]GA Resolution 41/128 of 4 December 1986.

the means and instruments, as the human rights approach focuses on norms and standards, while the human development approach focuses on poverty eradication, investing in human capabilities, and equitable economic growth.[2]

The relationship between migration and development has received wide attention, without reaching satisfactory conclusions (Papademetriou and Martin, 1991). While some emphasize the contribution that migration brings to both countries of origin and destination, others underscore the dependence that it creates and the additional migratory movement it generates. However, it is indubitable that migration is a function of development, as it originates as a result of displacement created during the development process and it delivers benefits for the development of both individuals and countries, if taking place under sound conditions. Therefore it can be seen as a component of the right to development, and as an instrument of development as it contributes to eradicate poverty and acquire human capabilities. At the same time, migration exposes the insufficient fulfillment of the right to development in the country where it originates from, and the consequent national and international responsibilities for it.

This approach leads to the affirmation of the right to migrate not only in the sense of the right to leave one's country and return to it, but also as part of the right to development. However, as development is such only if it occurs within the fulfillment of human rights, so migration can lead to development only if the human rights of migrants are recognized and protected. This requires substituting the economic approach, which is the prevalent and often exclusive criterion guiding migration policies, in favor of the human rights approach, for a broader and more humane management of migration.

The market approach, with its alleged "invisible hand" guiding it, leads to the exploitation of migrant labor as cheap and disposable; ultimately, it leads to the negation of the human rights of migrants. The human rights approach, instead, recognizes that migrants are more than just factors of production and recognizes that they can contribute to society; ultimately, it leads to human empowerment.

THE VULNERABILITY OF MIGRANTS

Human rights standards formulated in the various human rights instruments

[2]http://www.undp.org/hdro/Oslorep2.html

are available to migrants, except when explicit limitations are provided for. Nevertheless, migrants have become the object of special concern because they have been recognized as a category of persons rendered vulnerable. The vulnerability of migrants to abuse and exploitation is exemplified in countless cases touching the entire migration process.

At the recruitment stage, the desire, sometimes the urge, for a job overseas renders migrants vulnerable to exploitation by employment agencies. To ensure deployment, overseas migrants are led to accept substandard conditions, low salaries, and often sign contracts without the full knowledge of stipulations. Sometimes they agree to cooperate in obtaining forged documents to overcome specific regulations, such as age limits or entry restrictions. They are led to trust intermediaries who promise access to a country of immigration and to a job, and then be abandoned or inserted in a different occupation, perhaps of an illegal nature. Migrants are often charged exorbitant fees, exceeding what is stipulated in regulations, which they might pay with borrowed money. Loans create a situation of bondage, pushing migrants to accept exploitative arrangements.

Migrants are normally employed in low-skill occupations and encounter discrimination in access to employment. Migrant workers are tied to a specific job or a specific employer, at least for a period of time, without alternatives. They have limited or no contractual power to negotiate wages and working conditions. In most cases, collective bargaining is not possible. Retention or delay of wages is not infrequent. Insurance to cover for work accidents is not universally available and medical insurance is not provided.

Migrants encounter difficulties related to their stay in the country of immigration. Such difficulties derive from discrimination in access to housing, to education and to employment opportunities. Frequently migrants are subject to xenophobic and racist attacks. Migrant workers are severely hampered in their possibility to integrate by the strictly temporary nature of their stay. In some cases, women have to undergo pregnancy tests periodically. Insufficient knowledge of language and culture weakens their possibilities to obtain access to courts and seek redress for torts or abuse. Often they are not allowed to associate or to form organizations and need to rely on civil society in countries of immigration.

Some categories of migrants, like women and children, are rendered even more vulnerable. Migrant women are involved in occupations, such as domestic work, which are unregulated in most countries and are left to the discretion of the employer. Women and children are mostly the ones falling victim to trafficking. Unauthorized migrants are particularly vulnerable, as people take advantage of their fear of repatriation and impose exploitative conditions on them.

The precarious condition of migrants is expressed also in the insecurity of stay. Labor migration is utilized because of the flexibility it allows in the labor market. In times of crisis, governments regularly aim at diminishing the foreign workforce. During repatriation campaigns, the lack of due process and the possibility of arbitrary arrest are exacerbated.

The various aspects in which migrants are rendered vulnerable in the migration process have led the UN Working Group of Intergovernmental Experts on the Human Rights of Migrants to term their situation as "structural vulnerability."[3] It is essentially determined by the fact that migrants, because of their status, are in a lower position compared to nationals in regard to power and, because of cultural factors, they see violations of their rights go unpunished. "'Impunity' here is understood as the absence of economic, social or political costs for the violator of the human rights of a migrant."[4] Specific attention must be devoted to vulnerability resulting from the non-integration of migrants. In the case of migrant workers, who are institutionally discouraged from integrating, particularly through the prohibition to be joined by their families, vulnerability is enshrined in their status.

The vulnerability inherent to migrants' conditions justifies a specific concern for the protection of their human rights. At the same time, it must be emphasized that such vulnerability is not inherent in the persons who migrate, but in the economic, social and political organization of migration. The recognition and respect of their human rights create the premises for overcoming such vulnerability and eliminating the obstacles to full protection. In the words of the Special Rapporteur on the Human Rights of Migrants "the empowering function of human rights protection plays a fundamental role" to transcend vulnerability.[5]

THE HUMAN RIGHTS OF MIGRANTS

International Instruments

As human rights are universal, they are also applicable to migrants, who can-

---

[3]Report E/CN.4/AC.46/1998/5, paragraph 28.
[4]Ibidem, paragraph 30.
[5]Report E/CN.4/2000/82, paragraph 74.

not be discriminated against on the basis of nationality, except when explicitly provided for. The first reference to rights applicable to migrants must be made to the Universal Declaration on Human Rights (UDHR) and the two covenants: the International Covenant on Civil and Political Rights (ICCPR) and the International Covenant on Social, Economic and Cultural Rights (ICSECR). In addition to civil liberties and guarantees, the UDHR articles most specific to the migrant situation are art. 13 on the freedom of movement, art. 14 on the right to seek asylum, and art. 16 on the protection of the family as the fundamental group unit of society.

The same provisions become more specific in the ICCPR. Discrimination based on national origin is forbidden by art. 2, and, therefore, all rights in the covenant are applicable to all individuals in the territory of a state. Art. 12 concerns the right to leave any state and return to it. It provides the foundation for the right to migrate, which does not imply the right to enter another country, as it remains the sovereign right of a country to decide on admission of non-nationals. However, if a state is not obliged to admit particular individuals or categories of people, except in the case of asylees already in its territory, it has a general duty to admit foreigners to its territory. The same article limits the measures a state of origin can impose on the exit of nationals.

Art. 13 concerns protection against expulsion: it can be done only through a decision reached in accordance with law and after the alien is allowed to submit the reasons against it, except in situations concerning national security.

Social, economic and cultural rights are spelled out in the ICSECR. Among them are the right to work (art. 6), the right to equality of remuneration, equal opportunity in employment and safe and healthy working conditions (art. 7), the right to form and join trade unions and to strike (art. 8), and the right to education (art. 13). The traditional discussion on the progressive nature of these rights, which require resources to be implemented (art. 2), and which led people to consider them as second-generation rights, is increasingly considered outdated. The indivisibility of human rights entails that all obstacles to their attainment must be eliminated.

Although discrimination based on nationality is generally not admitted, it is contemplated in some cases. Political rights are reserved to citizens. Currently, art. 2(3) of ICSECR allows for some discrimination against non-nationals in regard to economic rights, but only to developing countries (Cholewinski, 1999). Even the International Convention on the Elimination of All Forms of Racial Discrimination allows for differential treatment between citizens and noncitizens, but not against any particular nationality.

Also particularly relevant for our subject are the Convention on the Elimination of All Forms of Discrimination Against Women (CEDAW) and the Convention on the Rights of the Child, which has obtained the highest number of ratifications (191). Concern for the implementation of CEDAW has led to specific attention on the issue of violence against women and the appointment in 1994 of a Special Rapporteur on this issue. Violence against migrant women was the specific concern of a UN Expert Group Meeting, held in Manila in 1996, particularly to establish indicators to better know the extent of the phenomenon (Shah, 1997).

In the Convention on the Rights of the Child, art. 10, concerning the reunification of children with the family, is particularly relevant as it urges states to deal with family reunification in a positive, humane and expeditious manner. The article was utilized to strengthen the language of the Plan of Action of the 1994 Cairo Conference on the family reunification of migrants in general.

The most explicit instrument for the protection of the human rights of migrants is the International Convention on the Protection of the Rights of All Migrant Workers and Members of Their Families (MWC), adopted on December 18, 1990. The initial objective of the convention was to ensure protection to unauthorized migrant workers. This explains the drafting of the convention by the United Nations rather than ILO. In fact, ILO had already adopted two conventions related to migrants: the Migrant for Employment Convention of 1949 (No. 97) and the Migrant Workers Convention of 1975 (No. 143). The first deals mostly with issues of recruitment and working conditions of migrants and establishes the principle of equality of treatment between migrants and nationals. The second was originated by the concern for unauthorized migration, which in the 1970s was becoming an issue. While obliging State Parties to take all necessary measures to eliminate unauthorized migration, it also provides for the protection of the human rights of migrants. However, such protection is granted not by formulating the human rights of migrants, but simply by pointing to the appropriate existing human rights instruments (art. 8).

The ILO approach was deemed insufficient for two reasons: first, ILO instruments were mostly dealing with migrants as workers and therefore did not emphasize the human rights perspective; second, ILO conventions were poorly ratified (Convention 97 is ratified by 41 countries and Convention 143 by 18 countries). In addition, the complexity of migration required extending protection to other categories of migrants.

The MWC provides protection to the human rights of all migrants, including unauthorized migrants, by explicitly formulating them in Part III. Those rights can be grouped in four categories: personal rights; legal guarantees; civil liberties; and social, cultural and economic rights. Political rights are not included in this part as they belong to the citizen, not to the migrant, let alone the unauthorized migrant.

The formulation of the human rights of migrants follows in most cases the language utilized in the covenants. In fact, articles are mostly taken verbatim from the ICCPR and in some cases from the ICSECR. In this sense there is little new ground broken. Rights are sometimes tailored to the migrant situation, as in the case of the right to communicate with consular or diplomatic authorities, or to be assisted by an interpreter in proceedings before court, if necessary without cost (art. 16). In case of detention, migrants should be held separately from convicted persons or persons detained pending trial. Failure to fulfill an obligation arising from the working contract should not lead to loss of residence or work permit or to expulsion (art. 17).

Some real improvements have been made on the issue of expulsion, which must be dealt with on an individual basis, but also excludes simultaneous expulsion of many individuals (art. 22). Equality of treatment with nationals in regard to remuneration, conditions of work and employment – enshrined in the ILO conventions – is extended to unauthorized migrants (art. 25). The right of access to education on the basis of equivalence with nationals is applicable also to children of irregular migrant workers (art. 29) and measures are provided to facilitate integration while respecting the culture of the country of origin.

Although not providing substantial improvements in the standards applicable to migrants, the MWC is very relevant for several reasons: it explicitly affirms the human rights of all migrants, including unauthorized migrants; it extends protection to categories of migrants previously left out; and it constitutes a general framework for an international management of migration. What the MWC lacks in efficacy (typically the convention is supervised by a committee to examine state reports on the implementation of the convention and, optionally, to accept state and individual claims), it can provide as an educational tool to be used in furthering the cause of migrant workers.

The major drawback in regard to the MWC is that it is not in force, as it lacks the necessary number of ratifications. Twenty ratifications are needed, while at the end of 2001, eleven years after adoption, only seventeen countries have ratified it (Table 1). In addition, it is not difficult to foresee that, when in force, it will have limited effectiveness. Only State Parties to the convention are bound by it and all of them are prevalently states of origin of migration. The major countries of destination do not intend to ratify the convention. Among the reasons put forward for not ratifying it was that it provided too much protection to unauthorized migrants, it required too complex an administrative mechanism to implement it, or that migration was not an area in which states wanted an international approach (Hune and Niessen, 1994; UN). In fact, the convention has suffered from the changing climate in regard to migration from the days when the drafting process started in the early 1980s to the present, when migration is perceived as a vehicle for importing terrorists. In addition to technical difficulties, because of new language introduced in human rights standards, the MWC has suffered also from lack of publicity and drive from powerful states (Cholewinski, 1997). Although the reluctance of countries to ratify the MWC reveals in clear terms the lack of international resolve to cooperate in the protection of migrants, it should not be forgotten that migrants remain covered by the other human rights instruments presented above.

The most recent instruments related to the protection of migrants are the two protocols to the United Nations Convention against Transnational Organized Crime. The Protocol to Prevent, Suppress and Punish Trafficking in Persons, especially Women and Children requires that some form of use of force, coercion, abduction, fraud, deception for the purpose of exploitation (for prostitution, or forced labor, or slavery or other) is involved to speak of trafficking.

The consent of the victim is immaterial. The Protocol Against the Smuggling of Migrants by Land, Sea and Air identifies smuggling as the procurement of illegal entry for migrants to obtain financial or material benefit. As the instruments aim at suppressing criminality, the impression could be derived that the human rights approach is shunned in favor of a police approach. However, it should be noted that in both instruments migrants are not criminally liable; rather, they are victims in need of protection.

Regional Instruments

In addition to human rights instruments of international validity, migrants can also appeal to regional human rights instruments. Among them are the 1950 European Convention for the Protection of Human Rights, the 1967 American Convention on the Protection of Human Rights, and the 1981 African Charter on Human and Peoples' Rights.

The Inter-American Human Rights System, which developed after the convention entered into force in 1978, did not have anything specific on the human rights of migrants. In 1996 the Organization of American States' General Assembly adopted a resolution to create a Special Rapporteurship on Migrant Workers and Members of Their Families, which called attention to the most common forms of abuse faced by migrant workers and the lack of due process guarantees (Laroche, 2001). At the Second Summit of the Americas, held in Santiago in 1998, governments committed to raise the awareness on violations of the rights of migrants and to ensure equality of treatment and protection from smuggling. At the same time, regional agreements took place, such as the Social and Labor Declaration of MERCOSUR and the North American Agreement on Labor Cooperation (NAALC). At the 2001 Quebec Summit, governments agreed to cooperate against trafficking of persons. However, in spite of these signs of progress, "states still tend to consider migration as a matter of national security" (Laroche, 2001).

The Council of Europe devoted attention to migration since the 1950s, with instruments mostly covering migrants coming from European countries. The development of the European Union, which comprises the major countries of destination in Europe, has overshadowed the Council of Europe initiatives. The Dublin Convention on Asylum (1997) and the Amsterdam Treaty (1999) have created the premises for a harmonized EU policy on refugees and migrants, which should be based on the European Convention on Human Rights.

RECENT DEVELOPMENTS

Although not much progress was achieved in the 1990s in ratification of instruments related to migration, various initiatives developed both at the international and regional levels. The protection of migrants was mentioned in the various international conferences, particularly the 1994 Conference on Population and Development held in Cairo, which emphasized that migrants should first of all have the option to remain in the country of origin, and the 1995 Fourth World Conference on Women held in Beijing, which included migrant women in various parts of the Platform for Action. However, such conferences, in spite of extensive intergovernmental consultation and the input of NGOs, have limited impact, except for furthering the thinking about specific subjects (Battistella, 1999). They also serve as indicators of the relevance migration has for the international community. There seems to be a reluctance to give prominence to migration in international events, as it is considered an issue to be dealt with at the national level. The most prominent example in this regard was the failure to convene an international conference on migration. Considered with UNGA resolution 49/127 of 19 December 1994, three attempts were made to obtain responses from governments: in 1995, 1997 and 1999. Nevertheless, 110 governments never replied. Of the 78 who responded, 47 were in favor of an international conference on migration, 5 indicated partial support, while 26 expressed reservations.[6] Thus, the idea was abandoned.

The most recent international event was the Conference Against Racism, Racial Discrimination, Xenophobia and Related Intolerance, held in Durban last September. The final declaration and program of action utilized standard language in which discrimination against migrants is condemned. Although not breaking new ground, the conference stated in various parts that policies toward migrants "should be consistent with applicable human rights instruments" (46). Furthermore, states were called upon "to review and, where necessary, revise any immigration policies which are inconsistent with international human rights instruments, with a view to eliminating all discriminatory policies and practices against migrants, including Asians and people of Asian descent" (37). Even without new formulations, it is important to register the insistence upon the human rights approach as the appropriate way to consider migration.

At the international level, however, the Human Rights Commission took the initiative of convening a Working Group of Intergovernmental Experts on the Human Rights of Migrants in 1997. The group was effective in revisiting

---

[6]Report A/56/157, 3 July 2001, paragraph 9.

the various issues affecting the protection of migrants and identifying obstacles to the effective and full protection of the rights of migrants. Obstacles were grouped in three categories: institutional (such as absence or nonapplication of standards in national law, failure to ratify international instruments, impunity and denial of justice); social (such as confinement in urban areas with substandard services and facilities, xenophobia, racism, prejudices); and economic (such as confinement to unskilled occupations, abuse of migrants in particular occupations, such as domestic workers and farmworkers, and those employed in the informal economy). In addition to the corresponding recommendations to eliminate the obstacles to effective protection of the rights of migrants, the Working Group also recommended preparing a compendium of provisions applicable to migrants under the relevant instruments of international law and appointing a special rapporteur for a three-year period.[7]

The Special Rapporteur was appointed by the Human Rights Commission in 1999[8] to solicit information from governments concerning violation of the rights of migrants, to formulate appropriate recommendations, to promote the application of relevant international norms, with a specific gender perspective and attention to violence against migrant women. The Special Rapporteur (Ms. Gabriela Rodriguez of Costa Rica) has since submitted two reports, calling attention to the need to clarify the definition of migrants and on the legal framework available to migrants. She can act through communications sent to countries calling attention to specific aspects or through official visits upon the invitation of governments.[9] It is difficult to assess the effectiveness of a special rapporteur, whose mandate is limited and who can at most call public attention to specific situations.

On the initiative of NGOs in Asia, December 18 was launched as International Migrants' Day in 1997.[10] The initiative was later supported by the Steering Committee for the Global Campaign for the ratification of the Migrant Workers Convention and through the Mexican delegation in Geneva it entered a resolution of the Human Rights Commission and eventually the General Assembly, which adopted it on 4 December 2000.[11] The initiative serves as an

[7]Report E/CN.4/1999/80, 9 March 1999.
[8]Resolution 1999/44.
[9]She visited Canada from 17 to 30 September 2000.
[10]The launching was done in Manila by the Philippines Migrants Rights Watch (PMRW) and the Asia-Pacific International Migration Network (APIM).
[11]Resolution A/55/93.

occasion for civil society activities calling attention to the plights of migrants.

Various intergovernmental activities have emerged in the 1990s at the regional level. Behind this flurry of initiatives is the concern for the increasing number of unauthorized migrants and the rise of trafficking and smuggling of persons. Cognizant of the inadequacy of national control measures, governments have embraced a regional approach, seeking cooperation with neighboring countries. The CIS Process, concerned with migration in the Commonwealth of Independent States, initiated in 1994. The Regional Conference on Migration, better known as the Puebla Process, concerning migration in North and Central America, was founded in 1996 and was followed in 1999 by the Lima Process for South America. The Dakar Process for Western and Central Africa was established in 2000, while the Migration Dialogue concerns migration to Southern Africa. In Asia, the Manila Process was later accompanied by the Asia-Pacific Consultations on Migration and Asylum (APC). One specific initiative of the Asia-Pacific consultation was the Bangkok Declaration of 23 April 1999, reached at the end of a ministerial conference and highlighting commitments to cooperate in addressing unauthorized migration. The Asian Regional Initiative Against Trafficking (ARIAT) was held in Manila in March 2000 on the initiative of the U.S. and Philippine governments to establish programs to cooperate against trafficking of women and children. The various initiatives, mostly utilizing IOM organizational support, have focused on aspects related to migration control, such as intelligence cooperation, border control, organized crime and cooperation for the return of migrants. Human rights have received little attention and NGOs do not have access to such initiatives, except for the Puebla process (Taran, 2000). An interesting result of these initiatives could be the increasing relevance of a regional approach to migration, considered more manageable than an international approach. However, are regional approaches human rights/human development-based approaches, or are they based on the objective of migration control? Regional cooperation can also spill over into local initiatives, established at the practical level, such as the anti-immigrant- victimization unit of the San Diego Police Department, which ensures the safety of unauthorized aliens without enforcing immigration laws, and its Grupo Beta counterpart in Tijuana (Martin, 2001).

Parallel to government action, civil society has been increasingly active and vocal in recent years on the issue of human rights, and the rights of migrants have progressively become an item of concern of major human rights groups such as Human Rights Watch and Amnesty International. Participation in the various international conferences has facilitated the networking and organization of initiatives across issues. It is practically impossible to provide even a summary of NGO programs. However, special mention must be given to the already- mentioned Global Campaign for the ratification of the Migrant Workers Convention, which emerged on the initiative of Migrants Rights International, based in Geneva.

THE CHURCH AND HUMAN RIGHTS

Most commentators agree that the Catholic Church has come a long way in its consideration of human rights. The Church did not provide specific contributions to the early formulations of human rights, whether in the 1776 American Declaration of Independence or in the 1789 Declaration of the Rights of Man and Citizen during the French Revolution. "The church, especially in France, experienced the proclamation of human rights in 1789 as a very cold and hostile wind, and it cannot claim for itself a significant place in either the theoretical or the practical struggle for human rights in the eighteenth and nineteenth centuries. Human rights theory in an explicit and politically dynamic form confronted Catholicism as an alien force, and it has taken Catholicism a long time to appropriate it" (Langan 1982). This is not the place for a detailed analysis of the reasons for such divergence. Mostly, human rights were an expression of liberal political philosophy. The Church argued that such an approach resulted in emphasis on the individual to the detriment of the common good; feared the freedom of expression and religious liberty as relativism; and argued that a free market economy would result in the demise of the poor (Baum, 2001).

Since then, the Church has become a staunch supporter of human rights. The turning point found solemn expression first in John XXIII's encyclical *Pacem in Terris*, in which he affirmed that "every human being is a person, that is, his nature is endowed with intelligence and free will. By virtue of this, he has rights and duties, flowing directly and simultaneously from his very nature. These rights are therefore universal, inviolable and inalienable" (9). In this short expression the Pope laid down the characteristics of the Catholic approach to human rights: an approach which is personalistic but also oriented at society; universalistic as it is derived from nature; and comprehensive, as it binds together both civil and economic rights (Langan, 1982).

The 1965 Vatican II declaration, *Dignitatis Humanae*, on religious freedom marked a definitive achievement in the recognition of freedom of conscience and an essential component in the Church's international relations. It also clarified its foundation, and, therefore, the foundation of all human rights. They are based "in the very dignity of the human person as this dignity is known through the revealed word of God and by reason itself" (2). The traditional foundation of human rights – the dignity of the human person created in the image of God – is derived both from natural law as well as revelation.

John Paul II has made the recognition and respect for human rights a central tenet of his pontificate. Already, in his first encyclical, *Redemptor Hominis*, he stressed the importance of respect for human rights. Such respect qualifies true humanism and limits the power of the state, which is at the service of the common good. "The common good that authority in the State serves is brought to full realization only when all the citizens are sure of their rights" (17). Among many other occasions, the Pope returned to the issue of human rights in his message for the 1999 World Day of Peace, on the occasion of the fiftieth anniversary of the Universal Declaration of Human Rights. He called respect for human rights the secret of true peace and identified the two foundations for dedication to human rights: promotion of the dignity of the person and search for the common good. Against the tendencies to limit the validity of human rights as a Western conceptualization and to separate civil and political rights from social, economic and cultural rights, he affirmed their universality and indivisibility as "essential for the construction of a peaceful society and for the overall development of individuals, peoples and nations" (3). Among the various human rights, he stressed the right to life, the right to religious freedom, the right to participate in the life of the community, the rights of ethnic groups and national minorities. He also emphasized rights of the second and third generation, as they are sometimes called, such as the right to self-fulfillment, which includes the right to education and work, and responsibility for the environment.

The Church's embracing of human rights is an expression of the anthropological shift that has occurred with Vatican II. In the affirmation of human rights, the Church finds consonance with its mission for salvation as revealed in Christ. It is utilizing a tool with which dialogue with the world is immediately established. At the same time, the Church maintains a specific human rights perspective. It remains critical of unbridled liberalism "at the expenses of the common good and the needs of the disadvantaged"; it leans toward a "third way" in the economic organization of society; and it continues to maintain a linkage between the neo-scholastic "natural law" foundation and a biblical foundation of human rights (Langan, 1982:35–36). The philosophical approach facilitates the dialogue with people of all faiths or no faith at all, while the biblical approach is instrumental for a dialogue with the Christian Churches.

The attempt to provide a theological foundation to human rights has received increasing attention,[12] but with contrasting results. David Jenkins, an Anglican theologian cited in Nelson (1982), wrote: "I do not believe that the notion of human rights is at all biblical." Nelson himself concluded that "the idea of naturally endowed rights is strange to the biblical writings" (1982:10). At the same time, the Scripture affirms without doubt the value of the human person and their possibility of fulfillment. "I came that they might have life, and have it abundantly" (Jn 10:10). A specific attempt at a theological foundation is provided by the Lutheran World Federation, which speaks of freedom, equality and participation as the framework which encompasses all persons. However, they are not to be considered idealistic goals but "the secular analogies to the essential terms of the Gospel by which all persons should be able to live" (Nelson, 1982:11). On the other hand, the World Alliance of Reformed Churches has adopted a more dynamic approach, speaking of the liberation by Jesus Christ of all human beings, created in the image of God and living in the hope of the coming of the Kingdom (ibidem). Both attempts underscore human rights as belonging to our redemption, not just to our creation.

As Churches refine their instruments toward a theological foundation of human rights, philosophers underscore that human rights ideology has no religious foundation. Henkins (1998) admits that religions also have human dignity as a cardinal theme, but its implications are not congruent with those deriving from human rights ideology. For instance, human rights support absolute freedom of conscience, while religions reject atheism; human rights require nondiscrimination, while religions admit distinctions based on religious adherence; human rights do not admit gender distinctions, while religions still maintain them. He concludes that religion is an alternative, and even competing ideology, to that of human rights. "Human rights are not, and

[12]See, e.g., Jean-François Collange, *Teologia dei diritti umani*. Brescia: Queriniana, 1991.

cannot be, grounded in religious conviction . . . . The human rights ideology is a fully secular and rational ideology whose very promise of success as a universal ideology depends on its secularity and rationality" (Henkins, 1998:238).

The response of the theologian is that because "the two normative worlds are in tension does not mean that they must be in opposition," and therefore asserts that "the relationship between theology and human rights reflection will inevitably be both competitive and cooperative" (Langan, 1998:253). In fact, even Henkins admits that "human rights are not a complete, alternative ideology, but rights are a floor, necessary to allow other values – including religions – to flourish." On that basis, religions "can devote themselves to the larger, deeper areas beyond the common denominator of human rights," providing what human rights do not provide: "the tensions between rights and responsibilities, between individual and community, between the material and the spirit" (1998:239).

A separate position on human rights within the Church was that taken by liberation theology. Engler (2000) has well summarized the development of the liberation theology position in three stages: in the early phase, human rights were ignored as a non-useful concept; in a second phase, they were criticized, because limited on civil and political rights, they were considered the rights of the elite; and the final phase, in which human rights are utilized, although in a specific reformulation as rights of the poor. Such reformulation is demanded for moral reasons (the poor demand a special need for liberation), for religious reasons (God shows special love for those who are dehumanized) and for cognitive reasons (the side of the poor provides a specific perspective for an approach to God and action).

After considering the various approaches, it is on the practical commitment of upholding the dignity of human person that cooperation is found. As the Catholic Bishops' Conference of England and Wales (1998) has stated, "the doctrine of human rights has become an essential tool" for the journey towards peace and justice, and "human rights have become central to the Church's mission in the world." Protecting the human rights of migrants is part of this general commitment.

THE CHURCH AND THE RIGHTS OF MIGRANTS

The approach of the Church to migration has increasingly emphasized its ecclesiological basis: migrants are viewed as icons of the Church, which is the people of God and the community of disciples at the service of the Kingdom, engaged in its exodus to overcome contingent realizations and, in recognizing each other, to recognize the Other who calls us into communion within diversity. The ecclesiological approach has led to overcoming an approach that only considered migrants as needy, both in society and the Church, and acknowledged instead their contribution both to church and society. The practical implications consist of upholding the rights of migrants, both in the Church and society. "Caring for migrants means striving to guarantee a place within the individual Christian community for his brothers and sisters coming from afar, and working so that every human being's personal rights are recognized" (WMD, 1998). The foundation of migrants' rights is their human dignity. "The migrant is to be considered not merely as an instrument of production but as a subject endowed with full human dignity" (WMD, 1991). Human dignity is to be understood in Christological terms. "The comprehension of the human being, which the Church acquired in Christ, urges her to proclaim the fundamental human rights" (WMD, 2001). Therefore, the Church "does not grow tired of affirming and defending the dignity of the human person, highlighting the inalienable rights that originate from it" (ibidem).

The Right to Migrate

Human rights also derive from the concept of universal common good, in the context of which the right to migrate should be understood. In fact, while the international community recognizes the right to leave one's own country and to return to it, the Church expresses the same right by explicitly speaking of a right to migrate. This was formulated in *Pacem in Terris* (25) "When there are just reasons in favor of it, he must be permitted to emigrate to other countries and take up residence there," and repeated by Paul VI, who advocated for migrants "a charter which will assure them a right to emigrate" (OA, 17). John Paul II has made it more explicit first by asking "what the right to emigrate is worth without the corresponding right to immigrate" (WMD, 1995) and then by articulating its dual implication. "The Church recognizes this right (to emigrate) in every human person, in its dual aspect of the possibility to leave one's country and the possibility to enter another country to look for better conditions of life." Obviously she also recognizes the right of the state to control migration, but such control should not be without responsibilities. In fact, "the more prosperous nations are obliged to the extent they are able to welcome the foreigner in search of the security and the means of livelihood which he cannot find in his country of origin" (CCC, 2241).

The Right Not to Migrate

While affirming the right to migrate, the Church also cautioned against making migration the only alternative to situations of injustice and conflict. "I consider it appropriate in this context to state once again that the fundamental right of a person is to live in its own land. However, this right can effectively be exercised only if the causes to migration are constantly kept under control" (IVWC, 1998). Such causes are of various nature and the Pope recommends the proper countermeasures, including balanced economic development. The linkage with the right to development, which must be integral human development and development not only of the individual but also of peoples (CA, 35), places the issue of migration in its proper context, as migration is both the result of inadequate development as well as a symptom of damages caused by development. A macro perspective is necessary to expose that "inequalities increase, poorer populations are forced into the exile of desperation, while the wealthy countries find they are prisoners of an insatiable craving to concentrate the available resources in their own hands" (WMD, 2000).

The Rights of Unauthorized Migrants

From the human rights concern of the Church, unauthorized migrants are not excluded. "His irregular legal status cannot allow the migrant to lose his dignity, since he is endowed with inalienable rights, which can neither be violated nor ignored" (WMD, 1995). The Church advocates the prevention of unauthorized migration, combating vigorously criminal activities and utilizing international cooperation for lasting results.

The Right to Live With the Family

The Church has always devoted specific attention to the family of migrants, in particular the right to family reunification. This is affirmed in the major documents, such as De Pastorali Migratorum Cura (7) and the Charter of the Rights of the Family (1983). It is then repeated in various messages, stressing the fact that "recognition of this right is often hindered by obstacles of various kinds that sometimes prevent it from being exercised" (WMD, 1993). The Pope specifically says that "one must reject the attitude of those who refuse it almost as though it were a claim with no juridical basis" (WMD, 1994). In fact, although the Bill of Rights speaks of protection to the family, this was never understood as to imply a right to family reunification. Such right is never formulated in international instruments, which only recommend states to facilitate reunification. Obviously, on this point the Church goes much further, mindful of what was already established in Vatican II: "in policy decisions affecting migrants their right to live together should be safeguarded" (AA, 11).

Cultural Rights

In the approach of the Church to migration, the protection of migrants' culture always occupied a prominent place. It is precisely because of their language and culture that migrants need a specific pastoral care (DPMC, 11). The Church sees the contribution that migration can give by creating societies which are culturally richer and more diverse. However, the opposite dangers of rejection and assimilation must be avoided by the receiving society, while migrants should avoid remaining enclosed in ghettos, refusing to integrate in the local society. The same principle applies also to the relationship with Christian communities. More societies are now experiencing a cultural pluralism, which is sometimes adopted as a specific government program, other times it is left to a more or less spontaneous intermingling of ethnic groups. The Church does not consider cultural pluralism as juxtaposition of closed realities but as participation in the search for the fundamental values of humankind (Tassello, 2001).

The Right to a Specific Pastoral Care

This is not a right mentioned in the traditional list of human rights, but it is fundamental in the Church. "Special concern should be shown for those among the faithful who, on account of their way of life, cannot sufficiently make use of the common and ordinary pastoral care of parish priests or are quite cut off from it. Among this group are the majority of migrants" (CD, 18). Unfortunately, the Code of Canon Law, although reflecting in various sections that those who cannot be attended to through ordinary pastoral care require specific attention (can. 383.1, 771.1) and providing for the possibility of specific institutions, such as personal parishes, missions, prelatures and the chaplain for migrants (can. 568), did not elaborate in the section on the rights of the faithful a specific section on the rights of migrants. This is redressed in the draft of the revised DPMC, which dedicates the first article to the right that migrants have to a specific pastoral care.

CONCERN FOR THE RIGHTS OF MIGRANTS: A PASTORAL CHALLENGE

One would assume that to the widespread attention to human rights by the Church, and specifically John Paul II, a similar attention would be found in the local Christian communities. This is probably true in the actual activities that communities organize for the welfare, protection and human promotion of migrants. It is not as evident in specific initiatives with migrants, both in raising awareness about their rights and violations they are suffering, as well as in providing referral to the proper mechanisms for redress, or in advocacy programs. It is in this specific practical approach of organizing pastoral activities that concern for the rights of migrants is a challenge. The challenge qualifies in that such activities diverge from the traditional pastoral approach, focused on evangelization and sacraments.

Specific initiatives could include the following:

Expanding coverage. In spite of the variety of instruments available for the protection of migrants, there remain lacunae in the coverage of all categories of migrants. For instance, the MWC (art. 16) provides for protection against violence. However, it does not address gender-based vulnerability. The lack of gender-specific provisions is also noted in regard to the non-differentiation between women's work and men's work. Also, trainee programs are often utilized as a substitute for migration programs. However, those trainees practically working like migrants are not protected. Building on specific cases, attention should be brought to representatives to ensure that lacunae are filled.

Expanding membership. As already mentioned before, instruments related to migrants (both UN as well as ILO instruments) do not enjoy a wide number of ratifications. As conventions normally oblige only the countries that are party to them (except when rights are already reflected in other instruments with higher ratification – such as the covenants on human rights – or when rights are already considered customary international law), it is important to ensure that as many countries as possible ratify such conventions. In this regard, specific initiatives can be organized at the local level in conjunction with international and national campaigns. What needs to be done is to expose the plan to maintain migrant labor as disposable, and, therefore, unprotected. Pushing for the ratification of international instruments, in particular the MWC, is pushing for the adoption of a human rights perspective into migration.

National legislation. International instruments lose much of their validity if their provisions are not adequately reflected in national legislation. In fact, human rights instruments lack effective mechanisms to ensure implementation. In particular, they often lack the individual complaint procedure. National legislation should contain, in particular, non-discrimination provisions, as discrimination in its various forms is a major area of abuse that migrants encounter.

Education. Education on the human rights of migrants needs to be pursued in various directions: first, with the migrants themselves, but also with employers and government officials. Instruments such as the MWC can be utilized in this regard, but other initiatives have been implemented, that can be replicated.[13] Concern for the human rights of migrants should be brought into schools and made part of the normal curriculum, so that fear or disrespect for the foreigner is eradicated at an early stage.

Networking. Local initiatives are undoubtedly necessary. However, their effectiveness increases when NGOs and migrants' organizations network for more general objectives, such as campaigns for the ratification of international instruments or initiatives utilizing December 18 as international migrants' day, or campaigns to support the pleas of migrants who are victims of abuse.

---

[13]For instance, the UN Interagency International Migration Policy Programme organized in Bangkok in 2000, the workshops in Asia of the Canadian Human Rights Foundation, which resulted in the training manual *UN Road Map*, and booklets produced by the Philippine Migrants Rights Watch.

Such networking can first be built at the local and national levels, to expand at the regional and international levels. The Internet has facilitated networking tremendously and various groups are offering information and services.

Participation in the Christian communities. Concern and commitment to human rights should begin at home, within the Christian communities. Specific issues that need to be addressed are: the capacity to be open and welcome all migrants in need; encouraging participation of migrants in the local communities as subject, not just object, of Christian mission; respecting diversity while building communion; empowering migrants to experience and facilitate the truth that "In the Church no one is a stranger, and the Church is not foreign to anyone, anywhere" (WMD, 1995).

However, the concern for the rights of migrants is a pastoral challenge in a more profound way, as a perspective in the mission with migrants. The concept of mission is rediscovered as independent from traveling and living overseas, as boundaries to be crossed can be very close at home. "Authentic mission is a movement from the center to the margin: from wherever our center may be to wherever our center is not; from wherever we are to wherever other people are" (Gittins, 2002). In this conceptualization, boundaries, like margins, become the place for mission. They are not ignored or easily erased, but they are instrumental for the shift that is required to accept membership in the Kingdom. Migration is about boundaries: boundaries that stop the flow, boundaries that are crossed, boundaries that are encountered after being crossed, boundaries that are taken with and remain for long time. The human rights perspective allows for boundaries to remain without barbed wire and fences and people to meet rather than remain divided, because those rights reveal the human dignity of all those who are at the margins as revealed in Christ, the Divine who went to the margin to meet the human.

This approach has long been espoused by the Church. Already, in 1971, the Synod of Bishops stated that "Her mission involves defending and promoting the dignity and fundamental rights of the human person" (JW, 1971). And John Paul II reminded us that "A commitment to peace, justice, human rights and human promotion is also a witness to the Gospel when it is a sign of concern for persons and is directed toward integral human development" (RM, 42). This is not an easy task. It is a true apostolate, the "apostolate of human rights," as he called it. It requires vigilance and an approach beyond our specific concerns, but it will generate hope and confidence. "It is therefore essential that there should be a global approach to the subject of human rights and a serious commitment to defend them. Only when a culture of human rights which respects different traditions becomes an integral part of humanity's moral patrimony shall we be able to look to the future with serene confidence" (WP, 1998).

This commitment has to be a critical one. The human rights ideology reveals some weaknesses. The most apparent emerges from a historical analysis, which unfolds the contradiction between the proclamation of human rights and the tolerance of abuses against human rights. This is often evident in the unequal access to human rights protection within countries and even more evident in the diversified policies adopted by Western powers toward countries accused of lacking respect for human rights. Regardless of rhetoric, it does not escape anyone's attention that, in the end, economic interests prevail over concern for human rights, particularly toward countries in the Middle East or China.

Although utilizing human rights in a critical way, it is also important to avoid downgrading civil liberties in favor of economic and social rights. Such approach, undermining the indivisibility of human rights, would only contribute to prolonging the rule of authoritarian regimes, without benefiting the poor, least of all the migrants.

REFERENCES

Battistella, G.
1999   "Protection of the Rights of Migrants," in *The Universal Declaration of Human Rights: Fifty Years and Beyond*. Ed. Y. Danieli *et al*. Amityville: Baywood Publishing Company.

Baum, G.
2001   "Catholic Foundations of Human Rights." <www.stthomasu.ca>, accessed January.

Catholic Bishops' Conference of England and Wales
1998   *Human Rights and the Catholic Church. Reflections on the Jubilee of the Universal Declaration of Human Rights*. London: Catholic Media Office.

Cholewinski, R.
1999   "International Human Rights Standards and the Protection of Migrant Workers in the Asia Pacific Region," *Asian Migrant*, Vol. 12, No. 1.

———
1997   *Migrant Workers in International Human Rights Law*. Oxford: Clarendon Press.

Engler, M.
2000   "Toward the 'Rights of the Poor.' Human Rights in Liberation Theology," *Journal of Religious Ethics*, Vol. 28, No. 3.

Gittins, A. J.
2002   *Ministry at the Margins. Strategy and Spirituality for Mission*. New York: Orbis Books.

Henkin, L.
1998   "Religion, Religions and Human Rights," *Journal of Religious Ethics*, Vol. 26, No. 2.

Hune, S. and J. Niessen
1994   "Ratifying the UN Migrant Workers Convention: Current Difficulties and Prospects," *Asian Migrant*, Vol. 7, No. 3.

International Organization for Migration (IOM)
2000   *World Migration Report 2000*. Geneva: IOM.

Langan, J.
1998   "Contrasting and Uniting Theology and Human Rights," *Journal of Religious Ethics*, Vol. 26, No. 2.

————
1982   "Human Rights in Roman Catholicism," *Journal of Ecumenical Studies*, Vol. 19, No. 3.

Laroche, I.
2001   "The Inter-American Human rights System and the Protection of the Rights of Migrants." <www.december 18.org>.

Martin, S.
2001   "Smuggling and Trafficking in Humans a Human Rights Issue," *People on the Move*, No. 86, September.

Massey, D., *et al.*
1998   *Worlds in Motion. Understanding International Migration at the End of the Millennium*. Oxford: Clarendon Press.

Nelson, R. J.
1982   "Human Rights in Creation and Redemption: A Protestant View," *Journal of Ecumenical Studies*, Vol. 19, No. 3.

Papademetriou, D. and P. L. Martin
1991   *The Unsettled Relationship. Labor Migration and Economic Development*. Westport, CT: Greenwood Press.

Shah, N. M. and I. Menon
1997   "Violence Against Women Migrant Workers: Issues, Data and Partial Solutions," *Asian and Pacific Migration Journal*, Vol. 6, No. 1.

Taran, P.
2000   "Human Rights of Migrants: Challenges of the New Decade," *International Migration*, Vol. 38, No. 6.

Tassello, G. G.
2001   "I documenti del magistero ecclesiale e le migrazioni," *Studi Emigrazione*, Vol. 38, No. 143.

United Nations Development Programme (UNDP)
2000   *Human Development Report 2000.* New York: Oxford University Press.

LIST OF ABBREVIATIONS

AS   Apostolicam Actuositatem

DPMC   De Pastorali Migratorum Cura

WMD   World Migrants Day

CA   Centesimus Annus

CCC   Catechism of the Catholic Church

OA   Optatam Totius

RM   Redemptoris Missio

JW   Justice in the World

IVWC   IV World Congress

TABLE 1
STATE SIGNATORIES AND PARTIES TO THE MIGRANT WORKERS
CONVENTION (END OF 2001)

Country	Ratification	Country	Signature only
Azerbaijan	11.01.99	Bangladesh	07/10/98
Belize	14.11.01	Burkina Faso	16/11/01
Bolivia	12.10.00	Chile	24/09/93
Bosnia & Herzegovina	13.12.96	Comoros	22/09/00
Cape Verde	16.99.97	Guatemala	07/09/00
Colombia	24.05.95	Guinea-Bissau	12/09/00
Egypt	19.02.93	Paraguay	13/09/00
Ghana	08.09.00	Sao Tome & Principe	06/09/00
Guinea	08.09.00	Sierra Leone	15/09/00
Mexico	08.03.99	Tajikistan	17/09/00
Morocco	21.06.93	Turkey	13/01/99
Philippines	05.07.95	Togo	15/11/01
Senegal	09.06.99		
Seychelles	15.12.94		
Sri Lanka	16.03.96		
Uganda	14.11.95		
Uruguay	15.02.01		

La humanidad peregrina viviente: Migración y experiencia religiosa

María Pilar Aquino
University of San Diego

Lunes 18 de junio del 2001. Se llamaba Carlota de la Cruz y era mexicana. Cuando nació, a nadie le fue dado el poder de premonición para decirle que su tierno cuerpo lleno de rebeldía y aspiraciones, terminaría a los escasos 19 años consumido por el sol, mientras hablaba con sus parientes ya muertos, quienes venían a susurrarle aliento con voces misteriosas y cercanas que sólo \ella podía reconocer. Su mente vagaba alucinando por las arenas ardientes del desierto y su cuerpo colapsó irremediablemente por las largas caminatas y los días sin comer entre los cardos secos y los piñacates. Su padre estuvo en vela hasta sus últimas horas, viendo cómo se le escapaba el aliento por que no podía hacer más, en medio de un dolor en el que sólo atinaba a clamar piedad del cielo. Pocos días antes habían cruzado la frontera clandestinamente, con ilusiones de un mejor futuro pero sin documentos de identidad. El cuerpo frágil sin vida de Carlota de la Cruz fue rescatado por la tarde, como a unas cincuenta millas al este de San Diego, donde existe el puro desierto cuya temperatura bien puede superar los 115 grados Fahrenheit (46.1° Celsius) en el tiempo de verano, incluso desde mayo hasta septiembre. Ella, su padre y otros dos parientes fueron abandonados en el desierto por "el coyote," quien siguió adelante con ocho migrantes más que llevaba y no se le volvió a ver.[1] La "institución del coyotaje" tiene como fin lucrarse con el tráfico y contrabando de gente indocumentada en la frontera,[2] no el de asegurar que la gente llegue sana y salva a su destino. Durante estos días, varias organizaciones sociales y religiosas interconfesionales de San Diego que luchan por los derechos humanos y de los migrantes, organizaron procesiones y marchas por la ciudad. Con justa indignación, exigían cambios en las leyes estadounidenses

---

[1]Gregory Alan Gross, "Dying immigrant hallucinated, talk of dead kin visiting," *San Diego Union Tribune*, San Diego, CA., Tuesday, June 19, 2001.

[2]Jorge Durand, "Origen es destino. Redes sociales, desarrollo histórico y escenarios contemporáneos," en *Migración México-Estados Unidos. Opciones de política*, coord. Rodolfo Tuirán, Consejo Nacional de Población-CONAPO, México, 2000, sitio en la red electrónica, <http://www.conapo.gob.mx>.

de inmigración y públicamente manifestaron su solidaridad con tantos migrantes anónimos que han muerto en la frontera méxico-estadounidense sin nadie que reclame sus cuerpos para darles digna sepultura. En una de estas marchas, la gente portaba al frente una enorme manta que decía en inglés: "¿Caminaría usted a través de montañas y desiertos para buscar trabajo? L@s Migrantes lo hacen; Cientos de ell@s mueren."

Miércoles 23 de Mayo del 2001. Era un grupo de 35 hombres mexicanos que incluía a adultos, jóvenes, y hasta un niño de diez años de edad. Después de caminar por cinco días en el traicionero desierto de Arizona, bajo la devastadora temperatura del verano, algunos se iban quedando a medio camino, y sólo 26 fueron encontrados cerca de Yuma, Arizona, a ciento cincuenta millas al este de San Diego. El "coyote," cuya identidad está en investigación, fue el responsable de la desventura de estos migrantes. Sin agua, sin pan, y sin sombra alguna, catorce hombres murieron por agotamiento y deshidratación, incluyendo a un jovencito de escasos 16 años de edad. La mayoría de los sobrevivientes padecieron severa insolación, colapso total de los riñones y quemaduras graves en la piel. Otros sobrevivieron consumiendo su propia orina y algo de líquido extraído del cactus propio de esta área. Puedo comprender la condición de vulnerabilidad y precariedad de estos hombres, jóvenes y niños por que yo crecí en esta frontera, a veinte millas al sur de Yuma. Se muy bien que sin la mínima protección, en este desierto la gente no puede escapar a la muerte ya sea por hipotermia en el invierno o por deshidratación en el verano. Desde el hospital a donde fue llevado, uno de los sobrevivientes dijo angustiosamente al personal que lo atendió: "Vine aquí con sueños e ilusiones, y en esto terminé. Soy buen trabajador. ¡Por favor, no me regresen!!" Pero su súplica no fue escuchada por las autoridades migratorias. Uno de los jóvenes que murieron fue regresado a Veracruz en una bolsa de plástico desechable, sólo para ser enterrado. De aquí había salido desesperado e impotente al ver que no podía ayudar a su familia con los escasos $8 dólares al día que le pagaban en la planta embotelladora de Coca-Cola. Otros difuntos cosechaban café para la compañía Nestlé, por miserables $4 dólares al día. Después de escapar del calvario de la explotación por estas compañías transnacionales, fueron presas de otra, para finalmente acabar en una tumba, sin ilusiones ni luz.[3]

---

[3]Pat Frannery, Christina Leonard, and Hernán Rozemberg, "Border Nightmare. U.S., Mexico vow justice in fatal desert trek," *The Arizona Republic*, May 25, 2001, sitio en la red electrónica,

Lunes 10 de Septiembre del 2001. Con escasos catorce años de edad, una jovencita mexicana cuyo nombre no fue revelado, fue rescatada ya moribunda, después de ser abandonada en el desierto junto con su padre, a diez millas al este de Nogales, Arizona. El "coyote" siguió de largo con el grupo que llevaba, sin preocuparse por el avanzado estado de deshidratación de esta jovencita. Su cuerpo desvalido fue arrojado al mordiente sol del desierto y ahí, sobre arenas hirvientes, languidecía en terrenos áridos sin agua, sin sombra y sin fin. El día anterior, domingo, la patrulla fronteriza había recogido a tres migrantes mexicanos que vagaban en círculos infinitos, perdidos en el desierto al oeste de Tucson. Sólo en el área de Tucson se registraron 75 muertes de enero a agosto del 2001, la mayoría a consecuencia de la insolación y la deshidratación. En esta área, la patrulla fronteriza detiene cada día entre 600 y 1,200 migrantes.[4]

Jueves 29 de Marzo del 2001. Se llama Oscar Reyes y es nicaragüense. Fue encontrado agonizando, encerrado en un furgón hermético junto a ciento ocho (108) migrantes más, en el desierto de Arizona cerca de Phoenix. En este grupo de migrantes iban mujeres y hombres, la mayoría de origen centroamericano. Sin agua, ni alimentos ni ventilación, el furgón literalmente se convirtió en un horno que puso sobre brasas invisibles a decenas de personas. A medio camino, ya dadas por muertas debido a la asfixia, estas personas fueron abandonadas por los "coyotes" como si fueran animales desahuciados o cadáveres despreciados. Otros cincuenta migrantes del grupo se habían quedado rezagados por los efectos de la deshidratación, condenados a vagar a través del sofocante desierto. Después de esta pesadilla innecesaria vivida a sus 23 años, Oscar sigue creyendo que solo la providencia Divina y la compasión de sus compañer@s le permitieron sobrevivir.[5] La mayoría de estas ciento ocho personas buscaba escapar de la pobreza que agobia a sus familias que viven en condiciones infrahumanas con salarios de sólo $1 dólar por día.

<http://arizonarepublic.com>; Migration Dialogue, "INS: Border Deaths, Trafficking," *Migration News*, vol. 8, no. 7, University of California Davis, July 2001, sitio en la red electrónica, <http://migration.ucdavis.edu/mn/archive_MN/>.
[4]Marcelo Bayliss Soto, "Rescata Migra a jovencita indocumentada," *La Prensa*, San Luis Río Colorado, Martes 11 de Septiembre de 2001; Douglas Carcache, "'Coyotes' pierden la noche," *La Prensa Digital*, Managua, Domingo 3 de Junio del 2001, sitio en la red electrónica, <http://laprensa.com.ni/nacionales/nacionales-20010603-10.html>.
[5]Douglas Carcache, "Indocumentados al borde de la muerte," *La Prensa Digital*, Managua, Domingo 3 de Junio del 2001, sitio en la red electrónica, <http://laprensa.com.ni/nacionales/nacionales-20010603-09.html>.

Como aves peregrinas vulnerables, no pudieron escapar las redes tendidas por un sistema de vida que los empuja a la aspereza del desierto. Nada se sabe sobre el destino final de toda esta gente, pero con seguridad, en decenas de hogares humildes desde México hasta Centro América, existe una madre, una hermana, un hijo o una hija que reza todos los días para que su ser querido regrese pronto sano y salvo.

Año 2000. Una mirada hacia el sur de América también arroja un perfil humano distorsionado. La Red de Casas del Migrante-Scalabrini dice que "la nueva actitud en el campo migratorio ha transformado a México en una interminable frontera vertical, sembrada de retenes, acosos, robos, asaltos y violaciones, hasta juntarse en la frontera Norte con los EE.UU. formando así una gran cruz de muerte. El cementerio de los migrantes se ha extendido desde las fronteras a grandes áreas del territorio donde parte de nuestra humanidad pide tan solo el derecho de transitar, como lo tienen los pájaros del cielo y los ríos de la tierra. En la franja fronteriza de México con Guatemala son incontables los muertos de este conflicto. En los últimos 3 años solamente en la zona entre el Departamento de San Marcos (Guatemala) y el estado de Chiapas (México) han muerto más de 250 migrantes centroamericanos. El camino de la migración en esta parte del continente americano se ha vuelto un campo minado, guerra de baja intensidad, con guerrilla de veredas y de leyes."[6]

Traigo ante ustedes estos eventos fatídicos que he escogido al azar, para que podamos ver que hasta hace poco existió un rostro querido, una mirada ilusionada, una sonrisa afectuosa, un cuerpo animado por energía vital que, en términos religiosos, es imagen de Dios y templo de presencia divina. Pero bien hubiera podido presentarles cuerpos diversos para cubrir cada día, porque su número supera todos los días del año. Solamente en el año 2000, la muerte de migrantes fue de aproximadamente 383 contando únicamente el lado estadounidense de la frontera.[7] Según varias fuentes, en el año 2000 fueron arrestados 1.6 millones de mexicanos que cruzaron la frontera desde México hacia los Estados Unidos de forma no-autorizada, sin documentos, o

---

[6]Red de Casas del Migrante Scalabrini, "El Clamor de los Indocumentados. Mensaje Jubilar," 22 May, 2000, sitio en la red electrónica, <http://www.sedos.org/spanish/ Scalabrini.htm>.

[7]Terry McCarthy, "The Coyote's Game," *Time Magazine*, Special Issue Welcome to Amexica, June 11, 2001, p. 57.

[8]Mary Jordan, "People Smuggling Now Big Business in Mexico," *Washington Post Foreign Service*,

"ilegalmente" en la versión de las leyes migratorias vigentes en este país.[8] Ya avanzado el año 2002, el 15 de junio Notimex reportó que sólo en el área de Tucson, Arizona, habían muerto ya 17 migrantes en menos de una semana.[9] El día anterior en la madrugada, en el área desértica ubicada aproximadamente a quince kilómetros al oeste de Calexico, California, un grupo de 23 migrantes – formado por 17 personas de El Salvador, 1 de Ecuador, y 5 de México – fue baleado por el Ejército mexicano que patrulla la zona. Entre los ocho migrantes heridos, únicamente el salvadoreño Manuel Murcia recuerda que en la oscuridad, escuchaba el ruido de las balas y los gritos aterrorizados de las mujeres migrantes, hasta que "cuando pararon de dispararnos nos bajamos corriendo de la camioneta y nos echamos a correr por todos lados sin saber a dónde ir porque no conocemos el lugar."[10] Ante tal agresión injustificada contra la población migrante, el Ejército mexicano ha optado por el hermetismo impune mientras continúa la violencia en la frontera.

Mi punto de referencia para esta presentación es la problemática que vivimos en la frontera méxicana-americana, y particularmente el área del oeste que conozco bien. Para nombrar esta frontera, usaré el neologismo "Amexica" porque me parece que expresa bien la aleación profunda y las ambivalencias de esta frontera.[11] Sin duda, la realidad de la migración pertenece estructuralmente a Amexica, es componente de su identidad y es

Thursday, May 17, 2001, A01. Ver también, Migration Dialogue, "INS: Border, Smuggling Border," *Migration News*, vol. 7, no. 2, University of California Davis, February 2000, sitio en la red electrónica, <http://migration.ucdavis.edu/mn/archive_mn/>.
[9]Notimex Internacional, "Reportan 17 indocumentados muertos en Arizona en menos de una semana," *Notimex Agencia Mexicana de Noticias*, Sábado 15 de Junio, 2002, sitio en la red electrónica, <http://www.notimex.com.mx/>.
[10]Abraham Nudelstejer, "Acusan Migrantes: 'Nos dispararon'. Silencio en lado mexicano. Violencia en la frontera," *LaCrónicaBC.com*, San Diego, California, 16 de Junio del 2002, sitio en la red electrónica, <http://lacronicabc.com/EdicionImpresa/>; Notimex, "Ocho heridos en un ataque contra 'ilegales," en San Diego," San Diego, 14 de junio 2002, publicado en *UNOM@SUNO en Línea*, Sábado 15 de Junio de 2002, Año 4 No. 49, sitio en la red electrónica, <http://www.unomasuno.com.mx/>; Carlos Lima y Samuel Murillo, "Tiroteo entre Ejército y 'Polleros,'" *LaCrónicaBC.com*, Mexicali, Baja California, junio 15 de 2002, sitio en la red electrónica, <http://www.lacronicabc.com/edicionenlinea/>.
[11]La revista *Time* exhibe este neologismo en una portada publicada en el año 2001, y explica su significado en estos términos: "It is often said the border is its own country, 'Amexica,' neither Mexican nor American. 'The border is not where the U.S. stops and Mexico begins,' says Laredo mayor Betty Flores. 'It's where the U.S. blends into Mexico.' Both sides regard their sovereign governments as distant and dysfunctional," Nancy Gibbs, "The New Frontier-La Nueva Frontera. A Whole New World," *Time Magazine*, Special Issue Welcome to Amexica, June 11, 2001, p. 42.

expresión de su historia, es memoria de una patria propia y es lucha diaria de espíritus rebeldes, es fuente de tragedia y también es fuente de salvación para quienes vivimos en terrenos transgresores de fronteras. Migración y Amexica están fundidas irremediablemente no sólo por la compleja entreveración de dos naciones, sino sobre todo y más agudamente, por las condiciones presentes de la globalización capitalista neoliberal. La pregunta que muchos nos hacemos es, ¿con qué medios y para qué fin podemos hacer de Amexica un espacio libre de calvarios tortuosos que destruyen a su propia gente? Sin una transformación radical de las condiciones que perfilan nuestras sociedades, esta frontera seguirá imponiendo la destrucción de vidas humanas como necesidad histórica para la continuidad de modelos sociales deshumanizantes. En las condiciones adversas del presente, ni Amexica ni ningún otro lugar similar en la tierra pueden ser lo que aspiran a ser, espacios comunicativos abiertos, renovados, libres y fértiles donde toda criatura viva feliz, incluyendo los desiertos porque también ahí crecen flores hermosas.

Quiero también que estos cuerpos me acompañen porque creo que son como un libro abierto donde podemos leer, interpretar, y conocer el actual perfil de la sociedad en que vivimos. Estoy convencida de que sólo viendo el mundo desde el lugar de estos cuerpos lánguidos, podemos poner al descubierto los mecanismos que la sociedad emplea para producir tales resultados. En estos cuerpos está la marca inconfundible del sistema en que vivimos, con sus estructuras e instituciones adversas a la dignificación de la vida, que conspira de diversas maneras en contra de la humanidad más vulnerable. Hablo aquí de una marca que en sus rasgos permite develar las características devastadoras de un modo de vida cuyo funcionamiento propio, arroja a la gente empobrecida hacia una peregrinación incierta, donde transita por un calvario infinito bañada en sudor y lágrimas. Entre los muchos métodos que existen para reconocer esa marca, está el de la retórica teológica feminista, que puede ser descrita como un lenguaje religioso para razonar analítica y críticamente sobre nuestra percepción de la actuación y presencia de Dios en medio de nuestras luchas plurales por la transformación social de alcance global. Con el lenguaje teológico argumentamos por una visión liberadora y emancipadora de la humanidad y de su actividad en el mundo. Debido a su contenido de dignidad humana basada en principios religiosos, y a su orientación hacia la justicia social, la igualdad y la integridad de la creación, este lenguaje quiere inspirar y sostener las luchas de todo movimiento social y religioso para rectificar el curso de la realidad histórica presente. En este marco, propongo mi reflexión en dos grandes partes tomando como eje organizador la humanidad migrante, en su dignidad, derechos, y trabajo. En la primera parte, me propongo explorar la problemática central, tanto de la vasta realidad llamada "migración" como la de los estudios sobre ella en el contexto actual de globalización de mercados. En la segunda parte presento algunos argumentos en favor de una reconceptualización teórico-política de la globalización, de la migración, y de la mujer u hombre migrante desde una postura crítico-ética que afirma la subjetividad viviente de la humanidad migrante, y a esta luz abordo algunas cuestiones espinosas que produce el sistema de las remesas. Termino mi reflexión con algunas propuestas de estrategia para la actividad y trabajo de las iglesias en su posible contribución a los movimientos y teorías que luchan por la actualización de la justicia e igualdad en un contexto sistemático.

LA PEREGRINACIÓN EN TERRENO DESNIVELADO

Según mi parecer, los actuales estudios sobre migración internacional constituyen un terreno vasto, dinámico y creciente, generalmente articulado por métodos académicos provenientes de la economía, de la demografía, de la alta estadística, de la antropología y de la sociología modernas. La gran mayoría de estos estudios hablan de números y de porcentajes que, con excesiva e indiscriminada confianza en las frías fórmulas de la razón teórica moderna, quieren acceder al conocimiento de la realidad migratoria mediante la cuantificación abstracta de los flujos humanos en términos estrictamente economicistas. Para mi, la dificultad mayor que presenta este modo de conocimiento tiene tres aspectos centrales. Primero, impide ver que la migración expresa procesos sociales formados por seres concretos que sienten, que sueñan, que luchan y que hablan incluso desde el silencio de su sepultura. Lo que esta gente clama en su humanidad dolida y lo que porta de ilusiones rebeldes, queda velado por el precario lenguaje de la clasificación economicista. Segundo, este modo de conocimiento oculta el análisis de los mecanismos que estructuralmente multiplican el trabajo, la opresión, la vulnerabilidad, y la ansiedad de las mujeres. La Organización Internacional de Migraciones (IOM, por sus siglas en inglés) bien señala que hasta muy recientemente, "los estudios y programas de migración tradicionalmente han estado enfocados en la experiencia de los hombres."[12] Tercero, los acercamientos académicos a la realidad migratoria carecen de códigos analíticos para exponer la identidad última de la marca causante de un *continuum* distintivo e infinito forjado con explotación y de deshumanización en términos sistemáticos. Por lo general, estos acercamientos convencionales exponen un conjunto de factores plurales e inseparables que posibilitan y mantienen la migración, pero no llegan a nombrar analíticamente a la globalización capitalista neoliberal como emisora primordial de esa marca en nuestros días, y así mutilan su propia capacidad para formular estrategias posibles y sistemáticas de transformación. Nadie puede confrontar a una entidad anónima y abstracta.

Desde el punto de vista de los gobiernos, la realidad vivida por la gente migrante queda reducida a un mero asunto laboral de carácter binacional, que tiene que ver con significativas transferencias de dinero y de fuerza de trabajo. Resumiendo, el Consejo Nacional de Población (CONAPO) de México entiende que "la migración entre México y Estados Unidos es un fenómeno esencialmente laboral, impulsado por la interacción de factores que tienen sus raíces en ambos lados de la frontera."[13] Para el Servicio de Inmigración y Naturalización (INS) estadounidense, la categoría "migrante" es simplemente definida en referencia a "una persona que deja su país de origen para buscar residencia en otro país," y aplica el término "inmigrante" a toda persona "extranjera" admitida en el país de forma legal como residente permanente, pero incluye también a quienes entran ilegalmente en el país o como indocumentados.[14] Por su parte, la IOM define la migración internacional como "el movimiento de la gente de un país a otro para adquirir empleo o establecer residencia, o buscar refugio de la persecución."[15] Si bien estas definiciones ayudan a acotar el terreno formal de las políticas gubernamentales con respecto a la migración, también parecen ser insuficientes para dar cuenta, tanto del

---

[12]International Organization for Migration (IOM), "Causes and Consequences of Migration," en *Overview of International Migration*, International Organization for Migration, Genova, Suiza, 1995, sitio en la red electrónica, <http://www.iom.int/migrationweb/>. Mi traducción del inglés.

[13]Rodolfo Tuirán, "Migración México-Estados Unidos. Hacia una nueva agenda bilateral," en *Migración México-Estados Unidos. Opciones de política*, coord. Rodolfo Tuirán, Consejo Nacional de Población-CONAPO, México, 2000, sitio en la red electrónica, <http://www.conapo.gob.mx>.

[14]Immigration and Naturalization Service of the United States, "Glossary & Acronym Page Title," sitio en la red electrónica, <http://www.ins.usdoj.gov/text/glossary2.htm>. Mi traducción del inglés.

[15]International Organization for Migration, "Migration Terminology and Patterns in Historical Context," en *Overview of International Migration*, op. cit.

perfil como del contenido de las luchas y demandas producidos por los
nuevos flujos migratorios que incursionan en el terreno gravemente desnive-
lado de la globalización.

Los procesos impulsados por la globalización contemporánea de los
mercados están trastocando mucho más que el componente económico en la
vida cotidiana de personas y sociedades enteras. De acuerdo al Profesor R.
Fornet-Betancourt, filósofo cubano, "la realidad de la globalización como
hecho histórico" constituye un complejo de procesos que está "cambiando el
rostro del planeta y nuestra manera de percibir el mundo y de ubicarnos en
él."[16] En cuanto tejido expansivo de mercados, este tipo de globalización des-
marca fronteras impulsado por los principios de la privatización, la competencia, la ganancia y rentabilidad, hasta resultar en la economización de toda
relación humana. Así, la comprensión misma de la vida, los mecanismos para
sostenerla, y los términos para nombrarla están en cuestión. Debido a que
estos principios son adversos a los intereses vitales de la gente, una creciente
población mundial enfrenta crecientes limitaciones en su acceso a los bienes
mínimos para sostener una existencia humana digna, y trastocan la actividad
práctica y cognitiva con la que poblaciones enteras organizan su existencia
diaria en el mundo. Los códigos éticos de la sociabilidad cotidiana y las políticas que la orientan están en franco proceso de cambio y readaptación. En este
contexto, la "migración" emerge como una categoría descriptiva del lenguaje
referida a grandes flujos humanos de alcance mundial que buscan encontrar y
dar sentido a su existencia diaria en un mundo que les niega la acogida.

Desde mi punto de vista, el término "migración" no es una categoría
analítica, sino meramente descriptiva de un tipo particular de actividad
humana que, aunque ha estado presente desde los orígenes de la historia, en
el actual capitalismo neoliberal obliga a repensar y redimensionar los marcos
vitales de la humanidad y cuanto la rodea. Así, creo que el término
"migración" es una construcción del lenguaje para describir, explicar y regular la movilidad humana alrededor del globo, que envuelve intereses sociales
de carácter económico y político, que está condicionada por circunstancias sistemáticas y contextuales asociadas a la posición social y la condición sexual y

---

[16]Raúl Fornet-Betancourt, *Transformación Intercultural de la Filosofía. Ejercicios Teóricos y Prácticos de
Filosofía Intercultural desde Latinoamérica en el Contexto de la Globalización*, Deslée de Brouwer, Bilbao,
2001, 332.

racial de la gente, y que conlleva repercusiones transformadoras del conjunto socio-cultural generador y receptor de la migración. Esta comprensión de "migración" implica la necesidad de superar las distinciones clásicas de la cultura moderna entre "nacionales" y "extranjer@s," y apoya los esfuerzos de mucha gente por resignificar y redimensionar conceptos heredados que ya muestran ser reductivos y caducos, tales como nación, estado, ciudadanía, etc.

A modo de ilustración para apoyar este argumento, quiero hacer notar que la definición moderna de *Estado* como poseedor de "una población permanente, un territorio definido, y un gobierno efectivo que ejercita soberanía interna y externa"[17] poco tiene que ver con lo que hoy existe en nuestros contextos, donde la población se mantiene en movimiento, los territorios están desdibujados o en disputa, y ningún gobierno de izquierda o derecha es efectivo para proteger a los grupos subalternos, ni mucho menos soberano frente a los poderes del mercado neoliberal.

De acuerdo con P. Hondagneu-Sotelo, "tanto los estudios feministas como los trabajos sobre raza y origen étnico contienen pistas importantes para una revisión analítica de la calidad migratoria."[18] Para estos estudios, los términos "migración" y "calidad migratoria" son construcciones socio-políticas que adquieren significado en contextos cambiantes de movilidad humana cuya motivación y momento puntual de emprenderla varían en la vida social e individual de las personas, y cuyo impacto ha ido en mayor detrimento para las mujeres y quienes de ellas dependen. Aunque esas categorías están formalmente definidas por la legislación moderna, las experiencias actuales de interacción socio-cultural y de reconceptualización de la actividad humana en el mundo – incluyendo la economía, la política, la cotidianidad, etc.– en términos democráticos de mayor justicia, muestran la urgencia de repensarlas para los fines de nuevos modelos sociales que aseguren el bienestar y los derechos de toda la gente. De hecho, la Organización Internacional de Migraciones señala que la legislación contemporánea sobre migración en el contexto de Estados particulares, es una adaptación de la legislación internacional sobre los derechos

---

[17]Para esta y otras definiciones relacionadas ver, International Organization for Migration. "International Migration Law," en *Overview of International Migration*, op. cit.

[18]Pierrette Hondagneu-Sotelo, "Trabajando 'sin papeles' en Estados Unidos: hacia la integración de la calidad migratoria en relación a consideraciones de raza, clase y género," en *Mujeres en las Fronteras: Trabajo, Salud y Migración (Belice, Guatemala, Estados Unidos y México)*, coord. Esperanza Tuñón Pablos, El Colegio de la Frontera Sur (ECOSUR), El Colegio de Sonora (COLSON), El Colegio de la Frontera Norte (COLEF), México 2001, p. 209.

humanos y tiene su raíz en las ramas de legislación internacional relativa a los derechos humanos.[19] Haciendo eco a numerosas organizaciones activistas estadounidenses que trabajan por los derechos de los migrantes desde las iglesias,[20] podemos decir que si la actual globalización de mercados ha roto barreras geográficas y culturales, es congruente y consistente con la razón humana abogar por nuevos marcos de sociabilidad político-cultural y de legislación que no sólo rompan el *continuum* de criminalización, de penalización, y de asesinatos fronterizos en serie, sino también que rompan los múltiples y crecientes desequilibrios que la globalización económica produce.

Con todo, el contexto presente también nos exige tomar en cuenta dos advertencias. La primera es señalada por el movimiento Alianza Social Continental, cuando reconoce que "la movilidad y el desplazamiento de los trabajadores y trabajadoras están excluidos de los acuerdos concernientes a la libre circulación de los capitales, de los bienes y de sus agentes."[21] Con esto, la población migrante y las organizaciones que con ella trabajan ven obstaculizada su influencia en la formulación y en la decisión sobre las políticas económicas que gobiernan el mundo. Más todavía, según indica la CEPAL, esta exclusión de los espacios donde las decisiones son tomadas, afecta notablemente a las mujeres pobres, a pesar de que ellas desempeñan luchas significativas en la reivindicación y defensa de los derechos humanos, así como en el desarrollo de estrategias para fines de supervivencia.[22] La segunda advertencia es argumentada convincentemente por el teólogo indio F. Wilfred al señalar que si el eje articulador de los derechos humanos es el principio de la igualdad, entonces la globalización capitalista neoliberal y los dere-

[19]International Organization for Migration, "International Migration Law," en *Overview of International Migration*, op. cit.

[20]Sobre esto ver, Leaders of faith-based and Human rights groups, "U.S.-Mexico Border Deaths Demand Policy Change," *Worldwide Faith News Archives y National Council of the Churches of Christ in the U.S.A.*, June 4, 2000, sitio en la red electrónica, <http://www.beta.wfn.org>, <http://www.ncccusa.org>.

[21]Alianza Social Continental, *Alternativas para las Américas. Hacia un acuerdo entre los pueblos del continente. Las Américas y la integración continental*, Segunda Cumbre de los Pueblos de las Américas, Québec, Abril 2001, sitio en la red electrónica, <http://www.cumbredelospueblos.org>.

[22]Comisión Económica para América Latina y el Caribe-CEPAL, "Desarrollo sostenible, pobreza y género. América Latina y el Caribe: medidas hacia el año 2000," *Séptima Conferencia Regional sobre la Integración de la Mujer en el Desarrollo Económico y Social de América Latina y el Caribe*, CEPAL, Santiago de Chile, 19 al 21 de noviembre de 1997, sitio en la red electrónica, <http://www.eclac.org/espanol/Reuniones/confmujer/l1064 e.htm>.

chos humanos son incompatibles. Desde su punto de vista, "el capitalismo transnacional con su mercado y comercio global invade todo sector de la vida humana y se ha convertido en un violador insidioso de los derechos humanos . . . de modo que, la gente empobrecida requiere hoy de nuevas rutas y medios para combatir y protegerse de este nuevo absolutismo económico que exige grandes sacrificios humanos."[23]

En la agenda de numerosos movimientos sociales y eclesiales por el cambio social, de nuevo emerge como ruta valiosa la lucha por presionar la observancia de los derechos de los migrantes estipulados por la Organización de las Naciones Unidas (ONU), junto con la revisión y reformulación de esos derechos para confrontar los nuevos escenarios impuestos por la globalización de mercados. Con esta idea, siguiendo el aporte de la socióloga feminista peruana Virginia (Gina) Vargas, la globalización pasa a ser comprendida como "nuevo terreno de disputa" en el cual, me parece, la migración se entiende como el nuevo sitio de lucha por los derechos de las mujeres y los hombres migrantes.[24] En este contexto, es interesante notar que mientras México y Estados Unidos se han comprometido a respetar y honrar el *Pacto Internacional de Derechos Económicos, Sociales, y Culturales* adoptado por la Asamblea General de la ONU desde 1966 y que aplica por igual a la población migrante, los Estados Unidos y otros países centroamericanos – con excepción de Guatemala y Belice – se han negado a firmar la *Convención Internacional sobre la Protección de los Derechos de todos los Trabajadores Migrantes y de sus Familiares,* adoptada por la Asamblea General de las Naciones Unidas en 1990.[25] De todas formas, aunque Estados Unidos ha aceptado implementar el *Pacto-66,* que habla de crear las condiciones para que cada persona pueda realizarse libre del temor y de la miseria, y goce de sus derechos económicos, sociales, culturales, civiles, y políticos, la evidencia indica que tales condiciones y tales

---

[23]Felix Wilfred, "Human Rights of the Rights of the Poor? Redeeming the Human Rights from Contemporary Inversions," *Service of Documentation and Studies-SEDOS,* Roma, Italia, sitio en la red electrónica, <http://www.sedos.org/english/Wilfred.html>. Mi traducción del inglés.

[24]Virgina Vargas, "Ciudadanías globales y sociedades civiles globales. Pistas para el análisis," Instituto de Comunicación y Desarrollo ICD, Mercosur, Montevideo, Uruguay, sitio en la red electrónica, <http://www.icd.org.uy/mercosur/forum/vargas.html>; Gina Vargas, "Nuevas dinámicas de la globalización," Feminismos Plurales: VIII Encuentro Feminista Latinoamericano y del Caribe, A Comunidad WWW de Movimientos Sociales, *Area de Mujeres ALAI,* Serie Aportes para el debate 7, sitio en la red electrónica, <http://www.alainet.org/mujeres/feminismos/>.

[25]Oficina del Alto Comisionado de las Naciones Unidas para los Derechos Humanos-UNHCHR, *Pacto Internacional de Derechos Económicos, Sociales y Culturales,* adoptado y abierto a la firma, rati-

derechos no son viables dentro y fuera de sus fronteras. Igualmente, desde marzo de 1999, México ha aceptado implementar la *Convención-90*, pero la violación de los derechos de los migrantes centroamericanos dentro de sus fronteras es permanente, como bien lo señala la Red de Casas del Migrante-Scalabrini. Desde el punto de vista de la migración, entonces, hemos de adoptar la postura de quienes señalan que su problemática central no radica principalmente en meras cuestiones laborales, sino en las graves y urgentes cuestiones del respeto a los derechos y dignidad fundamental de la persona humana. Esta postura ciertamente incluye la lucha por cambios en la legislación migratoria, pero como bien señala el PNUD en su *Informe 2000*, "la legislación por sí sola no puede garantizar los derechos humanos."[26]

De hecho, en el hoy de nuestros pueblos, esos derechos fundamentales de la persona humana que presuntamente le garantizarían una existencia digna, segura, estable, sana y buena, son los que ningún gobierno vigente tiene la capacidad de proteger ni dentro ni fuera de sus fronteras, y a menudo las élites políticas carecen de voluntad para hacerlo. El panorama para nuestros pueblos no tiene visos de mejoría en un futuro cercano. El Secretario Ejecutivo de la CEPAL señala en su reciente informe 2000–2001, que "la situación laboral es un área en claro deterioro"; que "en la mayoría de los países continuó la tendencia adversa en la distribución del ingreso"; que si bien las mujeres tienen una creciente participación "en la generación de ingreso familiar" y en la jefatura de hogares, su ausencia es notable en cuestiones de políticas públicas; y que "el problema esencial es incorporar efectivamente la equidad en la agenda social y , sobre todo, en la agenda económica."[27] En este panorama, la migración se convierte en la perspectiva única y decisiva a

ficación y adhesión por la Asamblea General en su resolución 2200 A (XXI), de 16 de diciembre de 1966, entrada en vigor: 3 de enero de 1976; Oficina del Alto Comisionado de las Naciones Unidas para los Derechos Humanos-UNHCHR, *Convención Internacional sobre la Protección de los Derechos de todos los Trabajadores Migratorios y de sus Familiares*, adoptada por la Asamblea General en su resolución 45/158, del 18 de diciembre de 1990; Oficina de la Alta Comisionada de Derechos Humanos, *Estatus de los principales instrumentos Internacionales de derechos humanos*, al 08 de Enero de 2002, Ginebra, Suiza. Todos estos documentos y otros de relevancia para este tema se encuentran en el sitio de la red electrónica de la UNHCHR, <http://www.unhchr.ch/spanish/>.

[26]Programa de las Naciones Unidas para el Desarrollo-PNUD, *Derechos humanos y desarrollo humano: Informe sobre Desarrollo Humano 2000*, PNUD, Nueva York, 2000, sitio en la red electrónica, <http://www.undp.org/undp/hdro2000>.

[27]José Antonio Ocampo, *Panorama Social de América Latina 2000–2001*, Comisión Económica para América Latina y el Caribe-CEPAL, Septiembre de 2001, sitio en la red electrónica, <http://www.eclac.org/>.

través de millones de personas que buscan aliviar su desesperada situación de pobreza, y la pobreza no es sino la expresión de las profundas desigualdades que directamente socavan la dignidad de la gente situada en los estratos más bajos de la actual jerarquía social y cultural. La desigualdad sistémica produce violencia entre los pueblos, grupos sociales, culturas, etnias, mujeres y hombres. La pobreza es generada por las desigualdades y las desigualdades provienen de la injusticia. Desde la perspectiva religiosa, las injusticias tienen su raíz en los poderes del mal que proceden de personas y sistemas que actúan en contra de la gente inocente. Como tal, el mal es un pecado que debe ser erradicado desde sus raíces para eliminar sus resultados. La eliminación del pecado, en cuanto actualización de la salvación, constituye la finalidad última de la experiencia religiosa y es la misión esencial de la iglesia. La erradicación del pecado pasa necesariamente por la transformación de los principios que gobiernan el mundo e implica, de suyo, cambiar el rumbo de la presente globalización mediante una transformación sistemática con miras a una nueva civilización sustentadora de la igualdad, la justicia, la libertad, el bienestar, la dignidad de toda la gente, y la integridad de la creación. Tanto la experiencia religiosa autónoma como la institucionalizada pueden y deben contribuir a esta transformación para igualar el terreno donde toda la humanidad es peregrina.

LA HUMANIDAD MIGRANTE PORTADORA DE REBELIÓN Y RESISTENCIA

Entre los varios métodos empleados por la IOM para estudiar las tipologías de la migración internacional, el método que identifica a los migrantes por causa o motivación señala tres tipos de ellos que, en mi opinión, son similares al migrante de nuestra región. Se trata de migrantes de sobrevivencia, quienes buscan escapar de la pobreza y el desempleo; migrantes de oportunidades, quienes buscan mejorar su calidad de vida; y migrantes ecológicos, quienes buscan escapar de alguna crisis ambiental o degradación de su medio ambiente.[28] Estas tres situaciones a menudo se empalman para delinear el perfil de la gente que peregrina motivada por un poder mayor que la mera razón esencialista moderna es incapaz de percibir o de explicar. Debido a su dependen-

---

[28]International Organization for Migration, "Migration Terminology and Patterns in Historical Context," op. cit.; ver también International Organization for Migration, "Causes and Consequences of Migration," op. cit.

cia de la retórica analítica secularista y economicista, la mayoría de analistas que estudian la migración, pasan por alto el hecho de que la gente cruza fronteras inspirada en visiones y sueños de bienestar que a menudo tienen raigambre religiosa. Para la gente migrante, cuando sus sueños de bienestar han sido rotos y traicionados una y otra vez, paradójicamente reapropian el poder conferido por sus visiones de bienestar, para autocomprenderse como actores y sujetos que luchan por una vida mejor, aunque su única ruta viable sea la migración. En esta lucha, mucha gente queda en el camino y entre sus opciones, sólo vislumbran morir de hambre en su tierra o morir luchando en el camino. Bien comenta A. Cedeño que "incontables son las historias de aquellas personas que se atrevieron a soñar y encontraron la muerte, la cárcel o fueron deportadas como si fuesen delincuentes."[29] De muchas maneras, en la lucha migrante persiste la marca que el PNUD-*Informe 2000* asigna a todas las civilizaciones, que es el respeto "a la dignidad y la libertad humanas. Todas las religiones y las tradiciones culturales celebran esos ideales. Pero han sido violados a lo largo de la historia."[30] La gran mayoría de migrantes aspiran a que la peregrinación que emprenden les brinde mayor dignidad y libertad humanas, y que encuentren la fuente de iluminación en sus propias visiones espirituales que ninguna ideología puede darles.

En esta misma línea, la debilidad del lenguaje dominante empleado por las elites educadas que estudian la realidad migratoria, bien sea desde plataformas gubernamentales o autónomas, radica en que ese lenguaje presenta a la gente migrante como meros objetos pasivos de estudio. Hablo aquí de un lenguaje que, además de ocultar las causas sistemáticas radicales de la migración, conceptualiza a la gente migrante no como sujetos de historia, sino como débiles actores escapistas que traicionan a sus Estados nacionales debilitados o que caen presa de la malévola política migratoria estadounidense. Así, esas elites ilustradas no sólo roban a la gente su capacidad de lucha y su poder de decisión transformadora, sino además la victimizan todavía más cuando la despersonalizan. Esas elites hacen discursos "sobre" la gente migrante, no desde ella ni sus intereses vitales, sin capacidad de atizar las luchas democráticas migrantes y sin poder para conferir fuerza a sus visiones

---

[29]Amalia Cedeño, "Remesas Familiares: ¿Granos de Arena o Pedacitos de Pan?" *Noticias Ideay*, Domingo 3 de marzo, 2002, sitio en la red electrónica, <http://www.ideay.net.ni/artículos/>.
[30]Programa de las Naciones Unidas para el Desarrollo-PNUD, *Derechos humanos y desarrollo humano*, op. cit.

de dignidad y bienestar. La persona migrante no es reducible a una mercancía ni a una estadística, ni la lucha migrante es un puro asunto de legislación laboral. Solamente entendiendo a la persona migrante como "mercancía" es como podemos justificar la idea de que "las naciones en vías de desarrollo se han transformado en exportadoras de mano de obra".[31] En cambio, solamente admitiendo que la persona migrante es fuente y portadora de espíritu creativo desde el cual lucha contra el sometimiento a la inercia de los mercados, es que podemos entenderla como sujeto de actividad práctica y cognitiva emancipadora. Aquí es donde adquiere sentido un lenguaje analítico-crítico comprometido con la dignidad y los derechos de las mujeres y los hombres migrantes.

La comprensión de la migración como nuevo terreno de lucha insertado en el espacio de la globalización neoliberal, tiene la posibilidad de energizar la fuerza activada ya por otros movimientos sociales como el feminista, el indígena, el estudiantil, o el ecológico, en sus luchas por otro tipo de globalización replanteada ahora en términos democrático-interculturales para influir en las posibles condiciones históricas que hagan viables la justicia social, la dignidad e igualdad humanas, y el bienestar de toda la gente. Esta comprensión, sin embargo, también exige un viraje de carácter filosófico, antropológico y ético en nuestra comprensión de la humanidad migrante. Para este viraje, encuentro sumamente valiosas las aportaciones hechas por R. Fornet-Betancourt quien, en el marco de una filosofía crítica intercultural, propone comprender la existencia humana desde "el principio subjetividad de la persona humana viviente."[32] Como explica Fornet-Betancourt, este es un principio articulador de reflexión y acción que, ubicado en la tradición del humanismo crítico-ético y con raíces en las corrientes liberadoras del cristianismo, entiende la subjetividad de la humanidad viviente en términos de rebelión y resistencia de esta forma:

> "Hablamos entonces de una subjetividad que carga con el programa de la *humanitas* para hacerse su vehículo de realización. Y es por eso que esta subjetividad participa de la memoria histórica que se condensa en la tradición

[31]Alianza Social Continental, *Alternativas para las Américas*, op. cit.
[32]Raúl Fornet Betancourt, "Aproximaciones a la globalización como universalización de políticas neoliberales, desde una perspectiva filosófica," *Revista Pasos DEI*, no. 83, sitio en la red electrónica, <http://www.dei_cr.org/Pasos832.html>. Ver una versión actualizada de este artículo en Raúl Fornet-Betancourt, *Transformación Intercultural de la Filosofía. Ejercicios Teóricos y Prácticos de Filosofía Intercultural desde Latinoamérica en el contexto de la Globalización*, Deslée de Brouwer, Bilbao, 2001, 309–347.

humanística liberadora con fuerza normativa y un imperativo de continuación; y es por eso también que esta subjetividad sabe valorar y discernir, levantándose como poder de elección y reclamando su autonomía frente a la 'ley' o frente al *curso legal* de las cosas. Y es por eso, finalmente, que esta subjetividad es la *formación* en la que la existencia humana conserva siempre – al menos como posibilidad – su carácter de foco irreducible de rebelión y resistencia. Cuando hablamos de subjetividad en la línea de la tradición filosófica del humanismo crítico-ético, nos referimos entonces a una subjetividad concreta y viviente que, alimentada por la memoria de liberación de todos los que han luchado por su humanidad negada, se funda como existencia comunitaria en resistencia para continuar dicha tradición de liberación."[33]

En mi opinión, la pertinencia del "principio subjetividad de la persona humana viviente" para la problemática migratoria puede ser apreciada desde varios ángulos. Primero, actúa como correctivo de los métodos dominantes de estudio sobre migración en su precario lenguaje economicista, sexista, y despersonalizante; segundo, corrige la comprensión de la persona migrante degradada a ser simple objeto de estudio en transacciones mercantiles; tercero, apuntala la actividad teórica que critica a la globalización neoliberal en su rumbo adverso a la igualdad y la justicia; cuarto, permite entender a la población migrante como subjetividad viviente participativa y valorante; quinto, supera la conceptualización reductiva de la persona humana que le niega el poder de engendrar espiritualidades emancipadoras; sexto, fortalece el desarrollo de los movimientos y teorías enfocadas en el empoderamiento de la población migrante con miras a la renovación democrática del todo social; séptimo y último, proporciona un marco teórico-político para enjuiciar éticamente las prácticas sociales con relación a la población migrante.

Más todavía, quiero subrayar que la comprensión del "principio subjetividad" como "foco irreducible de rebelión y resistencia" es especialmente relevante para el contexto vital de mujeres y hombres migrantes en cuanto que afirma positivamente los límites éticos de nuestra existencia personal y social desde una opción ética por la lucha en favor de la justicia. En palabras de Fornet-Betancourt,

"La definición de esta subjetividad en términos de rebelión y resistencia, no quiere decir que la entendamos negativamente en sentido de un rechazo

[33]Fornet-Betancourt, *Transformación Intercultural*, p. 312.

porque con su caracterización como foco fontanal de resistencia rebelde quer-emos resaltar más bien ese momento de fundación ética originaria como exis-tencia libre y solidaria con el destino del otro en cuanto es precisamente esta dimensión de afirmación 'subjetiva' o, lo que es lo mismo, esa capacidad de autodeterminación y autoestimación la que la lleva a poner la *humanitas* como el límite y/o la frontera que no podrán ser trasgredidos en ninguna persona humana, como tampoco violados por ninguna persona ni por ninguna prác-tica social ni sistema político o económico. La rebelión y/o la resistencia implican así el reconocimiento de la *humanitas* como valor último que debe ser realizado *en* y *por* cada uno. Es entonces la frontera donde se dice 'basta' y se protesta por el maltrato o se reclaman los derechos (humanos) negados. Dicho de otro modo, es la frontera que traza la misma lucha del sujeto por la justicia como compromiso solidario con la *humanitas* en y para todos."[34]

Estas reflexiones iluminan el camino para una reconceptualización de la mujer o del hombre migrante como personas vivientes, como focos de rebelión y resistencia, como sujetos de valoración ética, y como identidades que enjui-cian el todo del sistema en que vivimos. Desde la subjetividad viviente de la persona migrante queda expuesto que las luchas de los movimientos sociales por los derechos inherentes a la persona humana, además de incluir las "siete libertades" señaladas por el *PNUD-Informe 2000*,[35] igualmente exigen un vira-je hacia una comprensión más amplia de la población migrante en términos de rebeldía y resistencia, términos que envuelven necesariamente la dimensión ética y espiritual de la humanidad. Como bien señaló la célebre Comandante Dora María Téllez en su magnífica exposición sobre "Nicaragua: Inmigración y Sociedad," todo el trayecto de la ruta migrante, desde sus impredecibles principio y fin, revela el malestar y la protesta de la gente excluida contra las condiciones indignas e inhumanas que vivimos, pero también habla de una gran tenacidad y de la fuerza espiritual de la gente migrante, que ningún muro puede contener.[36] Y así es, el conjunto de las luchas envueltas en la pere-grinación migrante desde nuestra región, revela la protesta de la gente contra el fatalismo insidioso que la ideología neoliberal divulga en sus mensajes sobre el determinismo dogmático de los mercados. Pero también es resisten-

---

[34]Ibid., p. 313.
[35]Programa de las Naciones Unidas para el Desarrollo-PNUD, *Derechos humanos y desarrollo humano*, op. cit.
[36]Conferencia presentada por la Comandante D.M. Téllez ante la administración, facultad y alum-nado de la Universidad de San Diego (USD). Esta conferencia fue convocada por el Instituto Transfronterizo y el Social Issues Committee de la USD, Abril 23, 2001, San Diego, California.

cia contra la ideología dominante que justifica al mercado global como proveedor único y último de las más profundas aspiraciones humanas de dignidad y bienestar. Tales aspiraciones son no viables en el contexto presente.

A mi modo de ver, sugiero que la población migrante representa en toda su trayectoria el reclamo por participar en el curso de la historia con los medios que tiene a su alcance, aunque estos medios conlleven peores amenazas a su propia vida. De acuerdo a R. Gómez Arau y P. Trigueros, "los migrantes expresan su resistencia a situaciones sociales, políticas y económicas globales que los oprimen y marginan en ambas sociedades, incluso si se acomodan a vivir en condiciones de extrema vulnerabilidad e inseguridad."[37] De muchos modos, el mensaje que envía la humanidad migrante consiste en que hay que hacer algo frente a tanta pobreza, opresión, y miseria, y como indica F. Hinkelammert tomando ese dicho de la sabiduría popular, "vale más hacer algo que no hacer nada." Para Hinkelammert,

> "cuando hoy preguntamos por alternativas, lo hacemos dentro de una economía de mercado que cada vez más lo transformado en la única instancia totalizadora de las decisiones sociales . . . crear una sociedad en la que todos tengan cabida presupone, por consiguiente, disolver esas fuerzas compulsivas de los hechos que terminan por imponer una sociedad en la que nadie cabe . . . incluso en el caso extremo en que no aparece ninguna alternativa viable, eso no es ninguna razón para entonar el himno del suicidio colectivo de la humanidad. Tenemos que resistir asimismo aun cuando no haya una solución ya visible en el horizonte. Nunca es imposible no hacer algo. Y es mejor hacer algo que no hacer nada."[38]

A esta luz, la migración aparece como la única alternativa viable para miles de gentes y es así que pasa a ser, no solo sitio de rebelión, de resistencia y de protesta, sino también nuevo terreno de lucha por la dignidad y los derechos de la persona humana viviente. Por eso nos es dada la posibilidad de entender que la agonía vivida por miles de seres vivientes, simbolizados por Carlota de la Cruz y Oscar Reyes, no es sino el más degradante castigo que los

---

[37]Remedios Gómez Arnau y Paz Trigueros, "Comunidades transnacionales e iniciativas para fortalecer las relaciones con las comunidades mexicanas en los Estados Unidos," en *Migración México-Estados Unidos Opciones de política*, coord. Rodolfo Tuirán, Consejo Nacional de Población-CONAPO, México, 2000, sitio en la red electrónica, <http://www.conapo.gob.mx>.

[38]Franz Hinkelammert, *Cultura de Esperanza y Sociedad sin Exclusión*, Departamento Ecuménico de Investigaciones-DEI, San José, Costa Rica, 1995, pp. 158 y 325.

agentes del mercado les han impuesto a causa de su protesta, su rebeldía y su resistencia. En sus cuerpos vivientes torturados, como en un libro abierto, podemos leer que no fueron meros buscadores de fortuna tras una gratificación lucrativa, sino parte de esa rebelde y tenaz humanidad que habla de visiones de trascendencia. Las interminables cruces que penden a lo largo del muro de Amexica, o los rostros que vemos todos los días aquí cubiertos de ansiedad ante la inminencia de saltar el muro o de alcanzar la otra orilla del río, no pertenecen a las elites educadas, propietarias y bien acomodadas de nuestros países.[39] Estas elites cruzan Amexica en carro o llegan en avión protegidas por su visa, por su posición social, o por su estatus político protegido por la legislación estadounidense. Los rostros que vemos aquí son los de la población más pobre, los de esa humanidad excluida que lucha y sobrevive con el alimento de una espiritualidad forjada por la rebeldía y la resistencia.

Posiblemente, uno de los aspectos que mejor ilustra esa espiritualidad migrante de rebeldía y de resistencia lo encontramos en el sistema de las remesas generado y mantenido por la población migrante. Sin embargo, conviene también señalar que este sistema conlleva aspectos controvertidos porque las remesas juegan también un rol ambiguo, tanto para la humanidad migrante como para los estados nacionales y sus instituciones políticas. A pesar de que el asunto de las remesas está recibiendo un interés dramáticamente creciente por parte de las instituciones financieras internacionales y que tiene importancia capital para los gobiernos vigentes, este es el asunto menos conocido en las deliberaciones eclesiales y teológicas y es el menos abordado en las agendas de los movimientos sociales y religiosos por los derechos de los migrantes. De nuevo, para quienes subscribimos agendas de transformación emancipadora, más que un asunto de mera transacción de capitales, las remesas envuelven redes de subsistencia afincadas en la más profunda humanidad espiritual de la población migrante, aunque la realidad actual indica que estas redes pueden estar en proceso de cooptación y explotación por las gigantescas instituciones financieras mundiales y por las elites políticas de los Estados nacionales. Ciertamente, de esta cooptación y explotación no hablan las insti-

---

[39]Por ejemplo, tomando en cuenta el nivel educativo, el CONAPO informa que hasta 1996, "alrededor de 70 de cada 100 migrantes no tienen instrucción formal, o como máximo han terminado la primaria," Consejo Nacional de Población de México, "Nuevas orientaciones del flujo migratorio laboral México-Estados Unidos," Encuesta sobre migración en la frontera Norte de México (EMIF), Migración Internacional, Boletín no. 1, Mayo, 1997.

tuciones gubernamentales que estudian la migración. En cuanto a su definición formal, las remesas son los dineros que la población migrante regresa a su país de origen y que son enviados directamente a sus familiares sea en efectivo o en especie.[40] Como fruto del trabajo de la humanidad migrante, del cual viven millones de personas y el cual literalmente detiene el colapso de economías nacionales enteras, las remesas son reveladoras de una espiritualidad vivida que trasciende los pobres códigos mercantilistas. Como señala N. Lechner, investigador de la FLACSO, el trabajo "es no sólo la principal fuente de ingreso, sino igualmente el ámbito donde las personas hacen una experiencia vital de lo que puede ser la dignidad, el reconocimiento y la integración a una tarea colectiva.[41] En la enseñanza del Papa Juan Pablo II, el trabajo viene a ser "la clave esencial de toda la cuestión social" de la cual derivan consecuencias de naturaleza ética porque el primer fundamento del valor del trabajo es la persona misma, su sujeto, cuya actividad está en la dirección de "hacer la vida humana más humana."[42]

[40]Para estas definiciones ver, International Organization for Migration, "Causes and Consequences of Migration," op. cit.; Rodolfo Corona Vázquez, "Monto y uso de las remesas en México," en *Migración México-Estados Unidos Opciones de política*, op. cit.; José Gómez de León y Rodolfo Tuirán, "Patrones de continuidad y cambio de la migración hacia Estados Unidos," en *Migración México-Estados Unidos. Presente y Futuro*, coord. Rodolfo Tuirán, Consejo Nacional de Población-CONAPO, México, 2000, sitio en la red electrónica, <http://www.conapo.gob.mx>; Migration Dialogue, "Data. Remittances," Migration News, University of California Davis, sitio en la red electrónica, <http://migration.ucdavis.edu/Data/remit.on.www/remittances.html>; Fondo Multilateral de Inversiones, *Remittances as a Development Tool: A Regional Conference*, Conferencia auspiciada por el Fondo Multilateral de Inversiones-FOMIN y el Banco Interamericano de Desarrollo-BID, Mayo 17–18, 2001, Washington, D.C., sitio en la red electrónica, <http://www.iadb. org/exr/espanol/index_espanol.htm>. La definición más sofisticada de "remesa" la proporciona la Comisión Nacional para la Protección y Defensa de los Usuarios de Servicios Financieros-CONDUSEF de México en estos términos: "Las remesas familiares constituyen un tipo específico de transferencia unilateral de recursos entre dos economías, por lo que en la Balanza de Pagos las 'remesas familiares' se incluyen entre las transferencias unilaterales de recursos, registrados en la cuenta corriente . . . A partir de 1994, el Banco de México incorporó en la balanza de pagos el monto de las transferencias electrónicas y una estimación de las 'transferencias de bolsillo' tanto en efectivo como en especie (dinero o regalos llevados directamente por el migrante en su viaje de regreso o de visita a México)," CONDUSEF, "Transferencias de dinero EU-México," México, sitio en la red electrónica, <http://www.condusef.gob.mx>.
[41]Norbert Lechner, "Nuestros miedos," Conferencia Inaugural en la Asamblea General de la Facultad de Latinoamericana de Ciencias Sociales-FLACSO realizada en México, 1998. Esta conferencia fue publicada en *Perfiles Latinoamericanos* 13, FLACSO-México, diciembre 1998, sitio en la red electrónica, <http://mirror.undp.org/chile/desarrollo/textos/extension/indice.htm>.
[42]Juan Pablo II, *Laborem Exercens. Carta Encíclica sobre el Trabajo Humano en el 90 Aniversario de la Rerum Novarum*, Roma, 14 de septiembre de 1981, sitio en la red electrónica, <http://www.multimedios.org/bec/etexts/labore.htm>.

Para apreciar la magnitud de las remesas en cuanto a su potencial ilustrativo de trabajo rehabilitador y a la posible interpretación de su significado para el tema de una espiritualidad migrante de rebeldía y resistencia, conviene revisar algunas cifras, todas proporcionadas en moneda estadounidense. Por ejemplo, el presidente del Banco Interamericano de Desarrollo-BID, estima que sólo en el año 2000, la población latinoamericana inmigrante en los Estados Unidos envió a sus pueblos de origen un monto de $20 billones en remesas. En su opinión, en los próximos diez años esta población enviará una cantidad a sus hogares que puede superar los $300 billones, de los cuales aproximadamente el 80 porciento estará concentrado en México, Centroamérica y el Caribe.[43] Las remesas constituyen un flujo masivo e ininterrumpido de fondos que, en la región, excede las cantidades que los gobiernos asignan a los programas oficiales de desarrollo social. En el 2001, las remesas ascendieron a aproximadamente $23 billones. Mientras que la población migrante por décadas ha considerado las remesas como una estrategia de sobrevivencia para enfrentar condiciones de pobreza y exclusión, ahora el BID y otras corporaciones financieras similares están redoblando esfuerzos para incursionar en este "mercado multimillonario" de remesas mediante mecanismos de "intermediación financiera."[44] Para el BID, las remesas deben ser vistas como "instrumentos de desarrollo" y esos mecanismos buscan intervenir en el flujo de remesas para hacerlo más eficiente, pero esto conlleva un interés lucrativo de trasfondo en cuanto que también buscan apropiarse el porcentaje cargado por esos mecanismos en el envío y recepción de las remesas. Desde el punto de vista del BID, en nombre de la eficiencia para el desarrollo, es necesario diversificar estos "servicios" que el mercado ofrece a la persona migrante.

Sin embargo, para la persona migrante, el sistema de las remesas tiene una triple aplicación desligada del lucro. Primera y fundamentalmente, entre el 80 y 90 porciento de las remesas es usado por las familias para la subsisten-

[43]Enrique V. Iglesias, *Palabras del Sr. Presidente con Ocasión del Acto: Las Remesas como Instrumento de Desarrollo: Una Conferencia Regional*, Conferencia organizada por el Fondo Multilateral de Inversiones-FOMIN y el Banco Interamericano de Desarrollo-BID, Mayo 17–18, 2001, Washington, D.C., sitio en la red electrónica, <http://www.iadb.org/mif/eng/conferences/>; National Center for Policy Análisis, "Sending money home to Latin America," *Idea House Immigration Issues*, sitio en la red electrónica, <http//www.ncpa.org/pd/immigrat>.
[44]E. V. Iglesias, Ibid.; Banco Interamericano de Desarrollo, "Expertos de los sectores privado y público proponen mayor productividad en mercado multimillonario de remesas de emigrantes," Comunicado de prensa, Banco Interamericano de Desarrollo, 17 de mayo de 2001, sitio en la red electrónica, <http://www.iadb.org/exr/prensa>.

cia diaria, la satisfacción de sus necesidades básicas y la manutención cotidiana, que incluye alimentos, vestido, salud, transporte, educación, pagos corrientes de vivienda, etc. Del porcentaje restante, una cantidad es asignada a gastos de habitación, que pueden incluir la reparación, ampliación, compra o construcción de un techo donde vivir; y finalmente, la otra cantidad mínima es utilizada en la adquisición de insumos productivos, que incluyen ganado, tierras, maquinaria de trabajo, implementos de economía informal, y el ahorro.[45] El trabajo de la humanidad latinoamericana migrante, que sostiene la vivencia cotidiana de millones de hogares en sus pueblos de origen, puede ser bien sintetizado con la siguiente frase "las remesas son de gente pobre en Estados Unidos enviando dinero a gente pobre en Latinoamérica."[46] El impacto socio-económico de las remesas se describe en las siguientes cifras:

En el caso de México, este es el país más beneficiado con las remesas, seguido por República Dominicana y El Salvador. El monto aproximado de remesas enviado a México por la población migrante en Estados Unidos en 1999 se calcula en alrededor de 6,790 millones de dólares. Este monto demuestra que las remesas fueron superiores en ese periodo a las exportaciones agropecuarias, a los ingresos por concepto de turismo, y equivale al 60 por ciento de ingresos por exportación petrolera. En el año 2000, las remesas recibidas se aproximaron a los 7,000 millones, que equivale a dos tercios de las ventas de petróleo al exterior y supera todos los ingresos del turismo. Para el 2001, las remesas superarían los 9,000 millones.[47]

[45]Rodolfo Corona, "Monto y uso de las remesas en México," en *Migración México-Estados Unidos Opciones de política*, op cit.; José Gómez de León y Rodolfo Tuirán, "Patrones de continuidad y cambio de la migración hacia Estados Unidos," en *Migración México-Estados Unidos. Presente y futuro*, coord. Rodolfo Tuirán, Consejo Nacional de Población, México, D. F., 2000, sitio en la red electrónica, <http://www.conapo.gob.mx>; Jorge Castro y Rodolfo Tuirán, "Importancia de las remesas en el ingreso de los hogares," en *Migración México-Estados Unidos. Presente y futuro*, Ibid.; International Organization for Migration (IOM), "Causes and Consequences of Migration," op. cit.; Comisión Económica para América Latina y el Caribe-CEPAL, "Informe de la Reunión de Expertos sobre Uso Productivo de las Remesas en Nicaragua," *CEPAL y Naciones Unidas*, Managua, 6 de julio de 1999, sitio en la red electrónica, <http://cepal.un.org.mx/remesas.html>.

[46]Rosa Townsend, "Las remesas familiares, principal fuente de ingresos," *El País*, Miami, 23 de mayo de 2001, sitio en la red electrónica, <http://www.elpais.es/articulo.html>.

[47]Rodolfo Tuirán, "Migración México-Estados Unidos. Hacia una nueva agenda bilateral," en *Migración México-Estados Unidos. Opciones de política*, op. cit.; Comisión Nacional para la Protección y Defensa de los Usuarios de Servicios Financieros-CONDUCEF, "Transferencias de dinero EU-México," op. cit.; Moneda El Periódico Financiero, "Las Remesas: Fuente de financiamiento para la reconstrucción," *Moneda Centroamérica*, 29 de mayo-1 de junio de 2001, sitio en la red electrónica, <http://monedani.terra.com/moneda/noticias>; Graham Gory, "World Briefing. Americas: Mexico: a Lifeline From the U.S.," *The New York Times*, November 2, 2001, sitio en la red electróni-

En el caso de Guatemala, durante el período 1992 a 1997, las remesas a Guatemala pasaron de 172 millones a 350 millones, superando este último año las exportaciones individuales de azúcar, bananos, cardamomo y petróleo. Para 1999, las remesas recibidas alcanzaron un total de 535 millones, que casi igualaron las divisas obtenidas por la exportación de café.[48]

En el caso de El Salvador, este país depende principalmente de las remesas para sostener su economía. Tan sólo en 1999, el monto total de remesas estadounidenses para El Salvador superó los 1,500 millones, y en el 2000, las remesas superaron los 1,900 millones anuales, que representan un 12.5 porciento del producto interno bruto (PIB) salvadoreño y sigue siendo la principal fuente de ingresos externos, superando el monto de divisas generadas por la maquila, que es el principal rubro de exportación. En la economía salvadoreña, las remesas familiares cubren el equivalente al 85 porciento de su déficit comercial, y la proyección oficial es que este monto será superado en el 2001.[49]

En el caso de Nicaragua, para el año 1999, aunque hay discrepancia con las fuentes gubernamentales, varios estudios señalan que las remesas reales superaron los 600 millones, que representa dos tercios del valor de todas sus exportaciones. Fuentes conservadoras reportan que tan sólo de enero a junio del 2000, las remesas familiares alcanzaron los 138 millones, y ese monto ascendió en el mismo período a 159 millones en el 2001. En Nicaragua, las remesas exceden su producto interno bruto en un 14.4 porciento. De acuerdo a un estudio realizado entre la población migrante en Costa Rica, el porcenta-

ca, <http://www.nytimes.com>; Agencia de Noticias EFE, "BID propone que remesas de inmigrantes vayan al desarrollo," en Confederación Latinoamericana de Cooperativas de Ahorro y Crédito-COLAC, 15 de mayo de 2001, sitio en la red electrónica, <http://www.colac.com/noti_01.asp>; Fondo Multilateral de Inversiones-FOMIN, Latin_America & the Caribbean: Remittances by Selected Countries 1999 (US$ millions), FOMIN y Banco Interamericano de Desarrollo-BID, sitio en la red electrónica, <http://www.iadb.org/mif/>.

[48]Eduardo Antonio Velásquez Carrera, "Guatemala: Las remesas familiares, 1992–1998," Universidad de San Carlos de Guatemala, conferencia preparada para el Taller Centroamérica 2020, Migración y Transnacionalismo, San Salvador, El Salvador, julio 1999; Fondo Multilateral de Inversiones-FOMIN, Latin America & the Caribbean: Remittances by Selected Countries 1999 (US$ millions), FOMIN y Banco Interamericano de Desarrollo-BID, sitio en la red electrónica, <http://www.iadb.org/ mif/>.

[49]Moneda El Periódico Financiero, "Las Remesas: Fuente de financiamiento para la reconstrucción," Moneda Centroamérica, 29 de mayo-1 de junio de 2001, sitio en la red electrónica, <http://monedani.terra.com/moneda/noticias>; Notimex, "Preocupa en El Salvador baja en remesas familiares tras ataques a EU," Agencia Notimex, San Salvador, 23 de septiembre 2001; Agencia de Noticias EFE, "El Salvador recibió más de 900 millones de dólares en remesas," Noticias EFE, San Salvador, Agosto 21, 2000; Fondo Multilateral de Inversiones-FOMIN, Latin America & the Caribbean: Remittances by Selected Countries 1999 (US$ millions), FOMIN y Banco Interamericano de Desarrollo-BID, sitio en la red electrónica, <http://www.iadb.org/mif/>.

je de remesas enviadas al país es mayor entre las mujeres que entre los hombres, a pesar de que ellas obtienen salarios menores. Con el incremento en el monto de las remesas, este país podría cubrir el total de su deuda externa, calculada hasta el 2000 en 7,447 millones.[50]

En el caso de Honduras, tan sólo en el 2001, de enero a abril, Honduras recibió cerca de 150 millones en remesas enviadas por inmigrantes que viven es Estados Unidos, que es una cantidad similar por exportaciones de la industria ensambladora o maquila. Este país recibió en el año 1999 un total aproximado de 368 millones, y un estimado total superior a los 410 millones en el año 2000. Sus remesas anuales representan el doble de entradas por turismo y casi igualan al monto de asistencia oficial para el desarrollo. [51]

En el caso del Caribe, para Cuba, la agencia de noticias AFP reporta que mientras la CEPAL calcula en unos 800 millones anuales el monto de remesas enviadas a la isla por la población cubana en Estados Unidos, el Instituto Cubano de Economistas Independientes estima que las remesas sobrepasan los 1,000 millones anuales. En República Dominicana, el país recibe más de 1,740 millones anuales, lo cual triplica el valor de sus exportaciones agrícolas. La República Dominicana ocupa el tercer lugar, después de México y Brasil, como mayor receptora de remesas. En Haití, las remesas en 1999 llegaron a un total de 720 millones, que representan un 17 porciento de su producto interno bruto, el doble del total de divisas por concepto de importaciones, y cuatro veces más la cantidad que recibe en el rubro de asistencia oficial para el desarrollo.[52]

[50]Programa de las Naciones Unidas para el Desarrollo, *Informe sobre el Desarrollo Humano en Nicaragua 2000*, Programa de las Naciones Unidas para el Desarrollo-PNUD, 2000, sitio en la red electrónica, <http://www.undp.org.ni/idhnicaragua/>; Banco Mundial, "Countries: Nicaragua," The World Bank Group, sitio en la red electrónica, <http://www.worldbank.org/>; Edwin Saballos Rocha, "Remesas mantienen el mismo flujo," *Tiempos del Mundo*, Negocios, 13–19 de diciembre de 2001, sitio en la red electrónica, <http://www.tdm.com.ni/archivo/2001/>; Benjamín Blanco, "Mujeres envían más dinero a su familia," *La Prensa Digital*, 4 de abril del 2001, sitio en la red electrónica, <http://www.laprensa.com.ni/nacionales>; Fondo Multilateral de Inversiones-FOMIN, *Latin America & the Caribbean: Remittances by Selected Countries 1999 (US$ millions)*, FOMIN y Banco Interamericano de Desarrollo-BID, sitio en la red electrónica, <http://www.iadb.org/mif/>; Amalia Cedeño, "Remesas Familiares: ¿Granos de Arena o Pedacitos de Pan?" op. cit.

[51]La Prensa on the Web, "Honduras recibe 300 millones de dólares por maquila y remesas familiares," Agencia Informativa Acan-EFE, 19 de mayo de 2001, sitio en la red electrónica, <http://www.laprensahn/econoarc/0105/>; Fondo Multilateral de Inversiones-FOMIN, *Latin America & the Caribbean: Remittances by Selected Countries 1999 (US$ millions)*, FOMIN y Banco Interamericano de Desarrollo-BID, sitio en la red electrónica, <http://www.iadb.org/mif/>.

[52]AFP Noticias sobre Cuba, "Economistas Independientes calculan remesas a Cuba en más de USD 1.000 millones," *AFP La Habana*, Febrero 28, 2001, en Cuba Nueva, sitio en la red electrónica, <http://cubanueva.com/economia/>; Moneda El Periódico Financiero, "Las Remesas: Fuente de

Este panorama viene a confirmar la opinión de una periodista cuando dice que el "arma más eficaz para combatir la pobreza en Latinoamérica no proviene de los Gobiernos ni de la ayuda exterior, sino de las remesas de los emigrantes que viven en Estados Unidos."[53] Para la humanidad migrante, su prisma para ver el mundo comienza y termina con la determinación de romper el *continuum* de exclusión sistemática vivida cotidianamente, por eso su trabajo expresado en remesas, quiere hacer la vida humana más humana dentro y fuera de su lugar concreto. Sin embargo, la tendencia reciente adoptada por el BID y otras instituciones financieras paralelas, amenaza al sistema popular de remesas en cuanto quieren ahora concentrar los grandes mecanismos comerciales que obtienen beneficio directo de ellas con el fin de apropiarse más eficazmente del valor agregado que los actuales mecanismos adjuntan a los envíos y así controlar mejor el flujo de remesas. Esas instituciones, apoyadas por las elites locales del mercado y de los gobiernos en función, quieren controlar directamente las remesas como mera transacción de flujo comercial que viene a engrosar su balanza de capital. Si la humilde población migrante había sido considerada hasta hace poco como desechos humanos privados de valor y sólo merecedores de las penurias del desierto, los mercados depredadores globales la ven ahora como neto mercado multibillonario del que hay que extraer ganancia.[54]

Por eso, he sugerido interpretar las remesas en el marco de una espiritualidad de rebeldía y resistencia desde la humanidad migratoria viviente, justamente porque esta humanidad expone el verdadero "espíritu" de la globalización capitalista neoliberal. En palabras del Prof. Fornet-Betancourt,

financiamiento para la reconstrucción," *Moneda Centroamérica*, 29 de mayo-1 de junio de 2001, sitio en la red electrónica, <http://monedani.terra.com/moneda/noticias>; Agencia de Noticias EFE, "BID propone que remesas de inmigrantes vayan a desarrollo," op. cit.; Fondo Multilateral de Inversiones-FOMIN, *Latin America & the Caribbean: Remittances by Selected Countries 1999 (US$ millions)*, FOMIN y Banco Interamericano de Desarrollo-BID, sitio en la red electrónica, <http://www.iadb.org/mif/>.

[53]Rosa Townsend, "Las remesas familiares, principal fuente de ingresos," op. cit. En estos mismos términos se expresa A. Cedeño en su excelente artículo "Remesas Familiares: ¿Granos de Arena o Pedacitos de Pan?" op. cit.

[54]Deborah W. Meyers, "The Regional Map: Flows and Impact of Remittances in LAC," en *Remittances as a Development Tool: A Regional Conference*, organizada por el Fondo Multilateral de Inversiones-FOMIN y el Banco Interamericano de Desarrollo, Mayo 17–18, 2001, Washington, D.C., sitio en la red electrónica, <http://www.iadb.org/mif/eng/conferences/>; Banco Interamericano de Desarrollo, "Emigrantes de América Latina y Caribe Surgen como Importante Factor Para Desarrollo Económico y Social," *Comunicado de prensa*, Banco Interamericano de Desarrollo, 18 de mayo del 2001, sitio en la red electrónica, <http://www.iadb.org/exr/espanol/>.

"detrás de este 'espíritu' del neoliberalismo hay una antropología que define al ser humano como individuo, reduciéndolo a su capacidad de producir ganancias y de consumir," pero además pretende también "definir el horizonte desde el cual debemos comprender lo que somos y/o debemos ser" mediante la colonización de nuestras mentes con su espíritu que mercantiliza y monetariza todas las dimensiones humanas, y ahí lleva a cabo "un cambio en la sustancia misma de lo humano."[55] Mientras que la humanidad migrante busca hacer la vida humana más humana mediante su trabajo, los mercados están imponiendo una racionalidad y una espiritualidad corrupta que ve el mundo mediante el prisma único y decisivo de la economización rentable, la posesión excluyente, y la avaricia. Para las instituciones que mantienen al actual sistema y para los gobiernos neoliberales, todo empieza y todo termina con la avaricia. Por eso, desde una interpretación crítico-emancipadora, la racionalidad y la espiritualidad de quienes generan las remesas populares condensan el contra-espíritu de la globalización capitalista, y en su característica más profunda de rebelión y resistencia, subvierten el horizonte reductivo y degradado del mercado neoliberal. Este movimiento es expresado como "superación del paradigma de la posesión por el paradigma de la justicia."[56] Debido a que la humanidad migrante se atreve a subvertir el determinismo inhumano de los mercados y se rebela contra tal horizonte movida por la lealtad y compasión hacia los más pobres, para la Comandante D.M. Téllez, la humanidad migrante va edificándose así como "héroe" en las luchas por la justicia con su deliberada opción ética en favor de la dignidad humana y del bienestar común.[57]

También he sugerido en mi reflexión que las remesas son un arma de dos filos, de aquí su ambivalencia que es necesario rectificar. Por una parte, la sobrevivencia de nuestra gente sería mucho menos viable sin las remesas. Y es previsible que éstas aumenten porque la migración no va a terminar dadas las circunstancias sistemáticas presentes, y dadas las múltiples dependencias que el sistema estadounidense tiene de la fuerza de trabajo mal pagada que encuentra en la migración latinoamericana, y más notablemente en las mujeres.[58] Pero por otra parte, el sistema de las remesas también es utilizado

[55]Fornet-Betancourt, "Aproximaciones a la globalización," op. cit.; Fornet-Betancourt, *Transformación Intercultural*, pp. 340–342.
[56]Ibid., *Transformación Intercultural*, p. 317.
[57]D.M. Téllez, Conferencia presentada ante la administración, facultad, y alumnado de la Universidad de San Diego, op. cit.

por los gobiernos nacionales como un velo que oculta la rapacidad de sus funcionarios, quienes optan por proteger sus megasalarios a costa del desgaste de la humanidad migrante. Con las remesas, las instituciones gubernamentales erigen un poderoso muro de contención social que previene protestas sociales masivas contra su absoluta desidia e ineficacia ante los intereses y necesidades de nuestros pueblos, y así pueden perpetuar el alto nivel de vida de sus funcionarios, pero lo hacen a expensas de la miseria del pueblo y del trabajo de la humanidad migrante. Las remesas son un sistema de economía popular inventado por la gente migrante con fines de sobrevivencia, pero en él descansan los gobiernos para deshacerse de su responsabilidad por el interés común y para encubrir sus prácticas personales e institucionales corruptas. Las políticas corruptas de los gobiernos vigentes protegen a un limitado número de familias acaudaladas, a quienes benefician más incluso en las agendas de gasto social, porque como bien expone el Secretario Ejecutivo de la CEPAL, hoy día el 20 porciento más rico de la población obtiene inequitativamente un volumen superior en recursos de gasto social.[59]

Por su parte, el PNUD ha expuesto ya los graves impedimentos que acarrea la corrupción gubernamental y la de otras instituciones que incluyen la militar y la de seguridad social, para confrontar los problemas de la pobreza. Este organismo señala que, "las instituciones responsables encargadas de la gestión de los asuntos públicos suelen ser el eslabón perdido entre los esfuerzos contra la pobreza y la reducción de la pobreza . . . Hacer que los gobiernos sean responsables ante el pueblo es un requisito básico del buen gobierno . . . [pero] una fuente importante de la pobreza es la carencia de poder de la gente, no sólo su distancia del gobierno. La responsabilidad en el uso de los fondos públicos es fundamental para los esfuerzos de reducción de

[58]United States Catholic Bishops, *Welcoming the Stranger Among Us. Unity in Diversity*, A Statement of the U.S. Catholic Bishops, Office of Migration & Refugee Services, issued by the *National Conference of Catholic Bishops*, 15 de noviembre de 2000, Washington, D.C.; Jorge Santibáñez Romellón y Rodolfo Cruz Piñeiro, "Mercados laborales fronterizos," en *Migración México-Estados Unidos. Opciones de política*, op. cit.; National Center for Policy Analysis, "U.S. Dependents on Immigrant Workers," *Immigration Issues: Daily Policy Digest*, July 23, 2001, sitio en la red electrónica, <http://www.ncpa.org/pd/immigrat/>. Para un análisis feminista y datos sobre la situación laboral de las mujeres Latinas estadounidenses, ver María Pilar Aquino, "Latina Feminist Theology: Central Features," en *A Reader in Latina Feminist Theology. Religion and Justice*, ed. María Pilar Aquino, Daisy Machado and Jeanette Rodríguez, Austin, TX: University of Texas Press, 2002, 133–160.

[59]José Antonio Ocampo, *Panorama Social de América Latina 2000–2001*, op. cit.

la pobreza. Los pobres pagan un precio elevado por la corrupción . . . Si se eliminara la corrupción al mismo tiempo que los pobres se organizaran, muchos programas nacionales de lucha contra la pobreza indudablemente mejorarían su rendimiento al orientar los recursos a la gente que los necesita. Muchos problemas de orientación son en definitiva problemas de instituciones de gobierno irresponsables y que no responden a los intereses de los pobres."[60]

Y sí, hay que decirlo claramente, nos encontramos en un contexto en el cual, con las remesas, la golpeada humanidad migrante carga indebidamente con el peso de Estados nacionales debilitados, pero también altamente corruptos. De hecho, todo el sistema globalizador de mercados opera con gobiernos latinoamericanos y Caribeños que aceptan prácticas de corrupción para mantener escenarios económicos de doble estándar, uno que favorece a sus élites socio-políticas y otro que utiliza la pobreza de su gente para cabildear por ayuda externa y por la protección de remesas. Pero al mismo tiempo esos gobiernos vigentes mantienen un discurso público también de doble estándar en cuanto que, si bien proclaman su compromiso de lucha contra tales prácticas, su control del aparato legislativo prohíbe cambios en la legislación nacional hacia una práctica de gobernabilidad transparente y honesta. La magnitud de la corrupción hoy, tal como aparece en México, Argentina, Nicaragua, o en cualquier otro país en nuestra región, es tan medular y profunda que sería imposible ver su principio y su final. Lo que sí podemos ver claramente es el interés de los gobiernos para que las remesas sigan fluyendo e incrementándose ininterrumpidamente. A ninguno de estos gobiernos les interesa que cese el flujo de remesas porque bien saben que sin ellas, el tejido social de nuestros pueblos prácticamente colapsaría y porque cesaría ese catalizador clave de la pobreza masiva. Por eso tampoco les interesa impedir la migración.

En el marco de las deliberaciones sobre las nuevas políticas económicas del BID, encontramos ahora que en nuestro caso, también la Oficina Presidencial de México proclama como "héroes" a la humanidad migrante, justo por el mérito de que sigue enviando dinero a sus familias en cantidades masivas, alaba su lealtad insobornable y agradece su "compromiso real" y solidario que esta

---

[60]Programa de las Naciones Unidas para el Desarrollo, *Superar la pobreza humana. Informe del PNUD sobre la Pobreza 2000*, Programa de las Naciones Unidas para el Desarrollo-PNUD, Nueva York, 2000, sitio en la red electrónica, <http://www.undp.org/povertyreport/>.

humanidad viviente tiene con sus familiares en México.[61] Así, con esta retórica humanista de cuño espiritualista-neoliberal, sin evidencia irrefutable de administración gubernamental transparente, sin voluntad para empujar estructuras democráticas libres de avaricia, ni interés en ponderar a la humanidad excluida, es claro para mi que las fuertes asimetrías sistemáticas cultivadas por la corrupción van a continuar. Por eso es cada vez más urgente aunar las fuerzas de todos los movimientos sociales que luchan por la transformación del sistema, de modo que las visiones espirituales de nuestra gente por dignidad, bienestar y justicia no sigan siendo subvertidas. Por eso he sugerido también que hemos de reconceptualizar la globalización neoliberal como terreno de disputa porque, mientras las élites financieras y políticas que gobiernan nuestras sociedades la administran como terreno donde actualizan su avaricia y la justifican con una retórica espiritualista para fines de dominación, la humanidad migrante lucha por que sea gestionada como terreno donde la democracia radical es actualizada y justifican tal lucha con una retórica visionaria de dignidad, derechos y bienestar enraizada en sus experiencias de espiritualidad rebelde-emancipadora buscando de hacer la vida humana más humana. Por eso hemos de hacer el viraje hacia una comprensión de la migración como sitio de lucha que afirma y valida a la humanidad migrante en su agencia histórica propia como sujetos de cambio y de transformación. Desde una perspectiva de entera renovación democrática al interior de la persona y de la sociedad, esta es la única opción humana racional y espiritual que tenemos.

REFLEXIONES FINALES

En mi opinión, pisamos tierra firme cuando nuestra interpretación de la migración incluye factores religiosos, debido a que ésta es realizada por una humanidad viviente constituida también por dimensiones espirituales y religiosas que trascienden el mero código economicista utilitario. Para quienes hemos vivido los avatares de la migración familiar, la peregrinación migratoria envuelve de principio a fin, como premisa indisputable, un nivel inconmensu-

[61]Banco Interamericano de Desarrollo, "Emigrantes de América Latina y Caribe Surgen como Importante Factor Para Desarrollo Económico y Social," *Comunicado de prensa*, Banco Interamericano de Desarrollo, 18 de mayo del 2001, sitio en la red electrónica, <http://www.iadb.org/exr/espanol/>; Migration Dialogue, "Mexico: More Migration Remittances," *Migration News*, vol. 9, no. 1, January 2002; José Luis Ávila, Jorge Castro, Carlos Fuentes y Rodolfo Tuirán, "Remesas: monto y distribución regional en México," en *Migración México-Estados Unidos. Presente y futuro*, op, cit.

rable de confianza en la providencia, la fuerza y la gracia divina. Esta confianza no tiene explicaciones ni lugar en la racionalidad academicista y objetivante que domina en los estudios sobre migración, pero está presente constantemente en nuestras vidas como fuente de energía para seguir viviendo y luchando, especialmente en las condiciones más adversas. En el contexto de la migración, confrontamos la exigencia de desarrollar un lenguaje interpretativo que permita conocer críticamente nuestras vivencias cotidianas y que permita, al mismo, tiempo dar cuenta de las visiones que nos animan. Desde el lenguaje teológico que interpreta nuestras experiencias vitales en contextos socio-políticos cambiantes, como indica la Profesora E. Schüssler Fiorenza, la presencia Divina hemos de nombrarla "una y otra vez en las experiencias de lucha por el cambio y la transformación de estructuras opresivas y de ideologías y culturas deshumanizantes. Hemos de nombrar a Dios como activo 'poder de bienestar en nuestro medio' . . . [porque] es Dios quien nos acompaña en nuestras luchas contra la injusticia y por la liberación."[62] Hablar de la experiencia religiosa en el contexto de la migración, significa entonces dar nombre a esa percepción que tenemos de Dios como presencia activa y fuente última de gracia y de poder desde la misma humanidad migrante que confronta realidades opresivas para cambiarlas. Las dimensiones de rebeldía y de resistencia vividas por hombres y mujeres migrantes validan esta afirmación.

En el marco de toda teología liberadora, entiendo que el conocimiento religioso es un recurso de relevancia mayor para nombrar analíticamente, para iluminar críticamente y para dar sentido integral a las aspiraciones emancipadoras de la gente si queremos hacer que la vida humana sea más humana.

La religión es un factor que ha tenido siempre un papel central en nuestras sociedades y, si bien la racionalidad secularista de la modernidad la ha marginado, hoy adquiere una relevancia cada vez mayor en cuanto fuerza de gran peso en las políticas sociales y en cuanto forjadora de sociabilidad cotidiana. Pero también hemos de tomar en cuenta que la religión puede contribuir a frenar o a fortalecer visiones y prácticas de justicia e igualdad, puede alimentar fanatismos ciegos, puede paralizar luchas democráticas, o puede ser un espacio para cultivar y desarrollar la capacidad que tenemos de imaginar

---

[62]Elisabeth Schüssler Fiorenza, "Introduction. Feminist Liberation Theology as Critical Sophialogy," en *The Power of Naming. A Concilium Reader in Feminist Liberation Theology*, ed. Elisabeth Schüssler Fiorenza, Maryknoll, NY: Orbis Books y SCM Press, 1996, p. xxxiv. Mi traducción del inglés.

nuevas rutas humanizadoras para los procesos de cambio social. En esto, no olvidemos que las iglesias también son beneficiarias de las remesas en cuanto que, con ellas, la gente puede subvencionar las actividades parroquiales en sus varias celebraciones religiosas que pueden incluir el aniversario de templos, fiesta del santo o la santa patrona, funerales, reparación y mantenimiento de iglesias, e incluso sostener al clérigo con donaciones en limosna o en especie.[63]

Al mismo tiempo, muchos sacerdotes católicos latinoamericanos y mexicanos en particular, anualmente hacen su "peregrinación al Norte" con el fin de recoger dólares para sus parroquias entre la población Latina pobre a cambio de una "misita" o una bendición. A muchos he conocido en esta "peregrinación." Así que, hablar de la contribución de las iglesias a un futuro esperanzador desde la humanidad migrante, asume como presupuesto básico que las iglesias estén en disposición de optar deliberadamente para que el todo de su existencia sea consistente con su misión e identidad.

En este sentido, en la tradición cristiana entendemos que el contenido de la revelación Divina consiste en la salvación, expresada como emancipación radical o liberación integral de los poderes del mal para una participación plena en la vida de Dios. Entendemos, consecuentemente, que esta salvación ocurre y es anticipada desde dentro de la historia, que las iglesias encarnan el misterio de la salvación participando en la misión de Jesucristo por la gracia y poder del Espíritu-Sabiduría Divina, que la transformación del mundo y de la humanidad hacia el propósito de Dios es intrínseca a la misión de las iglesias, que éstas están llamadas a sanar a la humanidad herida y a reconciliar las relaciones sociales rotas, y que éstas tienen el imperativo evangélico de realizar esta misión desde la humanidad pobre y oprimida y a luchar a su lado por su liberación histórica y trascendente.[64] En términos de la humanidad migrante, esta comprensión no sólo es indiscutible, sino que además exige de las iglesias fortalecer deliberadamente sus actividades en favor de la eliminación del mal institucionalizado que engendra y resulta en injusticias del sistema. En este sentido, los rostros que acompañan mi reflexión desde su inicio como símbolos de la dramática desacralización de la imagen Divina en la persona humana, nos apremian como iglesia a confrontar activamente el pecado del

---

[63]Remedios Gómez Arnau y Paz Trigueros, "Comunidades transnacionales e iniciativas para fortalecer las relaciones con las comunidades mexicanas en los Estados Unidos," op. cit.

[64]Segunda Conferencia General del Episcopado Latinoamericano, *La Iglesia en la actual transformación de América Latina a la luz del Concilio. Conclusiones*, Librería Parroquial, México 1968; Concilio

mal y la injusticia que deterioran incesantemente la vida de nuestros pueblos y que encontramos expuestos ante el mundo entero en el libro abierto de la humanidad migrante. Para esto, como valientemente subraya el Consejo Mundial de Iglesias, "al afrontar las causas de la injusticia que lleva al desarraigo de las personas, la Iglesia debe estar dispuesta a pagar el precio que supone enfrentarse a los poderes establecidos y a los privilegios."[65] Con este mensaje, anoto aquí algunas tareas urgentes.

1) *Superar los miedos de nombrar la causa radical de las injusticias.* Como iglesia en acción conjunta entre el Pueblo de Dios y la jerarquía que gobierna la institución eclesiástica, tenemos la opción de construir marcos analíticos críticos que sirvan para nombrar la identidad emisora de las injusticias del sistema. Sólo así estamos en condiciones de forjar rutas cognitivas y organizativas para enfrentarlas. De aquí la necesidad de profundizar y divulgar el análisis crítico de la globalización capitalista neoliberal en sus expresiones y resultados plurales. Este análisis, para que sea sistemático e integral, debe incluir lo que en términos feministas identificamos como *globalización quiriarcal* precisamente porque es diseñada e impulsada mayoritariamente por élites de hombres educados y propietarios quienes controlan el complejo entero de la vida social, y ciertamente las élites de hombres son las que legislan y controlan la vida de las iglesias.[66] El poder que ejercen estas elites ha traído como resultado la exclusión de grandes poblaciones, pero más notable es la creciente y multiplicativa dominación y deshumanización de las mujeres. La nueva categoría analítica feminista de "quiriarcado" (del griego *kyrios*: señor, dueño, padre, esposo, maestro) supera las simples categorías descriptivas

Vaticano Segundo, *Gaudium et Spes. Constitución Pastoral sobre la Iglesia en el Mundo Actual*, Roma, 7 de diciembre de 1965, *Biblioteca Electrónica Cristiana*, sitio en la red electrónica, <http://www.multimedios. org/texts/>; Pablo VI, *Evangelii Nuntiandi. Exhortación Apostólica acerca de la Evangelización en el Mundo Contemporáneo*, Roma, 8 de diciembre de 1975, *Biblioteca Electrónica Cristiana*, sitio en la red electrónica, <http://www.multimedios.org/texts/>; Consejo Mundial de Iglesias, *La Naturaleza y Propósito de la Iglesia*, Lucerna, Suiza, noviembre de 1998, *Comisión de Fe y Orden del Consejo Mundial de Iglesias*, sitio en la red electrónica, <http://www.wcc-coe.org/wcc/what/faith/>.
[65]Consejo Mundial de Iglesias, *"Ha llegado el momento de optar por la solidaridad con losdesarraigados,"* Declaración Adoptada por el Comité Central del Consejo Mundial de Iglesias, 22 de septiembre de 1995, Lucerna, Suiza, sitio en la red electrónica, <http://www.wcc_coe.org/uprooted/momentsp.html>.
[66]Para un análisis más detallado de la "globalización quiriarcal" ver, María Pilar Aquino, "As

de "género" para efectuar un análisis sistemático que expone la compleja red de dominaciones interestructuradas y multiplicativas en las actuales sociedades y religiones.[67] Como iglesia, nos urge romper el miedo a las teorías críticas de análisis feminista que superen las limitaciones de las teorías, teologías y métodos analíticos quiriarcales. Y esto es especialmente cierto en el terreno de la migración, de aquí la relevancia que encuentro en los magníficos trabajos editados recientemente por E. Tuñón Pablos,[68] y D. Barrera Bassols y Cristina Oehmichen[69] quienes abren nuevas pistas teórico-metodológicas de cuño feminista dentro de un campo dominado por la racionalidad quiriarcal.

2)   *Activar y fortalecer las redes sociales para una transformación del sistema.* El análisis feminista de la globalización quiriarcal indica que los actuales procesos de globalización neoliberal han dejado de ser intocables. De hecho, existen numerosos movimientos sociales, eclesiales e intelectuales que luchan por transformarla hacia una globalización democrática emancipadora afincada en la justicia y en la dignidad humanas para el bienestar de la humanidad entera. La transformación sistemática de la *globalización quiriarcal* forma parte de la misión de las iglesias, pero para ello es necesaria una opción deliberada de la iglesia entera por unir nuestras energías y nuestros recursos con esos movimientos mediante el fortalecimiento de las redes sociales locales. Hoy en día, la transformación sistemática pasa igualmente por el cambio de los códigos que presiden la convivencia cotidiana, cuyo significado es fuertemente redimensionado debido a la migración. Aquí, como iglesia contribuimos más eficazmente al cambio social con nuestra labor educativa y organizativa enfocada en la

Dinâmicas da Globalização e a Universidade. Para uma transformação feminista, democrático-emancipadora radical," *Perspectiva Teológica* (Facultad de Teología, Centro de Estudos Superiores da Companhia de Jesus, Belo Horizonte, Brasil), Ano XXXIV, No. 92 (2002): 37–62.

[67]Elisabeth Schüssler Fiorenza, *Rhetoric and Ethic. The Politics of Biblical Interpretation*, Fortress Press, Minneapolis, 1999, p. 5; Elisabeth Schüssler Fiorenza, *Jesus and the Politics of Interpretation*, Continuun, New York, 2000, pp. 156–158.

[68]Esperanza Tuñón Pablos, ed., *Mujeres en las Fronteras: Trabajo, Salud y Migración* (Belice, Guatemala, Estados Unidos y México), El Colegio de la Frontera Sur-ECOSUR, El Colegio de Sonora-COLSON, El Colegio de la frontera Norte-COLEF, México, D.F., 2001.

[69]Dalia Barrera Bassols y Cristina Oehmichen Bazán, ed., *Migración y Relaciones de Género en México*, ed. Grupo Interdisciplinario sobre mujer, Trabajo y Pobreza-GIMTRAP e Instituto de Investigaciones Antropológicas, México, D.F., 2000.

construcción de una sociabilidad democrática que, enraizada en principios ético- religiosos, vaya rompiendo el *continuum* de violencia y deshumanización presente en nuestras vivencias domésticas y sociales.

3)   *Renunciar a privilegios y transformar las estructuras de la propia Iglesia.* En este punto, el Catolicismo Romano enfrenta desafíos mayores en los nuevos contextos de globalización. No es ningún secreto para nadie que, en la percepción de mucha gente, durante el papado de Juan Pablo II la gran mayoría de la jerarquía eclesiástica en la Iglesia Católica ha hecho un viraje hacia un eclipse de su conciencia social y hacia la negligencia en su responsabilidad frente a los clamores de la humanidad excluida por justicia, derechos y liberación.[70] En detrimento de la humanidad excluida, la mayoría de obispos ha renunciado a su obligación de impulsar la justicia y de participar en la transformación del mundo, a pesar de que claramente es una "dimensión constitutiva de la predicación del Evangelio, es decir, la misión de la Iglesia para la redención del género humano y la liberación de toda situación opresiva".[71] Este viraje sugiere que los principios fundantes de la iglesia apoyados por la profética conferencia episcopal reunida en la ciudad de Medellín (Colombia, 1968),[72] y revalidados por la conferencia episcopal reunida en la ciudad de Puebla (México, 1979),[73] han quedado sin efecto o en el olvido, y los pocos obispos sobrevientes de esta iglesia han

---

[70]Aunque esta percepción es un "secreto a voces" por temor a la represión de parte del Vaticano, por lo menos un estudio formal del PNUD la documenta en estos términos: "La Iglesia Católica, de fuerte trayectoria en la acción social y desarrollo de comunidades eclesiásticas de base, ha tendido a disminuir esa acción, replegándose a tareas de tipo sacramental y de difusión religiosa. Las iglesias evangélicas, en cambio, han modificado su práctica ligada a la prédica y a las reuniones de los fieles, hacia acciones vinculadas a la prevención de drogas, alcohol, prácticas deportivas y otras. La metodología de trabajo que utilizan les permite una amplia acogida personal a quienes carecen de otras oportunidades (laborales, sociales, y otras)," Programa de las Naciones Unidas para el Desarrollo-PNUD, *Desarrollo Humano en Chile 2000. Más Sociedad para Gobernar el Futuro. Parte III: Asociatividad y Capital Social*, Programa de las Naciones Unidas para el Desarrollo-PNUD, Santiago de Chile, marzo 2000, sitio en la red electrónica, <http://www.pnud.cl>.

[71]Sínodo de Obispos, *La Justicia en el Mundo*, Sínodo de Obispos, Roma, 1971, en Página principal de Cuenca, sitio en la red electrónica, <http://enete.gui.uva.es/>.

[72]Segunda Conferencia General del Episcopado Latinoamericano, *La Iglesia en la Actual Transformación de América Latina a la Luz del Concilio. Conclusiones*, Consejo Episcopal Latinoamericano CELAM, Bogotá, Colombia, 1968.

[73]Tercera Conferencia General del Episcopado Latinoamericano, *La Evangelización en el Presente y en el Futuro de América Latina*, Consejo Episcopal Latinoamericano CELAM, Bogotá, Colombia, 1979.

sido empujados a posiciones marginales. Para esa mayoría, la doctrina ratzingeriana ha adquirido primacía sobre la indigencia de nuestros pueblos, por lo cual creemos que su postura la está llevando al precipicio. Debido a la influencia que este grupo tiene en el conjunto de la Iglesia, bien podemos decir que la tendencia dominante del Catolicismo Romano actual es de sometimiento a la agenda ideológica del capitalismo neoliberal y de alejamiento radical de la agenda del evangelio liberador proclamado y actualizado por Jesucristo. Tal viraje pone en tela de juicio la capacidad de la Iglesia Católica para legitimizar su propia identidad y misión de salvación y liberación. Por eso he sugerido en el inicio de mi reflexión que la realidad de la salvación es cultivada hoy, igual que en el pasado, por la humanidad peregrina que lucha por modelos diferentes de sociedad y de iglesia impulsada por visiones siempre renovadas de emancipación. En este sentido, la humanidad migrante proporciona al Catolicismo dominante la oportunidad de volver al redil del evangelio, pero para ello, ha de transformar su conciencia y sus estructuras en el mundo. Sólo una Iglesia transformada y democrática está en condiciones de "pagar el precio que supone" la renuncia de sus privilegios en favor de la causa de la humanidad migrante.

4) *Redimensionar la tradición eclesial de enseñanza social y de compromiso por la justicia.* Las iglesias poseen una tradición inapreciable de enseñanza y de acción por la justicia social. Esta tradición, aunque es inherente a la misión de las iglesias y es componente intrínseco de la fe cristiana, en general es poco conocida y su influencia en la sociedad o en las políticas gubernamentales es escasa. La defensa de la dignidad humana, la opción por los pobres y oprimidos, y el bien común son los principios centrales que la caracterizan, y de éstos deriva el conjunto de orientaciones ético-prácticas que las iglesias ofrecen al mundo. No obstante, esta tradición que ha sido ampliada significativamente por la enseñanza social de la jerarquía eclesiástica, también ha permanecido en el campo de las buenas intenciones y de la pasividad de sus autores. La importancia de la enseñanza social de las iglesias es incuestionable, pero esta enseñanza debe ser juzgada a la luz de su fuerza para impulsar la transformación de actitudes y valores de la iglesia entera y de ésta al todo social. Desde una consideración de los grandes problemas que enfrenta-

mos hoy, parece ser claro que esta tradición no ha tenido la habilidad de estar a la altura de los desafíos que nos confrontan como iglesia. Pero también, como señala M. Shawn Copeland, la comunidad teológica ha fallado en su responsabilidad de crear nuevos lenguajes y significados transformadores mas allá de la mera enseñanza doctrinal contenida en la tradición de enseñanza social.[74] Por otra parte, la vida de la humanidad migrante no puede esperar. Si las luchas de esta humanidad no nos dicen nada sobre la urgencia de redimensionar e impulsar esta tradición en términos cognitivos y organizativos, entonces no tenemos nada que hacer aquí. Antes de que esta humanidad perezca, tenemos la opción de redimensionar desde ella el significado e implicaciones practico-políticas de la dignidad humana, del bien común, de la igualdad, de la participación, de la solidaridad, y de los otros grandes principios que conforman esta tradición. El compromiso serio de las iglesias por redimensionar e impulsar su tradición de enseñanza social nos coloca en la ruta espiritual de la humanidad viviente, para la cual la religión opera como fuente sustentadora y segura de fuerza abundante y esperanza. Como reconoce Katie G. Cannon, la tradición religiosa de la justicia ha dotado a las mujeres migrantes con la fuerza espiritual para seguir luchando a pesar de tantos obstáculos en su camino.[75]

5)   *Impulsar la actuación integrada para la organización y visibilidad de las luchas migrantes.* El principio de "actuación integrada" sugerido por Dora María Téllez como eje articulador en la búsqueda de soluciones para confrontar la problemática que nos afecta y luchar contra la pobreza, muestra ser imprescindible y urgente en el trabajo entero de las iglesias. Para ella, las condiciones actuales exigen "trascender el campo económico o la simple coordinación diplomática o policial" ya que las nuevas realidades exigen "una actuación integrada que incluya no solamente los gobiernos o las entidades estatales, sino también y especialmente la movilización de la sociedad civil . . . en la búsqueda de soluciones, de nuevos rumbos de gob-

---

[74]M. Shawn Copeland, "Method in Emerging Black Catholic Theology," in *Taking Down Our Harps. Black Catholics in the United States,* ed. Diana L. Hayes y Cyprian Davis, O.S.B., Maryknoll, N.Y: Orbis Books, 1998, 132–133.
[75]Katie G. Cannon, "The Emergence of Black Feminist Consciousness," en *Feminist Interpretation of the Bible,* ed. Letty M. Russell, Philadelphia: The Westminster Press, 1985, 30–40.

ernabilidad democrática y convivencia, de nuevas formas de luchar contra la pobreza."[76] A la luz de este principio, si el trabajo con la humanidad migrante es entendido como sitio de lucha, el trabajo de las iglesias supone la conjunción de estrategias plurales en ambos lados de la frontera, que incluye actividades de tales como:

Apoyo crítico a las propuestas de las organizaciones internacionales y de las no-gubernamentales que impulsan los derechos y dignidad de la humanidad migrante;

Participación activa en los movimientos sociales y eclesiales que trabajan por la organización política de la humanidad migrante y su fortalecimiento como sujetos y actores de cambio social;

Sostenimiento continuo de actividades de denuncia y de presión social y eclesial por un cambio en la legislación migratoria, con miras a los métodos de control policíaco fronterizo, en el desmantelamiento de la creciente industria multibillonaria del coyotaje,[77] y de las prácticas de corrupción gubernamental y policial;

Impulso de la presencia eclesial que valide en términos religiosos a los movimientos y organizaciones de la sociedad civil comprometidas en el fortalecimiento de las mujeres migrantes para erradicar su exclusión de todos los ámbitos de las sociedades e iglesias ya que, como todos los estudios señalan, las condiciones de vulnerabilidad y de desigualdad afectan mayormente a las mujeres migrantes;[78]

Fomento de actividades académicas y pastorales en los ámbitos donde incursionamos para incrementar el conocimiento y la concientización de nuestras comunidades sobre las realidades de la humanidad migrante para cambiar los estereotipos intolerantes y altamente dañinos que la cultura dominante divulga sobre ella;

Mayor diálogo entre las comunidades teológicas Latina y la latinoameri-

---

[76]Dora María Téllez, "Nicaragua: Entorno económico y social," en *Gobernabilidad Democrática y Seguridad Ciudadana en Centroamérica: El caso de Nicaragua*, comp. Andrés Serbin y Diego Ferreyra, Coordinadora Regional de Investigaciones Económicas y Sociales-CRIES, Managua, 2000, 73.

[77]Para mayor información sobre esta industria, ver Mary Jordan, "People Smuggling Now Big Business in México," *Washington Post Foreign Service*, Thursday, May 17, 2001; Page A-01.

[78] Consejo Nacional de Población-CONAPO, "Mujeres en la Migración a Estados Unidos," *Boletín Migración Internacional-CONAPO* 13, año 5, no. 13, 2000; Comisión Económica para América Latina y el Caribe-CEPAL, "Desarrollo sostenible, pobreza y género. América Latina y el Caribe: Medidas hacia el año 2000," op. cit.

cana que apoye la conceptualización intercultural y feminista de la teología, particularmente de la antropología teológica y de la espiritualidad. Con este diálogo, queremos afirmar nuestra disposición y nuestra voluntad para ayudar a superar, tanto las comprensiones reduccionistas de las identidades interculturales fronterizas, como las actitudes arrogantes de teólogos y teólogas de América Latina y del Caribe quienes veladamente o no, desprecian e subestiman a quienes vivimos y trabajamos desde "el Norte." En mi intercambio con estas comunidades teológicas, a menudo encuentro que un grupo de ellas sigue apoyando el mito de que la gente pobre forzada a migrar "al Norte" y quienes vivimos *geográficamente* en los Estados Unidos, automáticamente al cruzar la frontera formamos parte de "la gente rica". El mito de que la gente Latina vive en la abundancia, de que no tiene identidad, y de que ha renegado de sus raíces culturales latinoamericanas y caribeñas simplemente es eso, un mito e insostenible basado en la ignorancia. Para ese grupo, en el que también participan teólogos y teólogas afiliadas a la Asociación Ecuménica de Teólogos del Tercer Mundo (ASETT), no somos completamente *latinoamerican@s*, y así con sus marcos reduccionistas nos excluyen de los foros de intercambio teológico local y continental. Sin un diálogo intercultural abierto y sincero, nuestra actividad teológica en ambos lados de la frontera queda trunca para los fines de liberación.

Finalmente, quiero decir que para mi, hablar de la migración y la experiencia religiosa no es sino hablar de las experiencias y visiones emancipadoras que la humanidad peregrina viviente comunica al mundo en sus luchas y procesos hacia una civilización diferente donde la dignidad humana, la igualdad y la justicia sean viables y gratuitas. Pero hablar así presupone que las condiciones de posibilidad para esta civilización provienen de la erradicación de los poderes quiriarcales en nuestras sociedades, culturas y religiones. Desde la humanidad peregrina viviente podemos hablar de una experiencia religiosa que es fuente de poder para liberar a la gente, no para paralizarla o victimizarla todavía más, y por eso asume una clara determinación ético-política. Esta experiencia es posible porque está arraigada en una comprensión religiosa del mundo como morada de la Sabiduría Divina y entiende a la humanidad como semejanza de Dios en su gracia y presencia creativa. La experiencia religiosa de la humanidad migrante nos habla de la Sabiduría Divina, arquitecta del universo, quien despliega vigorosamente su inteligencia creadora por todos los confines de la tierra y gobierna excelentemente el mundo con rectitud y equidad. En ella, esta humanidad encuentra resguardo, cobijo, consuelo, protección y fuerza, porque su "fuerza es el principio de su justicia" (Sab 12:16).

The Experience of Migration in the United States as a Source of Intercultural Theology

Peter C. Phan
Georgetown University

Migration has been an ever-present world-wide fact of life, but currently demographers are talking of it as a new global phenomenon, given the increasing large-scale number of people who leave their homelands, by force or by choice, because of economic poverty, violence, war, and political and/or religious persecution, in search of better living conditions and freedom elsewhere, with or without proper documents.[1] Migration is a highly complex phenomenon, with significant economic, socio-political, cultural, and religious repercussions for the migrants, their native countries, and the host societies.[2] It has been the subject of research in different disciplines, primarily soci-

[1]For a recent study of world migration, *see The Cambridge Survey of World Immigration,* ed. Robin Cohen (Cambridge: Cambridge University Press, 1995). Douglas S. Massey distinguishes four periods of international migration: the mercantile period (1500–1800), the industrial period (1800–1925), the period of limited migration (1925–1960), and the postindustrial period (1960–). This last period constitutes a sharp break with the past in that migration now is "a truly global phenomenon": "Rather than being dominated by outflows from Europe to a handful of former colonies, immigration became a truly global phenomenon as the number and variety of both sending and receiving countries increased and the global supply of immigrants shifted from Europe to the developing world." *See* his "Why Does Immigration Occur? A Theoretical Analysis," in *The Handbook of International Migration: The American Experience,* ed. Charles Hirschman, Philip Kasinitz, and Josh De Wind (New York: Russell Sage Foundation, 1999), 34.

[2]For a discussion of the feasibility of a "grand theory" of immigration, especially to the United States of America, *see* Alejandro Portes, "Immigration Theory for a New Century: Some Problems and Opportunities," in *The Handbook of International Migration,* 21–33. Portes argues that a unifying theory purporting to explain the origins, processes, and outcomes of international migration would be so abstract as to be futile and vacuous. Rather he suggests that mid-level theories explaining the origins, flows, employment, and sociocultural adaptations of immigrants in specified areas are preferable to all-encompassing theories. For further theoretical studies on migration, *see New Approaches to the Study of Migration,* Rice University Studies, vol. 62, no. 3, ed. David Guillet and Douglas Uzzell (Houston: William Marsh Rice University, 1976), especially the essay by Sylvia Helen Forman, "Migration: A Problem in Conceptualization," pp. 25–35 and *Migration Theory: Talking across Disciplines,* ed. Caroline B. Brettell and James F. Hollifield (New York and London: Routledge, 2000), especially Chapter 5, Caroline Brettell, "Theorizing Migration in Anthropology: The Social Construction of Networks, Identities, Communities, and Globalscapes," pp. 97–123.

ology, anthropology, political science, and economics. Recently it has also engaged the attention of social ethicists[3] and systematic theologians.[4]

It is a common practice to distinguish between internal and external (or transnational) migrants, the former seeking safety and shelter within their own countries, and the latter in foreign lands. It is also common to single-out among the latter the special category of refugees. Refugees are those whose emigration from their homelands is not motivated by economic reasons but caused by war, or political and/or religious repression, and as a consequence are limited in their ability to set up transnational networks in their homelands until there is a change in the political situation there.

In this essay, the focus is more on transnational migrants of whatever reason, including refugees, since, generally speaking, their existential condition provides a greater source for theological reflection than that of internal migrants, though what is said of the former also applies to the latter, albeit perhaps not to the same extent. Furthermore, special attention will be given to recent transnational migrants in the United States of America, not only because the U.S. is quintessentially a country of immigrants, but also, as will be shown shortly, immigrants into the U.S. in the last quarter of the twentieth century bring with them challenges and problems as well as resources and traditions quite different from those brought by the earlier immigrants from Europe.[5] The first part of the essay will explore the existential condition of recent non-European immigrants in the U.S. as the new context for doing theology. The second part examines how this existential condition of the immi-

---

[3]For the challenges of migration to ethics, see Migrants and Refugees, ed. Dietmar Mieth and Lisa Sowle Cahill (Maryknoll, NY: Orbis Books, 1993). The editorial summarizes well these challenges: "Taken as a whole, and seen in its varied aspects, this topic [migration] represents a challenge to social ethics. The moral grounding of rights and duties, the working out of a conception between autonomy and integration, the balancing out of the various claims and the consequences of structural help on the basis of the analysis of structural 'sins,' the conceptualization of prejudices and aggressions, the anthropological and ethical significance of the foreignness and a native land, all these are key themes for ethics" (vii). In this essay I will prescind from the ethical aspects of migration.

[4]Even though an explicit focus on migration is still scarce in systematic theology, related themes such as exile and the land as theological symbols have been extensively studied.

[5]For helpful work on refugees and immigrants in the U.S., see Dictionary of American Immigration History, ed. Francesco Cordasco (The Scarecrow Press: Metuchen, NJ, 1990). A collection of older essays is still useful: American Immigration & Ethnicity, ed. George E. Pozzetta (New York: Garland Publishing, Inc., 1991). From the Catholic standpoint, there is a useful collection of primary sources on Asian-American Catholics in Keeping Faith: European and Asian Catholic Immigrants, ed., Joseph M. Burns, Ellen Skerret and Joseph M. White (Maryknoll, NY: Orbis Books, 2000), 229–307.

grant determines the interculturality of theology in terms of its epistemology, hermeneutics and methodology. The third part attempts to survey the resources made available by these non-European immigrants for a U.S. intercultural theology.

A NEW WAVE OF IMMIGRANTS AND THEIR EXISTENTIAL CONDITION

Contrary to the predictions of most demographers that the flow of immigrants into the U.S. would trickle down after the restrictive laws of the 1920s, the country now receives near record numbers of legal immigrants each year, and the second generation – those born in the U.S. with one or both parents born abroad – is larger than ever before. This dramatic increase of immigration is due to the Hart-Celler Act of 1965 and recent amendments to it, especially the Immigration Reform and Control Act of 1986 and the Immigration Act of 1990. Between 1920 and 1965 legal immigration to the U.S. averaged about 206,000 per year, most of it from northern and western Europe. On the contrary, between the mid-1960s to the mid-1990s, the number of immigrants averaged over 500,000 per year, not counting undocumented immigrants.[6]

Non-European Immigrants in the U.S. and Contextual Theologies

What is of great significance in this unexpected phenomenon is that these new immigrants hail from parts of the world other than Europe and therefore bring with them challenges as well as resources vastly different from those of the still- dominant white, Anglo-Saxon Americans, whether Catholic or Protestant.[7] Recently much publicity has been made of the findings of the 2000 census regarding the dramatic growth of the minority groups and their impact on American society. With regard to the influx of Hispanics (Latinos/as) into the

[6]Under the 1986 Immigration Reform and Control Act any undocumented resident who could demonstrate that he or she had lived in the U.S. before 1982 was eligible to apply for citizenship. Three million undocumented aliens took advantage of this opportunity. At the end of the amnesty program in October 1988, it was estimated that 2.7 million undocumented residents remained in the country who would provide the social networks for the coming of more undocumented immigrants. During the decade of 1990–2000, according to the Immigration and Naturalization Service (INS), another 2.4 million immigrants have entered the U.S. without proper documents. The INS estimates that as of October 1996 there were five million undocumented aliens living in the U.S.
[7]Before 1925, 85 percent of all international migrants originated in Europe, but since 1960 there has been a dramatic increase in emigration from Africa, Asia, and Latin America.

U.S., in 1989 Allan Figueroa Deck referred to it as "The Second Wave."[8] According to the 2000 census, the Hispanic population increased by more than 50 percent since 1990, of whom Mexicans constitute 58.5 percent, Puerto Ricans 9.6 percent, Cubans 3.5 percent, Central Americans 4.8 percent, South Americans 3.8 percent, Dominicans 2.2 percent, Spaniards 0.3 percent, and all other Hispanics 17.3 percent.[9] Native Mexicans aside, Hispanic immigrants came mainly from Mexico, Cuba, Puerto Rico, and the countries of Central America (in particular, El Salvador).

The number of Asians has increased enormously in the past decades. Prior to 1965, immigration from Asia, especially from the so-called Asian Pacific Triangle, had been prohibited on the basis of prejudices about the racial and ethnic inferiority and cultural unassimilability of Asians.[10] But things have changed drastically since then. During the last decade the Asian-American population grew nearly 50 percent to reach a little more than 10 million in 2000. The five largest groups as reported by the 2000 census are: Chinese (2.4 million), Filipino (1.8 million), Indian (1.6 million), Vietnamese (1.1 million), and Korean (1.0 million). In addition to Hispanics and Asians, mention should be made of a significant number of immigrants from the Caribbean and the Pacific Islands.

The changes in the origin, size, and composition of these newer immigrants have contributed to what has been called the "browning of America." As the authors of a recent study on these new immigrants put it, "These so-called new immigrants – those arriving in the post 1965-period – are phenotypically and culturally distinct from the old immigrants, who more closely resembled Anglo-Americans in terms of their physical characteristics and cultural patterns .... Moreover, research shows that the new immigrants are less inclined than the old immigrants to blend fully into American society. Most prefer, instead, to

---

[8]Allan Figureroa Deck, *The Second Wave: Hispanic Ministry and the Evangelization of Cultures* (New York: Paulist Press, 1989).

[9]These figures are taken from the U.S. Census Bureau, compiled by Betsy Guzmán in an essay entitled "The Hispanic Population" (May 2001). In the census, by "people of Hispanic origin" are meant those whose origin was Mexican, Puerto Rican, Cuban, Central or South American, or some other Hispanic origin. The terms "Hispanic" or "Latino" are also used interchangeably.

[10]Anti-Asian immigration legislation culminated in the Tydings-McDuffe Act of 1934 which can be traced back as far as the 1882 Chinese Exclusion Act, the Gentlemen's Agreement of 1908, and the 1917 and 1924 Immigration Acts. For an exposition of the American anxiety about the "Yellow Peril," *see* David Palumbo-Liu, *Asian/American: Historical Crossings of a Racial Frontier* (Stanford: Stanford University Press, 1999), 31–42.

preserve and maintain their own cultural heritages and identities . . . ."[11] This shift is evidenced in the fact that instead of speaking of "assimilation," research on recent immigrants now refers to their "adaptation" to and "incorporation" into the American society which no longer possesses a single core culture but much more diverse cultural matrices.[12]

It goes without saying that this recent immigration has had a profound and extensive impact on all sectors of the American society, not only in terms of what the U.S. as the receiving country has to do for these migrants, whether short-term, cyclical, or permanent,[13] but also in terms of the multiple benefits they indisputably bring to the American society. For good or for ill, the shape of the U.S. political, social, economic, cultural, and religious landscape has changed as the result of the massive presence of these non-European immigrants.

With regard to the religious arena in particular, it is well known that a great majority of Latinos/as are Roman Catholic, though the Protestant, especially Pentecostal, presence is growing. Among Asian Americans, Roman Catholicism, though a tiny minority in Asia, except in the Philippines (some three percent of the total Asian population), has a significant membership. It is estimated that in the U.S. 19 percent of Chinese (393,000), 65 percent of Filipinos (1.4 million), 30 percent of Vietnamese (329,000), and 8 percent of Koreans (91,000) are Catholic. There is little doubt that the American churches, and the Roman Catholic Church in particular, have been significantly affected in different ways by these new arrivals.

In terms of theology as an academic discipline, at least as it is practiced in the U.S., the presence of non-European immigrants should have, and has

---

[11]James H. Johnson, Jr., Walter C. Farrell, and Chandra Guinn, "Immigration Reform and the Browning of America: Tensions, Conflicts, and Community Instability in Metropolitan Los Angeles," in *The Handbook of International Migration*, 391.

[12]*See* Richard Alba and Victor Nee, "Rethinking Assimilation Theory for a New Era of Immigration," in *The Handbook of International Migration*, 137–160; Herbert J. Gans, "Toward a Reconciliation of 'Assimilation' and 'Pluralism': The Interplay of Acculturation and Ethnic Retention," ibid., 161–71; Rubén G. Rumbaut, "Assimilation and Its Discontents: Ironies and Paradoxes," ibid., 172–95; and Min Zhou, "Segmented Assimilation: Issues, Controversies, and Recent Research on the New Second Generation," ibid., 196–211.

[13]A study published by the Rand Corporation in November 1985 entitled *Current and Future Effects of Mexican Immigration in California* suggests that there are three types of Mexican immigrants: short-term (usually tied with agricultural, seasonal jobs), cyclical (with regular returns to the same employers), and permanent (usually with families settled in the U.S.). *See* Allan Figueroa Deck, *The Second Wave*, 12–15.

begun to have, a significant impact on how theology is done, since theology, as is widely acknowledged today, must be contextual, and in this case, inter-cultural.[14] The issue here is not simply the unfamiliar sources and resources, which are very different from those hitherto used by Western theologians, and from which intercultural theology will have to draw its materials, as will be examined in the next part of the essay, but more fundamentally, the very exis-tential condition of the immigrants themselves. In other words, the theologi-cally important question concerns first and foremost the very nature of being an immigrant and refugee. This existential ontology of the immigrant entails a distinct epistemology and hermeneutics, a particular way of perceiving and interpreting reality; that is, oneself, others (in particular, the dominant others and fellow groups of immigrants), the cosmos, and ultimately, God. Conse-quently, if the experience of immigration is to constitute the context for theol-ogy, then it is vitally important for the theologian to ascertain the contours of the existential predicament of the immigrant and its attendant epistemology. This existential predicament provides, as it were, a perspective – the *objectum formale quo*, to use a Scholastic expression – for the elaboration of a theology not merely about but *out of* the migration experience.

The Experience of Immigration: Displacement and Suffering

What then is the existential condition of a transnational immigrant and refugee? From the findings of various social-scientific research, it is clear that its most obvious features include violent uprootedness, economic poverty, anxiety about the future, and the loss of national identity, political freedom and personal dignity. What Teresa Okure writes of African refugees applies as well to those of other countries, though of course not necessarily to the same degree of severity:

> Refugees basically seek safety in their lives, survival, food and shelter. They
> nourish a strong hope of returning one day to their homes or homelands. In

[14]On the multicultural and intercultural character of contemporary theology, *see* the following works: Robert Schreiter, *Constructing Local Theologies* (Maryknoll, NY: Orbis Books, 1985); idem, *The New Catholicity: Theology Between the Global and the Local* (Maryknoll, NY: Orbis Books, 1997); and Stephen Bevans, *Models of Contextual Theology* (Maryknoll, NY: Orbis Books, 1992. It is well known that Hispanic/Latino theology, with its own professional association and journal, has emerged as a voice to be reckoned with. To a lesser extent, Asian-American theology has begun to contribute to the theological enterprise in the U.S.

refugee camps, they encounter hunger and disease, poor sanitary conditions, cultural alienation heightened by ignorance of the language of the host country, the loss of a sense of identity, rejection of the host country or confinement to camps, and exploitation in terms of hard labor for low pay. Children are separated from parents, husbands from wives; women are exploited and violated, often by the very persons who are expected to be their saviors. Children grow up without a sense of identity, roots, culture. They have poor educational facilities, if any. Confined to camps, if they are lucky to be in one, like animals in a cage they grow up in an artificial context. This leaves a negative psychological impact on them, sometimes for life. Refugees experience uprootedness, the lack of a sense of belonging, abuse, ignominy and general dehumanization.[15]

A theology out of the context of migration must begin with personal solidarity with the victims of this abject condition of human, often innocent, suffering. Theologians speaking out of the migration experience must "see" for themselves this "underside of history" (Gustavo Gutiérrez), "listen" to the "stories" of these victims (Choan-Seng Song), preserve their "dangerous memory" (Johann Baptist Metz), and to the extent possible, "accompany" them in their struggle for liberation and human dignity (Roberto Goizueta).[16]

The Experience of Immigration: Being Betwixt-and-Between

In addition to this dehumanizing condition, transnational migrants also exist, from a cultural perspective, in a "betwixt-and-between" situation that is the hallmark of marginalization. They live and move and have their being between two cultures, their own and that of the host country. In this "in-between" predicament they belong to neither culture fully, yet participate in both. As I have pointed out elsewhere, to be betwixt and between is to be neither here nor there, to be neither this thing nor that. Spatially, it is to dwell at the periphery or at the boundaries, without a permanent and stable residence. Politically, it means not residing at the centers of power of the two intersect-

---

[15]Teresa Okure, "Africa: A Refugee Camp Experience," in *Migrants and Refugees*, 13.

[16]On the first step of liberation theology, that is, concrete solidarity with the poor and the marginalized, *see* Leonardo Boff and Clodovis Boff, *Introducing Liberation Theology*, trans. Paul Burns (Maryknoll, NY: Orbis Books, 1987), 1–6; 22–24 and Peter C. Phan, "Method in Liberation Theologies," *Theological Studies* 61 (2000): 42–50. On the theology of "accompaniment," *see* Roberto Goizueta, *Caminemos con Jésus: Toward a Hispanic/Latino Theology of Accompaniment* (Maryknoll, NY: Orbis Books, 1995), especially pp. 1–46.

ing worlds but occupying the precarious and narrow margins where the two dominant groups, *i.e.*, those of the homeland and those of the host country, meet, and consequently being deprived of the opportunities to wield power in matters of public interest. Socially, to be betwixt and between is to be part of a minority, a member of the marginal(ized) group. Culturally, it means not being fully integrated into and accepted by either cultural system, being a *mestizo/a* or *mulato/a*, a person of mixed race. Linguistically, the betwixt-and-between person is bilingual but usually does not achieve mastery of both languages and often speaks with a distinct accent. Psychologically and spiritually, the immigrant does not possess a well-defined and established self-identity, but is constantly challenged to forge a new sense of self out of the resources of the two, often conflicting, cultural and spiritual traditions.[17]

This betwixt-and-between predicament, while a source of much soul-searching and suffering, can be an incentive and resource for a creative re-thinking of both cultural traditions, the native and the foreign. Being in-between is, paradoxically, being *neither* this *nor* that but also being *both* this *and* that. The immigrants belong fully to neither their native culture nor to the host culture. By the same token, however, they also belong to both, though also not fully. And because they dwell in the interstices between the two cultures, they are in a position to see more clearly and to appreciate more objectively, both as insiders and outsiders ("emically" and "etically"), the strengths as well as the weaknesses of both cultures, and as a result, are better equipped to contribute to the emergence of a new, enriched culture. Hence, to be in-between as an immigrant is to-be-*neither*-this-*nor*-that, to-be-*both*-this-*and*-that, and to-be-*beyond*-this-and-that.[18]

---

[17]See *Journeys at the Margins: Toward an Autobiographical Theology in American-Asian Perspective*, ed. Peter C. Phan and Jung Young Lee (Collegeville, MN: Liturgical Press, 1999), 113. For this understanding of marginality, *see* Jung Young Lee, *Marginality: The Key to Multicultural Theology* (Minneapolis: Fortress Press, 1995), 29–79. *See also Behaviors in New Environments: Adaptation of Migrant Populations*, ed. Eugene Brody (Beverly Hills, CA: Sage Publications, 1979), especially Eugene Brody, "Migration and Adaptation," pp. 12–21 and Henry P. David, "Involuntary International Migration," pp. 73–95.

[18]This predicament is not dissimilar to what Fernando Segovia describes in his evocatively-titled essay, "Two Places and No Where on Which to Stand: Mixture and Otherness in Hispanic American Theology," in *Mestizo Christianity: Theology from the Latino Experience*, ed. Arturo L. Bañuelas (Maryknoll, NY: Orbis Books, 1995), 29–43. From an anthropological point of view, this "in-betweenness" is equivalent to a liminal situation as described by Victor Turner. As such, "in-betweenness" intimates anomaly, insofar as people in liminality are no longer what they were ("neither-this") nor are they yet what they will be ('nor-that"); however, they are not stuck in the

Such an existential predicament lends itself well to an articulation of an intercultural theology that responds to the needs of our times determined by the all-encompassing process of globalization. Contemporary immigrants in the U.S. more often than not came from an underdeveloped country and now have to find their way in a technologically advanced country. Economically, in many cases, they were supported by the socialist or state economy of their native countries, whereas now they have to earn their livelihood in a neo-capitalist system and a market economy. Politically, they were deprived of the most basic human rights, and now they live in a society whose constitution guarantees all sorts of freedoms. Culturally, they were victims of Western colonization and now have to retrieve their cultural heritage, which more often than not is pre-modern, in a modern and post-modern age. Spiritually and morally, they were guided by a vision of life and ethics that privilege the family and the community and now they are part of a society permeated by a highly individualist ethos. The inevitable and at times tragic collision among these contradictory forces and systems *within* the persons of the immigrants themselves and often among the different generations of the immigrants' families makes the immigrants the privileged sites of intercultural encounters. They embody the *tiempos mixtos* – pre-modernity, modernity, and post-modernity – that form the matrix of an emergent multi-cultural, inter-cultural theology.[19]

AN INTERCULTURAL THEOLOGY FROM THE IMMIGRANTS' EXPERIENCE OF CULTURES AS A GROUND OF CONTEST IN RELATIONS

In light of the in-between predicament of the immigrant, a theology out of the experience of migration cannot but be intercultural. More importantly, in the U.S., given the many, culturally diverse ethnic groups that increasingly make up its population, theology must be *inter-multi-cultural*. That is to say, a North

---

present but project themselves toward the future ("beyond-this-and-that"). They live between memory and imagination. On memory and imagination as two inseparable modes of doing theology, *see* Peter C. Phan, "Betwixt and Between: Doing Theology with Memory and Imagination," in *Journeys at the Margins*, ed. Peter C. Phan and Jung Young Lee, 113–33.

[19]On the notion of *"tiempos mixtos,"* see Fernando Calderon, "America Latina, identidad y tempos mixtos, o cómo ser boliviano," *Imagenes desconscidas* (Buenos Aires: CLASCO, 1988), 225–29.

American intercultural theology is not only a theology shaped by the encounter between *two* cultures, *i.e.*, the dominant (Anglo/European/White) culture and one other minority culture (*e.g.*, Latino), but by the much more complex and challenging encounter of *several* cultures at the same time (*e.g.*, Anglo, Latino, black, Asian, Native American, and so on).[20] To express this point with prepositions, the encounter is not *between* but *among* cultures. The complexity of this theology will appear all the more daunting when one calls to mind that there are not monolithic cultures called Anglo, Latino, black, Asian, and Native American but rather that each culture contains within itself several significant varieties and is itself an ever-changing and dynamic reality. Throw into this ethnic and cultural mix the gender component, and the shape of this intercultural theology becomes even more unwieldy.

Inter-Multi-Culturality of Theology

Despite its complexity, this inter-multi-cultural character must be accepted as the epistemological, hermeneutical, and methodological vantage point for the yet-to-emerge intercultural theology in the U.S. In this respect, a North American intercultural theology promises to be far more interesting, and by the same token, exceedingly more difficult to construct, than a monocultural or even duocultural theology. To delineate the contours of this emerging intercultural theology, in this section I will reflect further on the epistemological, hermeneutical, and methodological implications of the existential ontology of the immigrants for intercultural theology and the resources it brings to such a theology.

The multi-cultural dialogue that shapes a theology out of the experience of migration is fortunately not foreign to many groups of immigrants in the U.S. but is an intrinsic part of their collective history. As Virgilio Elizondo has argued, the reality of *mestizaje* (the mixing of the Spanish and the Amerindian) and *mulataje* (the mixing of the Spanish and the African) is the fundamental characteristic of many Hispanics and thus makes interculturality a necessary

---

[20]This point has been made by María Pilar Aquino in "Theological Method in U.S. Latino/a Theology: Toward an Intercultural Theology for the Third Millennium," in *From the Heart of Our People: Latino/a Explorations in Catholic Systemic Theology*, ed. Orlando Espin and Miguel H. Díaz (Maryknoll, NY: Orbis Books, 1999), 24–25: "U.S. Latino/a theology may not renounce its intercultural cradle. This is a theology born within a reality where a number of religious traditions and several theological formulations converge. European, Latin American, European-American, Afro-Latin and African American, Native American, and feminist traditions and elaborations have been welcome and critically embraced."

matrix for Hispanic theology and church life.[21] This is no less true of African Americans, that is, Americans of African descent whose ancestry dated back to the period of slavery in the U.S., and whose cultural lineage is traced, through the history of the slave trade, back to Africa (in particular West Africa), as well as of black Americans, including recent immigrants from Africa, Central and South America, and the Caribbean. Their cultural and religious identity has been shaped by a long and painful encounter with the white supremacist culture and religion.[22] Asian Americans, too, bear within their history the mixture of cultures, in particular the Japanese, Koreans, and Vietnamese, who have absorbed, often by force, the Chinese/Confucian culture. Of course, this in-between cultural standing of these new non-European immigrants is exacerbated as they try to make their home in the U.S., since they have to contend not only with the dominant Anglo/European/white culture but also with the cultures of fellow immigrant groups.

A North American intercultural theology from the perspective of migration will take this pre-existing multicultural experience of these new arrivals as the vantage point from which to perceive and know reality (*epistemology*), to interpret it (*hermeneutics*), and to guide the articulation of a Christian understanding appropriate for and relevant to the betwixt-and-between predicament of immigrants facing multiple cultures (*methodology*). The resulting theology would then be truly "inter-multi-cultural."[23]

[21]See Virgilio Elizondo, *The Galilean Journey: The Mexican-American Promise* (Maryknoll, NY: Orbis Books, 1983); *The Future is Mestizo: Life Where Cultures Meet* (Oak Park, IL: Meyer-Stone Books, 1988); original French edition, *L'Avenir est au métissage* (Paris: Nouvelles Éditions Mame, 1987). *See also* his earlier two-volume work, *Mestizaje: The Dialectic of Cultural Birth and the Gospel* (San Antonio, TX: Mexican American Cultural Center, 1978), which is the English translation of his doctoral dissertation presented at the Institut Catholique, Paris, *Métissage, Violence culturelle, Announce de l'Évangile: La Dimension interculturelle de l'Évangelisation*. It is interesting to note that the mixed race (*mestizaje*) – the *raza cósmica* – had been proposed by José Vasconcelos as a new era of humanity occurring in the Aesthetic Age. Such a *raza cósmica*, according to Vasconcelos, is already present in the peoples of Latin America insofar as they incorporate in themselves the Indian, European, and African "races." *See* his *The Cosmic Race/La raza cósmica*, trans. with introduction D. T. Jean (Baltimore and London: The Johns Hopkins University Press, 1979).

[22]See in particular Gayraud S. Wilmore, *Black Religion and Black Radicalism: An Interpretation of the Religious History of African Americans*, 3rd edition (Maryknoll, NY: Orbis Books, 1998) and *Black Theology: A Documentary History, Volume I, 1966–79*, ed. James H. Cone and Gayraud S. Wilmore (Maryknoll, NY: Orbis Books, 1993) and *Black Theology: A Documentary History, Volume 2, 1980–1992*, ed. James H. Cone and Gayraud S. Wilmore (Maryknoll, NY: Orbis Books, 1993).

[23]Because this neologism is too cumbersome, in this essay, the term "intercultural" is sometimes used instead of it, but only in the sense intended by "inter-multi-cultural" as explained above.

Epistemology of Inter-Multi-Cultural Theology: Seeing from the Margins

Epistemologically, intercultural theology must be multi-perspectival. It must look to several cultures for insights and validation. It is understandable that theologians at first turn to the cultures of their own ethnic groups as the context in which to construct a theology in dialogue and even confrontation with the dominant theology. Thus black theology, Latino/a theology, and Asian-American theology have emerged in the U.S., in this chronological order. Recently, there have been auspicious attempts at crossing the ethnic as well as denominational boundaries to construct an inter-multi-cultural theology and to articulate a common theological method.[24]

In this effort, however, intercultural theology must be aware that for the immigrant, who embodies the *tiempos mixtos* and often feels torn among competing cultures, culture is experienced not as an integrated and integrating whole (as in pre-modernity and modernity) but primarily as a ground of contest in relations (as in post-modernity). In recent years the modern concept of culture as an integrated and integrating whole into which members of the society are socialized has been subjected to a searching critique. The view of culture as a self-contained and clearly bounded whole, as an internally consistent and integrated system of beliefs, values, and behavioral norms that functions as the ordering principle of a social group and into which its members are socialized, has been shown to be based on unjustified assumptions.[25]

Against this conception of culture it has been argued 1) that it focuses exclusively on culture as a finished product and therefore pays insufficient attention to culture as a historical process; 2) that its view of culture as a con-

---

[24]Works that attempt to carry out this multi-partnered theological dialogue include: *A Dream Unfinished: Theological Reflections on America from the Margins*, ed. Eleazar S. Fernandez and Fernando F. Segovia (Maryknoll, NY: Orbis Books, 2001), which brings together African-American, Asian-American, and Hispanic-Latino/a theological voices; and *The Ties that Bind: African American and Hispanic American/Latino/a Theologies in Dialogue*, ed. Anthony B. Pinn and Benjamin Valentin (New York: Continuum, 2001), which includes articles by African-American theologians with responses from Latino/a theologians and vice versa. For reflections on ethnic theologies in the U.S. and a common methodology, *see* Peter C. Phan, "Contemporary Theology and Inculturation in the United States," in *The Multicultural Church: A New Landscape in U.S. Church* (New York: Paulist Press, 1996), 109–30; 176–92 and "A Common Journey, Different Paths, the Same Destination: Method in Liberation Theologies," in *A Dream Unfinished*, 129–51.

[25]*See* Pierre Bourdieu, *Outline of a Theory of Practice* (Cambridge: Cambridge University Press, 1977); James Clifford, *The Predicament of Culture* (Cambridge, MA: Harvard University Press, 1988); George Marcus and Michael Fischer, *Anthropology as Cultural Critique* (Chicago: University of

sistent whole is dictated more by the anthropologist's aesthetic need and the demand for synthesis than by the lived reality of culture itself; 3) that its emphasis on consensus as the process of cultural formation obfuscates the reality of culture as a site of struggle and contention; 4) that its view of culture as a principle of social order belittles the role of the members of a social group as cultural agents; 5) that this view privileges the stable elements of culture and does not take into adequate account its innate tendency to change and innovation; and 6) that its insistence on clear boundaries for cultural identity is no longer necessary since it is widely acknowledged today that change, conflict, and contradiction are resident *within* culture itself and are not simply caused by outside disruption and dissension.[26]

Rather than as a sharply demarcated, self-contained, homogeneous, integrated, and integrating whole, culture today is seen as a ground of contest in relations and as a historically evolving, fragmented, inconsistent, conflicted, constructed, ever-shifting, and porous social reality. In this contest of relations the role of power in the shaping of cultural identity is of paramount importance, a factor that the modern concept of culture largely ignores. In the past, anthropologists tended to regard culture as an innocent set of conventions rather than a reality of conflict in which the colonizers, the powerful, the wealthy, the victors, the dominant, the host can obliterate the beliefs and values of the colonized, the weak, the poor, the vanquished, the subjugated, the immigrant, so that there has been, in Serge Gruzinski's expression, "la colonization de l'imaginaire."[27] This role of power is, as Michel Foucault and other masters of suspicion have argued, central in the formation of knowledge in general.[28] In the formation of cultural identity the role of power is even more

Chicago Press, 1986); Ulrich Beck, *Risk Society: Toward a New Modernity* (London: Sage, 1992); Homi K. Bhabha, *The Location of Culture* (London: Routledge, 1994); Jonathan Friedman, *Cultural Identity and Global Process* (London: Sage, 1994); Mike Featherstone, *Undoing Modernity: Globalization, Postmodernism and Identity* (London: Sage, 1995); Kathryn Tanner, *Theories of Culture: A New Agenda for Theology* (Minneapolis: Fortress, 1997).

[26]For detailed articulations of these six objections against the anthropological concept of culture, see Kathryn Tanner, *Theories of Culture*, 40–56.

[27]Serge Gruzinski, *La Colonisation de l'imaginaire: Sociétés indigènes et occidentalisation dans le Mexique espagnol XVIe-XVIIIe siècle* (Paris: Gallimard, 1987). English translation, *The Conquest of Mexico* (Cambridge: Polity, 1993).

[28]See Michel Foucault, *The Archaeology of Knowledge*, trans. A. M. Sheridan Smith (New York: Pantheon Books, 1972); *Discipline and Punish: The Birth of Prison*, trans. Alan Sheridan (New York: Vintage Press, 1975); *Critique and Power: Recasting the Foucault/Habermas Debate*, ed. Michael Kelly (Cambridge, MA: MIT Press, 1994); *Madness and Civilization: A History of Insanity in the Age of Rea-

extensive, since it is constituted by groups of people with conflicting interests, and the winners can dictate their cultural terms to the losers.

This predicament of culture is exacerbated by the process of globalization in which the ideals of modernity and technological reason are extended throughout the world (globalization as extension), aided and abetted by a single economic system (*i.e.*, neoliberal capitalism) and new communication technologies.[29] In globalization, geographical boundaries, which at one time helped define cultural identity, have now collapsed, especially for the immigrants. Even our sense of time is largely compressed, with the present predominating and the dividing line between past and future becoming ever more blurred (globalization as compression). In this process of globalization, a homogenized culture is created, consolidated by a "hyperculture" based on consumption, especially of goods exported from the United States, such as clothing (*e.g.*, T-shirts, denim jeans, athletic shoes), food (*e.g.*, McDonald's and Coca Cola), and entertainment (*e.g.*, films, video, and music). U.S. immigrants, especially the young ones, are daily enticed, even assaulted, by this hyperculture.

Such a globalized culture is not, however, accepted by local cultures hook, line and sinker. Between the global and the local cultures there takes place a continuous struggle, the former for political and economic dominance, the latter for survival and integrity. Because of the powerful attraction of the global culture, especially for the young, local cultures often feel threatened by it, but they are far from powerless. To counteract its influence, they have devised several strategies of resistance, subversion, compromise, and appropriation. And in this effort religion more often than not has played a key role in alliance with culture.

son, trans. Richard Howard (New York: Vintage Books, 1988); *Language, Counter-Memory, Practice: Selected Essays and Interviews*, ed. Donald Bouchard and trans. Donald Bouchard and Sherry Simon (Ithaca, NY: Cornell University Press, 1977); *Power/Knowledge* (New York: Pantheon Books, 1987); *Politics, Philosophy, Culture: Interviews and Other Writings*, ed. Lawrence D. Kritzman and trans. Alan Sheridan (New York: Routledge, 1988).

[29]For a discussion of the historical development of globalization, *see* the works of Immanuel Wallerstein, *The Modern World-System I: Capitalist Agriculture and the Origins of the European World-Economy in the Sixteenth Century* (New York: Academic, 1974) and *The Modern World-System II: Mercantilism and the Consolidation of the European World-Economy, 1600–1750* (New York: Academic, 1980); Anthony Giddens, *Modernity and Self-Identity: Self and Society in the Late Modern Age* (Stanford: Stanford University Press, 1991); and Roland Robertson, *Globalization: Social Theory and Global Culture* (London: Sage, 1992). In general, Wallerstein attributes an exclusively economic origin to globalization, while Giddens sees it rooted in four factors, namely, the nation-state system, the world military order, the world capitalist economy, and the international division of labor, and Robertson highlights the cultural factors in globalization.

Moreover, globalization affects not only non-Western countries but also, like a boomerang, returns to hit the thrower. This is seen, for example, in France, Britain, and Portugal, where people of their former colonies come to live and thereby create a multicultural and multiethnic situation unknown hitherto. The same situation occurs also in the United States, where because of economic and political pressures, people from South America and Asia, as we have seen above, have come in recent decades to settle in large numbers, as legal or illegal immigrants, and thus diversify the racial, ethnic and cultural composition of the population.[30]

Like the anthropological concept of culture as a unified whole, the globalized concept of culture as a ground of contest in relations has its own strengths and weaknesses. On the positive side, it takes into account features of culture that are left in the shadow by its predecessor. While recognizing that harmony and wholeness remain ideals, it views culture in its lived reality of fragmentation, conflict, and ephemerality. Cultural meanings are not simply discovered ready-made but are constructed and produced in the violent cauldron of asymmetrical power relations. It recognizes the important role of power in the formation of cultural identity. Furthermore, it sees culture as a historical process, intrinsically mutable, but without an a priori, clearly defined *telos* and a controllable and predictable synthesis. On the debit side, this post-modern concept of culture runs the risk of fomenting fundamentalistic tendencies, cultural and social ghettoization, and romantic retreat to an idealized past.[31]

Hermeneutics of Inter-Multi-Cultural Theology: Suspicion, Retrieval, and Reconstruction

In light of this post-modern understanding of culture as a ground of contest in relations, which is fortified and spread by globalization, an inter-multi-cultural theology will no longer be able to start from a universalized concept of cul-

---

[30]For a brief discussion of globalization, *see* Robert Schreiter, *The New Catholicity*, 4–14. Social scientist Arjun Appadurai lists five factors that have contributed to the "deterritorialization" of contemporary culture: "ethnoscape" (the constant flow of persons such as immigrants, refugees, tourists, guest workers, exiles), "technoscape" (mechanical and informational technologies), "finanscape" (flow of money through currency markets, national stock exchanges, commodity speculation), "mediascape" (newspapers, magazines, TV, films), "and "ideoscape" (key ideas such as freedom, welfare, human rights, independence, democracy). *See* his "Disjuncture and Difference in the Global Economy," *Public Culture* 2/2 (1990): 1–24.

[31]On these three tendencies or cultural logics dubbed as antiglobalism, ethnification and primitivism, *see* Robert Schreiter, *The New Catholicity*, 21–25.

ture or culture in general, inevitably shaped by the dominant culture, and then proceed to an application of it to ethnic cultures. Rather, hermeneutically and methodologically, it must begin with what Fernando Segovia has aptly termed "minority studies."[32] Taking a cue from Gilles Deleuze's and Félix Guattari's proposals for a "minor literature" as a deterritorialized, political, and collective discourse embedded within every literature and critically appropriating the insights of Abdul JanMohamed and David Lloyd on "minority discourse" (as opposed to "ethnic discourse"),[33] Segovia proposes, as I understand him, an intercultural theology as a "minor literature" and "a Christian minority discourse."[34]

1.   Such a Christian minority discourse will obviously start with a "hermeneutics of suspicion," unmasking the asymmetrical relation between the dominant and minority cultures and the forces of power at work in such a relation.[35] With regard to the immigrants in the U.S., this hermeneutics will seek to show that the American ideal of the melting-pot is far from being "a highly successful model of a multiethnic, multicultural, multireligious, and polyglot society."[36] As Benjamin Schwarz has argued, in its past history America successively engaged in swallowing up peoples and cleansing ethnics, subscribed to a project of

---

[32]See his insightful and challenging essay, "Introduction: Minority Studies and Christian Studies," in A Dream Unfinished, 1–33.

[33]"Ethnic culture" is sharply contrasted with "minority culture" insofar as the former "faces inward – toward its own internal concerns and problems, its own traditions and histories, its own projects and dreams," whereas the latter "faces outward – toward a dominant state formation, capable of bringing destruction upon it either by violence or by assimilation . . . . Out of this confrontation emerges a minority discourse – an appositional discourse marking the actual or potential destruction in question at the hands of the dominant culture, but also offering the grounds for a critique of this culture in terms of its own internal logic and projects" (A Dream Unfinished, 23).

[34]Segovia calls this field of study "multipolar and multilingual, cacophonous and conflicted" (A Dream Unfinished, 30). It is similar to what I have called "inter-multi-cultural theology" in a culture as a ground of contest in relations.

[35]This hermeneutics of suspicion – inspired by the three great "masters of suspicion," Nietzche, Marx, and Freud – is a familiar feature of Latin American liberation theology and feminist theology. For the use of this hermeneutics in black Catholic theology, see M. Shawn Copeland, "Method in Emerging Black Catholic Theology," in Taking Down Our Harps: Black Catholics in the United States, ed. Diana L. Hayes and Cyprian Davis (Maryknoll, NY: Orbis Books, 1998), 128–29; and in Latino/a theology, see María Pilar Aquino, "Theological Method in U.S. Latino/a Theology," in From the Heart of Our People, 11–14.

[36]Benjamin Schwarz, "The Diversity Myth: America's Leading Export," The Atlantic Monthly 275/5 (May 1995), 60, quoted in Fernando Segovia, "Melting and Dreaming in America: Visions and Revisions," in Dreams Unfinished, 242.

imperial expansion, was involved in a nationalist-separatist conflict between its North and South, and adopted a policy of racial exclusion and maltreatment toward a sizeable segment of its population.[37] Furthermore, Segovia has shown that even the recent and more enlightened views of Arthur M. Schlesinger Jr., David Kennedy, and Samuel P. Huntington still take the assimilation of the new immigrants into the American society as the goal – which is, in fact, turning them into "born-again Anglo-Americans."[38] A hermeneutics of suspicion will provide an intercultural theology with a more complete and complex history of immigration, one that involves, as Segovia puts it, "intertwined accommodation and conflict, ever-present and ever-expanding hybridity, and a mangled project of exalted principles and despicable behavior."[39] Thus, in this story the immigrants' "success stories" must be placed in the context of their suffering from opposition, prejudice, discrimination, exploitation, and marginalization at the hands of the dominant society. These two inseparable sides of the immigrants' experience must be allowed to complement and illumine each other.

2.   The next step is to retrieve this "underside of history" as lived by the immigrants, their stories of hard struggle for physical survival and for human dignity, especially stories of women who are triply discriminated against – because they are poor and minority and female – stories of how their faith in the God who vindicated Jesus and gave him a new and transcendent life over death inspired and sustained them to overcome bouts of self-doubt and despair; stories of hope against hopes; stories of effective solidarity of immigrants with each other in a community of love and mutual acceptance, of shared spiritual and material resources, of common work to build a more just and equitable society across gender, racial, ethnic, economic, and political differences; and, yes, even sto-

[37]See the summary of Schwarz's essay in Fernando Segovia, "Melting and Dreaming in America," in *Dreams Unfinished*, 242–43.
[38]See Fernando Segovia, "Melting and Dreaming in America," in *Dreams Unfinished*, 245–61. The works he examines are: Arthur M. Schlesinger Jr., *The Disuniting of America: Reflections on a Multicultural Society*, revised and enlarged edition (New York and London: W.W. Norton & Co., 1998); David Kennedy, "Can We Still Afford to Be a Nation of Immigrants," *The Atlantic Monthly* 278/5 (November 1996): 42–68; and Samuel P. Huntington, "The Erosion of American National Interests," *Foreign Affairs* 76/5 (September-October 1997): 28–49.
[39]Fernando Segovia, "Melting and Dreaming in America," in *Dreams Unfinished*, 267.

ries of immigrants' mutual suspicion and jealousy, of self-reliant "model immigrants" over against public welfare-dependent ones, of earlier immigrants scapegoating and discriminating against more recent ones, for fear that the American pie would be cut into too many slices.

Furthermore, the hermeneutics of retrieval must also pursue archival "archeology" into the immigrants' cultural, moral, religious, and ritualistic traditions and customs, their language and myths, often marginalized by the dominant society, or forgotten, or even ridiculed by the immigrants themselves for their quaint, pre-modern appearance in a modern and post-modern society. But this archeology must not be undertaken out of a romantic nostalgia for the good old days, nor out of a purely historical interest to serve the academy; rather, its goal is to re-discover the abiding truths and values inherent in the immigrants' cultures capable of sustaining them in their struggle for full humanity. Consequently, these cultures should be subjected to the same critical scrutiny and evaluation, as stringent and rigorous as the one applied to the dominant culture.

3. Lastly, the hermeneutics of reconstruction aims at shaping, out of the resources of the immigrants' cultures and those of the dominant one, a new culture, a *tertium quid*. This step is necessary because, as pointed out above, the immigrants are not only betwixt-and-between cultures but also *beyond* them. Of course, the contours of this emerging culture remain blurred and hazy. Nevertheless, however indistinct the shape of such a culture still is, it is clear that, because of the morally mixed history of the U.S., made of both lights and shadows, a U.S. intercultural theology is forbidden, as Segovia has correctly pointed out, to make the three claims of "American exceptionalism" that have been made by an earlier theology inspired by the "Manifest Destiny" myth. That is, it must renounce "any and all claims to national election (a "chosen people"), a national promise (a "promised land"), and national mission (a "light to the nations")."[40]

Inter-Multi-Cultural Theology: Method

1. As is clear from what has been done so far, an intercultural theology out of the experience of migration must first of all make use of the social sci-

---

[40]Fernando Segovia, "Melting and Dreaming in America," in *Dreams Unfinished*, 267.

ences, in particular of sociology, political science and economics as well as of the history of American immigration, in order to obtain as accurate a portrait as possible of the immigrants in the U.S. and to trace the various factors that contribute to their oppressive plight. This first methodological step has been called by Clodovis Boff the "socio-analytic mediation" of theology.[41] This mediation has also been called for by Latino/a and black theologians.[42]

In addition to socio-political analysis, intercultural theology must, as has been argued above, dig deep into the humus of the immigrants' lives to find resources for their reflection. This is what Latino/a theology refers to as *lo cotidiano*.[43] The stories of these lives are often not recorded in history books written by victors but must be retrieved from the forgotten and oppressed past to form the "dangerous memory" (Johann Baptist Metz) by which the stimulus for social transformation may be nourished and sustained. The telling, of course, often takes the verbal form, in prose or poetry, but is not limited to it. It can also be done in songs,

[41]*See* Clodovis Boff, *Theory and Praxis: Epistemological Foundations*, trans. Robert Barr (Maryknoll, NY: Orbis Books, 1987) and *Teoria do Método Teológico* (Petropolis, Brazil: Vozes, 1998). For analysis of the three mediations of liberation theologies, of which intercultural theology is a subset, *see* Peter C. Phan, "Method in Liberation Theologies," *Theological Studies* 61 (2000): 40–63. Among liberation theologians the one most insistent upon the need for theology to dialogue with the social sciences is Juan Luis Segundo whose theological project is to dialogue with the social sciences in order to "deideologize" the customary interpretation of the Christian faith and its language that hide and legitimate oppression or social injustice. For a helpful collection of Segundo's writings, *see* Juan Luis Segundo, *Signs of the Times: Theological Reflections*, ed. Alfred Hennelly and trans. Robert Barr (Maryknoll, NY: Orbis Books, 1993), especially his two essays "Theology and the Social Sciences" (7–17) and "The Shift Within Latin American Theology" (67–80). It is important to note that in the last-mentioned essay Segundo was critical of his colleagues for having made the poor rather than the deideologizing of Christian tradition the primary locus or source of theology.
[42]*See* Orlando Espín, *The Faith of the People*, 3: "... historical and cultural studies had to be engaged, that the social sciences had to become partners in dialogue." *See also* Shawn Copeland, *Taking Down Our Harps*, ed. Diana L. Hayes and Cyprian Davis, 129–30. For further reflections on the relationships between theology and the social sciences, see Peter C. Phan, "Social Science and Ecclesiology: Cybernetics in Patrick Granfield's Theology of the Church," in *Theology and the Social Sciences*, ed. Michael H. Barnes (Maryknoll, NY: Orbis Books, 2001), 59–87. Clearly, then, intercultural theology is by necessity a multi-disciplinary enterprise. Furthermore, this dialogue of intercultural theology with the humanities must include philosophy as a partner, a point well argued by Alejandro García-Rivera, "The Whole and the Love of Difference: Latino Metaphysics as Cosmology," in *From the Heart of Our People*, ed. Orlando Espín and Miguel Díaz, 54–83.
[43]On *lo cotidiano* as a source for intercultural theology, *see* María Pilar Aquino, "Theological Method in U.S. Latino/a Theology," in *From the Heart of Our People*, ed. Orlando Espín and Miguel Díaz, 38–39.

drama, dance, ritual, symbolization, visual art, and folklore.[44]
One of the results of story-telling as a theological method is contextual-
ization. Story-telling makes intercultural theology concrete, rooted in
real life experiences, and historical. Through stories the narrator
acknowledges her or his inescapable social, political, and economic location and implicitly affirms the validity of his or her experience. By the
same token, in recognizing the contextuality of their own theologies,
intercultural theologians also carry out, at least indirectly, an ideology
critique in so far as they reject the claims to universality of the dominant
or official theology and show that it too is inescapably located in a particular social, political, and economic context. On the other hand, story-
telling helps bridge the gap inhibiting communication among people of
diverse cultures because stories create a communal fund of wisdom
from which intercultural theologians can draw inspiration for their
reflection. In this way story-telling contributes to building up a kind of
concrete universality, out of particular stories and histories, from below
as it were, rather than the kind of abstract universality and normativity
that the dominant theology attempts to impose on others from above.[45]

2.   The socio-analytic mediation is followed by the "hermeneutical mediation" by which the sociological and historical data and their theoretical
constructions are given a properly theological interpretation by using
appropriate biblical symbols and doctrinal traditions. It is important to
note that this interpretation does not seek a one-to-one equivalence
between the biblical symbols and their doctrinal interpretations (*e.g.*, the
Hebrew exiles and the theological interpretations of their deportation)
on the one hand and present-day data and their sociological theories
(*e.g.*, the U.S. immigrants and the various theories about migration) on
the other. Nor does it seek to establish a direct correspondence between
the ratio between the biblical events and their historical contexts (*e.g.*,
the Hebrew exiles and their Babylonian context) and the ratio between

---

[44]Miguel H. Díaz highlights this narrative quality of Latino/a theology in his essay "*Dime con quién andas y te diré quién eres* (Tell me with whom you walk, and I will tell you who you are): We Walk-with Our Lady of Charity," in *From the Heart of Our People*, ed. Orlando Espín and Miguel Díaz, 153–71.

[45]Orlando Espín argues for this sort of "universality" which he terms "universal relevance" in con-trast to "universal validity." *See* his "An Exploration into the Theology of Grace and Sin," in *From the Heart of Our People*, ed. Orlando Espín and Miguel Díaz, 143, note 6.

our political events and their historical contexts (*e.g.*, the immigrants and their U.S. context). Such attempts would be prone to biblicism, fundamentalism and eisegesis which would lead to applying to present-day immigrants what happened to and what was said of the Hebrew exiles, without due regard to their vastly different contexts. Clearly, the exiled Hebrews are not identical to the U.S. immigrants, nor is the former's deportation in the sixth century B.C.E. identical to the latter's migration in the twenty-first century C.E. Furthermore, how the Hebrew exiles were related to their Babylonian context is not identical with how the U.S. immigrants are related to their U.S. context.

Rather the goal of the hermeneutical mediation is to discover the possible *relationship* between the relationship obtaining between one set of terms (*e.g.*, the Hebrew exiles and their context) and the relationship obtaining between another set of terms (*e.g.*, the U.S. immigrants and their context). In other words, the hermeneutical mediation seeks the relationship between/among relationships obtaining between two or more sets of terms rather than an identity or correspondence between these sets of terms. In this mode of hermeneutical mediation, intercultural theology is not on the one hand bound by a deadening conformity to past interpretations but rather enjoys a creative freedom to risk novel interpretations, and on the other hand is not buffeted by fanciful, context-free and text-free lucubrations of post-modern deconstruction.[46]

There is however a new aspect in the hermeneutical mediation of a U.S. intercultural theology that has so far not been given adequate attention, and that is the increasing presence of Asians among U.S. immigrants. It is well known that Christians in Asia form but a tiny minority of the Asian population (some 4 percent). They live and move and have their

---

[46]For a more detailed explanation of the hermeneutical mediation, *see* Peter C. Phan, "Method in Liberation Theologies," *Theological Studies* 61 (2000): 50–57. On Latino/a biblical interpretation, *see* Jean-Pierre Ruiz, "The Bible and U.S. Hispanic American Theological Discourse: Lessons from a Non-Innocent History," in *From the Heart of Our People*, ed. Orlando Espín and Miguel Díaz, 100–20. Fernando Segovia, in his helpful survey of Hispanic ways of reading the Bible, distinguishes five approaches to the Bible as represented by Virgil Elizondo, Ada María Isasi-Díaz, Harold Recinos, Justo González, and himself. *See* his "Reading the Bible as Hispanic Americans," in *The New Interpreters' Bible*, vol. 1 (Nashville: Abingdon, 1994), 167–73. *See also* Justo González, "Scripture, Tradition, Experience, and Imagination: A Redefinition," in *The Ties That Bind*, ed. Anthony Pinn and Benjamin Valentin, 61–73.

being among followers of other religions that, contrary to past mission-aries' predictions, have not been vanquished by Christianity but rather have lately experienced a remarkable renaissance. Interreligious dia-logue for them is not a luxury but an absolute necessity.[47] This multi-reli-gious context, which is unique to Asian Christian immigrants, is not shared by black and Latino/a immigrants but is increasingly becoming a permanent fixture of the U.S. religious landscape.[48] Just as feminism has thrown, as it were, a monkey wrench into intercultural theology, so interreligious (and not merely ecumenical, intra-Christian) dialogue has made life exceedingly complicated for U.S. intercultural theologians who have hardly embarked upon this task.

With respect to hermeneutics, intercultural theology must practice what has been called "multifaith hermeneutics." In this hermeneutics, which takes into account of the fact that the sacred Scriptures of other religions are also revered and read as revelatory of the divine, the Christian Bible is not a priori granted a universal validity and normativity, "fulfilling" and abolishing in a kind of *Aufhebung* the other Scriptures. Nor is it read simply side-by-side with other Scriptures as if they have nothing to com-plement, correct, and enrich each other. Rather, in multi-faith hermeneu-tics, each of the sacred books of all religions is first allowed to be unique and to speak on its own terms, without pretension to superiority and universal validity, and then all of them are bought to bear on each other to correct, validate, prolong, and complement the religious insights of each.[49] In this way, retrieving a universal wisdom from and out of par-ticular wisdom traditions, a U.S. intercultural theology is not only multi-ethnic (or better, multi-minority) but also multi-religious.

[47]This point has been repeatedly emphasized by Asian theologians and the Federation of Asian Bishops' Conferences. See *For All Peoples of Asia: Federation of Asian Bishops' Conferences. Documents from 1970 to 1991*, ed. Gaudencio Rosales and C. G. Arévalo (Quezon City, Philippines: Claretian Publications, 1002) and *For All Peoples of Asia: Federation of Asian Bishops' Conferences. Documents from 1992 to 1996*, ed. Franz-Josef Eilers (Quezon City, Philippines: Claretian Publications, 1997).

[48]It may be argued that the American religious context has always included the presence of Judaism and, lately, Islam. However, while there are many historical and doctrinal commonalities among these three "Religions of the Book," such a thing cannot be said of the relationship between Christianity and other Asian religions such as Buddhism, Confucianism, Taoism, and so on.

[49]See *Voices from the Margin: Interpreting the Bible in the Third World*, ed. R.S. Sugirtharajah (Mary-knoll, NY: Orbis Books, 1991).

3.   The third and last mediation of a U.S. inter-multi-cultural theology is the
"practical mediation." By this mediation is meant not only the socio-
political commitment of individual theologians in terms of the "option
for the poor,"[50] but also as, in Clodovis Boff's terminology, "pistic criteriology." Praxis (orthopraxis), he rightly points out, cannot be used as a
criterion for the truth of a *theological* doctrine (orthodoxy); the "theological criteriology" is only constituted by both internal consistency and
coherence with what the community believes (faith). On the other hand,
"pistic criteriology" refers to the inherent capacity of faith for socio-
political transformation.[51] This transformation is not something explicitly sought out by the praxis of faith as its goal; in other words, faith is not
subordinated to and instrumentalized for socio-political transformation.
Rather, faith itself is performed for its own sake, "aesthetically," as, in
Roberto Goizueta's words, "receptivity" and "response" to God's gift of
life. In this way, "praxis" is distinct from "poiesis."[52] But praxis as aesthetics is not authentic if it is not productive of socio-political transformation, and then it forces us to call into question the alleged truth of the
doctrines upon which such a praxis is based. Thus, there is a dialectical
tension between praxis and theory: praxis exerts pressure on theory to
critically examine itself; theory, in turn, reacting, modifies praxis; then
theory and praxis are transcended; and the spiraling never-ending circular movement goes on and on.

PULLING THE RESOURCES TOGETHER FOR AN
INTERCULTURAL THEOLOGY

In this final part of the essay I would like to draw up a list, by no means
exhaustive, of the resources that Latino/a and Asian (and to a lesser extent,
black) theologies can and should make use *together* to construct a U.S. inter-

---

[50]On this practical mediation in Latino/a theology, *see* María Pilar Aquino, "Theological Method
in U.S. Latino/a Theology," in *From the Heart of Our People*, ed. Orlando Espín and Miguel Díaz,
28–32. Aquino speaks of the three principles of this mediation: beginning with the "faith of the
people," adoption of the "option for the poor and oppressed," and practicing a "liberating praxis."

[51]*See* Clodovis Boff, *Theology and Praxis*, 198.

[52]On praxis as aesthetics, *see* Roberto Goizueta, "Fiesta: Life in the Subjunctive," in *From the Heart
of Our People*, ed. Orlando Espín and Miguel Díaz, 84–99. Goizueta has developed this idea in his
earlier work, *Caminemus con Jesús*, 89–131.

multi-cultural theology from the perspective of migration.[53] Such as theology is by necessity a *teología de conjunto*, one done not only collaboratively by theologians with and in the midst of the community but also across racial and ethnic communities in a culture as a ground of contested relations. Most of these resources are well known and have already been used in various ethnic theologies.[54] My point in listing them is to cross-reference them so that their parallels and similarities may be foregrounded.

1. With respect to the past, since missionary activities have played an essential role in shaping Christianity in Latin America and Asia, a careful study of the work of Christian mission in both continents since the sixteenth century is necessary for a better understanding of the late-Medieval, Iberian Catholicism that Hispanic and Asian immigrants in the U.S. have inherited. This common historical root will provide interesting parallels between these two U.S. groups of immigrants.[55]

2. With respect to the present, another source that binds Hispanic and Asian immigrants together is *lo cotidiano*. An inexhaustible source for intercultural theology, *lo cotidiano* includes the daily lives of immigrants as cultural hybrids (*mestizo/a* and *mulatto/a*), their shared histories of economic and political marginalization, their experiences of living betwixt-

---

[53]*See* Sixto J. Garcia, "Sources and Loci of Hispanic Theology," in *Mestizo Christianity*, ed. Arturo Bañuelas, 105–123.

[54]Two brief but helpful overviews of the developments of Black and Latino/a theologies with bibliographies are available in Anthony Pinn, "Black Theology in Historical Perspective: Articulating the Quest for Subjectivity," and Benjamin Valentin, "Strangers No More: An Introduction to, and an Interpretation of, U.S. Hispanic/Latino/a Theology," and their mutual responses in *The Ties That Bind*, ed. Anthony Pinn and Benjamin Valentin, 23–57. Beside several anthologies on Latino/a theology, two analyses of Latino/a theology deserve mention: Eduardo C. Fernández, *La Cosecha: Harvesting Contemporary United States Hispanic Theology (1972–1998)* (Collegeville, MN: Liturgical Press, 2000) and Miguel H. Díaz, *On Being Human: U.S. Hispanic and Rahnerian Perspectives* (Maryknoll, NY: Orbis Books, 2001). For Asian-American theologies, *see Journeys at the Margins*, ed. Peter C. Phan and Jung Young Lee (with a selected bibliography); Andrew Sung Park, *Racial Conflict & Healing: An Asian-American Theological Perspective* (Maryknoll, NY: Orbis Books, 1966); and Peter C. Phan, "The Dragon and the Eagle: Toward a Vietnamese-American Theology," *Theology Digest*, forthcoming.

[55]*See, e.g.*, Moises Sandoval, *On the Move: A History of the Hispanic Church in the United States* (Maryknoll, NY: Orbis Books, 1990); and *The Notre Dame History of Hispanic Catholics in the U.S.: Issues and Concerns*, ed. Jay Dolan and Allan Figueroa Deck (Notre Dame: University of Notre Dame Press, 1994). On the Iberian roots of Vietnamese Christianity, see Peter C. Phan, *Mission and Catechesis: Alexandre de Rhodes & Inculturation in Seventeenth-Century Vietnam* (Maryknoll, NY: Orbis Books, 1998).

and-between with nowhere to stand, and their struggles to live the Christian faith in the everyday situations.[56] Incidentally, it must be noted that these "stories," at least in the U.S. (and, increasingly everywhere else, given the spread of the media culture) are not told only by the *abuelitas* but massively by songs, popular novels, and especially the electronic media, at least for youth.

3.   In rooting itself in *lo cotidiano*, intercultural theology must pay special attention to the role of women in both Latino/a and Asian communities. On the one hand, women have been frequent victims of *machismo* prevalent in Latin cultures and of patriarchalism in societies influenced by Confucianism. Women in a Confucian society are taught to be bound by "Three Submissions" (*tam tong*): when a child, she must submit to her father; in marriage, to her husband; in widowhood, to her eldest son. Their behavior is to be guided by Four Virtues (*tu duc*) that are designed to restrict women's role to the sphere of domesticity: assiduous housewifery (*cong*), pleasing appearance (*dung*), appropriate speech (*ngon*) and proper conduct (*hanh*).[57]

This subordination of women is most often aggravated for women immigrants. While in their native countries their work, though heavy, is mostly confined to the home, in the U.S., for economic survival, they have to work at a full-time job outside the home *and* take care of household chores which their men consider beneath them.

On the other hand, as is well known, women play a key role in the transmission of cultural and religious values. Orlando Espín concludes his study of Latino/a anthropology with the following statement: ". . . if we were to seek out and identify the more crucial daily relationships (and indeed the key protagonists in Latino/a popular Catholicism), mature women would easily appear as *the* leaders and interpreters of that religion and, most importantly, as *the ones with whom Latinos/as sustain the*

---

[56]On *lo cotidiano* as source of intercultural theology, *see* María Pilar Aquino, "Theological Method in U.S. Latino/a Theology," in *From the Heart of Our People*, ed. Orlando Espín and Miguel Díaz, 38–39. For an example of the theology of grace and sin, *see* Orlando Espín, "An Exploration into the Theology of Grace and Sin," ibid., 121–52. *Lo cotidiano* also plays a key role in *mujerista* theology.

[57]*See* Hue-Tam Ho Tai, *Radicalism and the Origins of the Vietnamese Revolution* (Cambridge, MA: Harvard University Press, 1992), 52–53 and David G. Marr, *Vietnamese Tradition on Trial 1920–1945* (Berkeley: University of California Press, 1981), 190–99.

most meaningful and deepest of daily relationships."[58] Similarly, despite patriarchal and androcentric Confucianism, Asian women have held the highest political offices in their countries. A U.S. intercultural theology must therefore make its own the reflections of womanist, *mujerista*, and Asian-American feminist theologies.[59]

4.   Within *lo cotidiano* what has been called "popular Catholicism," that is, Catholicism as lived by the "people" and as distinct from (not opposed to!) the Catholicism of religious specialists and of the official, hierarchical members of the Church.[60] Even though popular Catholicism should not be identified with the sum of devotional practices, there is no doubt that Marian piety plays a large part in it, especially the devotion to our Lady of Guadalupe. Devotion to Mary also looms large in Asian popular Catholicism.[61] *Religiosidad popular* may very well be one of the strongest ties that tie Latino/a and Asian-American Catholics together.[62]

5.   Popular devotion brings up a distinctive source for a U.S. intercultural theology, namely, the religious practices of Asian religions with which

---

[58]Orlando Espín, "An Exploration into the Theology of Grace and Sin," in *From the Heart of Our People*, ed. Orlando Espín and Miguel Díaz, 141, italics in the original.

[59]For a dialogue between womanist and *mujerista* theologies, *see* Ada María Isasi-Díaz, "Preoccupations, Themes, and Proposals of *Mujerista* Theology," and Chandra Taylor Smith, "Womanist Theology: An Expression of Multi-Dimensionality for Multi-Dimensional Beings," in *The Ties That Bind*, ed. Anthony Pinn and Benjamin Valentin, 135–66.

[60]The writings of Orlando Espín on popular Catholicism are well known. For a dialogue between black and Hispanic theology on popular religion, *see* Dwight N. Hopkins, "Black Theology on God: The Divine in Black Popular Religion" and Harold J. Recinos, "Popular Religion, Political identity, and Life-Story Testimony in an Hispanic Community," and their mutual responses, in *The Ties That Bind*, ed. Anthony Pinn and Benjamin Valentin, 99–132. For an excellent overview of Hispanic theology of popular Catholicism and critique, especially with regard to liturgical inculturation, *see* James L. Empereur, "Popular Religion and the Liturgy: The State of the Question," *Liturgical Ministry* 7 (Summer 1998): 107–20; Mark Francis, "The Hispanic Liturgical Year: The People's Calendar," *ibid.*, 129–35; Keith F. Pecklers, "Issues of Power and Access in Popular Religion," *ibid.*, 136–40; Robert E. Wright, "Popular Religiosity: Review of Literature," *ibid.*, 141–46; Arturo Pérez-Rodríguez, *Popular Catholicism: A Hispanic Perspective* (Washington, DC: The Pastoral Press, 1988); and Arturo Pérez-Rodríguez, *Primero Dios: Hispanic Liturgical Resource* (Chicago: Liturgy Training Publications, 1997).

[61]*See* Peter C. Phan, "Mary in Vietnamese Piety and Theology: A Contemporary Perspective," *Ephemerides Mariologicae*, forthcoming.

[62]In privileging popular Catholicism as a source for a U.S. intercultural theology, attention should be paid to Justo Gonzalez's well-taken warnings about how it (especially in its Marian manifestations) is still rejected by many Protestants as rank superstition. *See* his "Reinventing Dogmatics: A Footnote from a Reinvented Protestant," in *From the Heart of Our People*, ed. Orlando Espín and Miguel Díaz, 217–29.

Asian-American Catholics are familiar. These include, beside the reading of the sacred books of Asian religions, widespread practices such as meditation, monastic traditions, prayers, fasting, and sacred dance. Among these devotional practices, of great significance is the cult of ancestors which had a three-century long controversy in the history of Christian mission in Southeast Asia known as the Chinese Rites Controversy. An Asian-American theology cannot afford ignoring these religious practices and the cult of ancestors in particular.[63]

6. Finally, it is necessary to point out that a U.S. inter-multi-cultural theology must foster a dialogue not only among various minorities theologies but also with the dominant Euro-American theology. Without this dialogue, there is the danger that the latter and the academic and ecclesiastical powers that support it will regard ethnic or minority theologies at best as an interesting but harmless exercise, to be tolerated within a pluralistic context but without posing any challenge to itself, and at worst as a theological aberration to be suppressed. More positively, without this open dialogue between the dominant Anglo-European theology and minority theologies, in which none is granted a superior and normative status and a rigorous critique is directed to all, a U.S. theology will not be a full and faithful articulation of the "joy and hope" (*gaudium et spes*) of all Americans.

[63]*See* Peter C. Phan, "The Christ of Asia: An Essay on Jesus as the Eldest Son and Ancestor." *Studia Missionalia* 45 (1996): 25–55; "Jesus the Christ with an Asian Face." *Theological Studies* 57 (1996): 399–430; "Jesus as the Eldest Brother and Ancestor? A Vietnamese Portrait." *The Living Light* 33/1 (1996): 35–44; and "Culture and Liturgy: Ancestor Veneration as a Test Case." *Worship*, forthcoming.

Theology's Contribution to (Im)migration

Robert Schreiter, CSSP
Catholic Theological Union, Chicago and
The University of Nijmegen in the Netherlands

Can theology contribute to an understanding of migration and immigration today? What kind of support might it be able to offer, either by way of providing a theological foundation for understanding the experience of migration, or to offer a theological motivation for those who migrate and those who work with them? The purpose of this brief presentation is to outline some possibilities which theology might offer. These possibilities are not worked out in detail here, but are intended to serve as a stimulation for thought and discussion.

The theological literature for supporting an understanding of migration and immigration is not extensive, and is of relatively recent origin.[1] I would like to propose here three general approaches toward thinking about a theology of and for migration and immigration. The first approach would seek some biblical frameworks for understanding migration and immigration. A second approach would take up some larger theological themes which may be of use in understanding this phenomenon better. A third approach would use a theological stance to investigate some of the countervailing narratives about migrants and immigrants.

BIBLICAL THEMES OF MIGRATION AND IMMIGRATION

A number of biblical figures and biblical narratives suggest themselves as potential sources for a theology of migration and immigration. As a backdrop to all of this, one should recall that nomadism and pastoralism play a significant role, especially in the early history of Israel. Thus, the crossing of boundaries is part and parcel of many of the founding narratives found in the Hebrew Scriptures. Among the many possibilities upon which one could draw, let me single out six here for consideration.

---

[1] An early attempt can be found in Giacomo Danesi, "Per una teologia delle migrazioni," *Per una pastorale dei migranti* (Roma: Direzione Generale dei Missionari Scalabrini, 1980), 75–128.

Stories of Abraham and Sarah

The founding narrative of the Hebrew people is that of the call of Abraham out of Ur (Gen 12:1–9). Abraham, himself a pastoralist, is no stranger to moving. But in this passage he is called to leave his own country and go to a new place. The call is linked with blessing: there he will be given land. Although Abraham is already seventy-five years old, he makes the trek.

This story reminds us of the courage and the strong motivation which brings people into migration. Even for someone used to moving around, as was Abraham, there was great risk involved in leaving his homeland to go to a strange place where he would not be protected because he was not known. To do this at an advanced age only underscores the level of risk, on the one hand, and the commitment to move, on the other. One of the things which will eventually emerge out of this narrative is that a new people will be born. Those who receive immigrants are often hostile to them; yet it is through migration that cultures are cross-fertilized and new possibilities come into being.

A second story of Abraham and Sarah bears mentioning in this context as well. This is the story of their receiving three strangers and offering them hospitality (Gen 18:1–15). The extending of hospitality is a law in many cultures, and is especially strong in pastoralist settings, where the hostile character of the environment requires offering protection and care to sojourners. The story emphasizes here that the hospitality extended to the three strangers was extraordinary in its abundance. In response to this hospitality, Abraham and Sarah are given the blessing which has eluded them throughout their long lives: the birth of a child.

Not all hospitality is so generously reciprocated as that in this story. Yet hospitality is certainly incumbent upon any Christian toward the migrant and the immigrant. For the migrant and immigrant are often highly vulnerable to the territory through which they are passing. As strangers, they are often not accorded the rights given to citizens. As being different, they can be the object of hostile projections on the part of local populations. Abraham, himself a migrant, perhaps feels more keenly than others the responsibility of hospitality.

Joseph and His Brothers in Egypt

The story of Joseph receiving his brothers in Egypt provides another set of possibilities for reflection (Gen 42–45). There are many rich themes embedded in this narrative, but let me single out just a few. First of all, it is famine which causes the brothers of Joseph to leave their homeland and go to Egypt in search of food. This element in the story reminds us that the motivation for a migrant is not always the "pull" of better possibilities elsewhere, but the "push" of desperation in one's homeland. The fact that they were pushed out of the homeland by the need for survival puts them in a different posture for entering Egypt from those who have decided to go there to seek opportunity. The survival mentality which drove them would continue to dominate their consciousness, putting them on the defensive, as it were, toward any new experience. When Joseph demands to see their youngest brother who had been left behind, this would have struck them even more keenly than might otherwise have been the case.

Second, Joseph's own memory of how he got to Egypt was necessarily triggered by the sight of these desperate men before him. In his case, he had been betrayed by his own brothers, and had come to Egypt as a slave. His migration had been forced as well, but forced in a much different way than that of his brothers. Did memory of that experience help or hinder him in dealing with these men? The surface of the narrative is of course dominated by the fact that he recognized this group as the very brothers who had betrayed him and sold him into slavery. But beneath or alongside this theme we can explore another: namely, how does one's own experience of crossing boundaries affect how we come to treat others? A not uncommon experience is one where immigrants who have been badly treated in turn maltreat those who arrive after themselves. This grows out of not having had the opportunity to deal with the wounds which had been created by crossing the border. Certainly, part of the ministry among migrants and immigrants is one of knowing what those who minister bring to the situation – how the wounds of the past help or hinder in ministry.

Moses

The story of Moses is the story of the second founding of the people of Israel. It is a story criss-crossed by borders, ranging from Moses as a foundling, to his death within sight of the final border of the Promised Land. Let me note just three of those border crossings which might inspire us here.

The first is Moses' awareness as a young man that, although having been brought up in Pharaoh's household, he is really of the people who have been enslaved by Pharaoh (Ex 2:11). One thinks here of the young migrants who grow up in a country, strangers in their own land, caught between two cultures. The ferocity of Moses' response, first to the maltreatment of one of his kinfolk by an Egyptian, and then to an altercation between two Hebrews, may well have been conditioned by his own "third culture" experience, *i.e.*, of not being fully Hebrew or Egyptian. Yet later in the story, when he returns to confront Pharaoh on behalf of the Hebrew people, it becomes apparent that it is precisely his location in this third culture reality which makes it possible for him to do what he does.

The second is his exile in Midian after he flees Egypt. There, within the liminality of yet another betwixt-and-between situation, he receives his call from God to become the leader of his people (Ex 3). The liminal state in which migrants and immigrants find themselves can be viewed as a problem or as an opportunity. The material and social burdens which liminal living usually entails usually cause people to fasten upon liminality as a problem. But we know that certain things often cannot occur unless we find ourselves without the accustomed protection of routine and the sense of safety in our own context.

The third is Moses' leadership of the Hebrews through the wanderings in the Sinai desert. Here one finds ample material for reflection upon the dangers and travails of migration, especially in those situations where the movement from one place to another is hazardous and uncertain. The growing disheartened of the people; Moses' own frustration, both with the people and with the possibility of leading them; the constant risks of starvation, of physical danger; and the final fact that Moses himself will not be the one to lead them across the border into the Promised Land – all of this and much more in the long narrative of the Exodus and wanderings supply many themes which illuminate the experience of migration and immigration.

Ruth

The story of Ruth is one of the great narratives of migration and immigration in the Bible. The story begins with famine, and the need to migrate from Judah to Moab. The deeply touching story of how Naomi, a vulnerable widow who has also lost her two sons, decides to return to Judah, is made even more poignant by the insistence of her Moabite daughter-in-law that she will accompany Naomi on that trek. As the story unfolds, Ruth remarries and becomes one of the progenitors of the future King David.

This is one of the few stories where the plight of migration and immigration is seen through the eyes of a woman. Here we see how care overcomes the codes of kinship, as Ruth accompanies her mother-in-law on the trip back to Judah. We see too her constancy through a number of different situations. We see also how, as a foreigner, she becomes an essential link in the establishment of the monarchy in Israel. Again, here is a story replete with themes of migration and immigration.

Daniel

The story of Daniel is the story of forced migration. He is essentially a hostage in the court of Nebuchadnezzar in Babylon. They endured what such forced migration: they had to learn a foreign language and foreign ways (Dan 1:4); they were given strange food to eat (1:5); and they were given new names (1:7). Daniel resists the food, and finds help from God in doing so (most foreigners are not so lucky!). As a forced migrant, he is constantly vulnerable and at risk, as the story of the fiery furnance makes abundantly clear. It might be also noted that, once again, his liminal position contributes to his ability to interpret for the King.

As a story, the Book of Daniel provides a picture of much of the anguish which surrounds those in exile. The outcome of the story is, of course, far more positive than it is for most people who find themselves in this situation. But that there is material here once again for reflection on the experience of exile, of being in a strange land where one is at once not in control of one's own existence and constantly at risk makes the story of Daniel a source for reflection.

Jesus

The story of Jesus as given us in the Gospels is filled with themes pertinent to migration and immigration. Let me just note some of them here.

First off, there is the story of the flight into Egypt after the birth of Jesus (Matt 2:13–23). That Jesus himself was a refugee and an exile has been a source of comfort to many today who find themselves in the same position. Second, one can point to the very itinerancy of Jesus' ministry which, while carried out mainly in Galilee and for the sake of the House of Israel, did take him into foreign areas and to Jerusalem. There, away from home (in at least one sense), he was to meet his death. Third, one can point to his dealing with foreigners, such as the centurion (Matt 8:5–13), the Syrophoenician woman (Mark 7:24–30), and the Samaritan woman at the well (John 4:1–42). The story of the encounter with the Samaritan villagers (Luke 9:51–56) provides yet another example.

One could single out other elements as well, such as those dealing with strangers and with people who are considered enemies because they are foreign. The story of Jesus is one of crossing boundaries, be those social, religious, or political. As such they can be approached for reflection on what it means to be involved with migration and immigration today.

THEMES CONTRIBUTING TO A THEOLOGY OF MIGRATION AND IMMIGRATION

A second way to approach theology's possible contribution to migration and immigration is to look at some larger themes within theology and see how they might contribute to this project. I wish to note four here. Again, little more can be done than call them to our attention and suggest how they might be further elaborated.

Stranger and Guest

The biblical concern for the alien and the stranger, underscored so often in the classical prophets and reiterated in the word and ministry of Jesus, is a well-known theme. A theology of the stranger is grounded in Christian anthropology, namely, that all are made in the image and likeness of God (Gen 1:27). As we have already seen above in a variety of biblical stories, the role played by people coming into our setting from the margins provides one of the ways in which God's working in the world can be discerned. In offering hospitality to the stranger we may indeed be entertaining angels.

Welcoming the migrant and immigrant as a guest is thus one of the bases for a theology of ministry in such settings.[2] Hospitality is a sign of the com-

[2]See the letter of the United States Catholic Bishops' Conference, *Welcoming the Stranger* (Washington, DC: USCCB, 2001), issued through the Office for the Pastoral Care of Migrants and Refugees. For some reflections on what welcome to strangers means in the context of migration, *see* Francesco Gioia, "L'accoglienza dello straniero ieri e oggi," *Migration at the Threshold of the Third Millennium* (Rome: Pontifical Council for Migrants and Refugees, 1999), 125–137; Kurt Koch, "Aufnahme des Fremden als ein Zeichen der Kultur: Von der Feindlichkeit zur Gastfreundlichkeit," *idem*, 115–124.

munion which marks the life of the Trinity. The experience of graciousness is the experience of the grace of God.

Pilgrimage and Paroikia

If the previous theme focused upon those who welcome the migrant and the immigrant, the themes of pilgrimage and *paroikia* center upon those who are travelling themselves. Seeing life itself as pilgrimage is a theme which has pervaded Christian belief, from the wanderings of great figures in the Hebrew Scriptures, through the New Testament reminders that we have in this world no lasting dwelling place (Heb 13:14), through great works of Christian literature, such as John Bunyan's *Pilgrim's Progress*. The theme of the Christian as a pilgrim grows out of the covenant experience, whereby we live in a posture of promise and fulfillment, with our eyes set upon the future God holds for us. In view of this, even those most settled in their day-to-day existence are people on the move. Within such a framework, we should be able to appreciate and situate the experience of those who are on the move, either voluntarily or involuntarily, in our world today.

The liminality which is connected to being a pilgrim is expressed in a slightly different way in the concept of *paroikia*, that is, being outside the household – a stranger. It is a term used for the addressees of the First Letter of Peter (1:1). It is implied in the words addressed to the Gentiles in Ephesians 2, as people who had been strangers without a home, but are now citizens in the household of God. That experience of being outside the household is certainly one which marks the migrant and immigrant – of not belonging, and especially of being made to feel not to belong. To realize that the state of *paroikia* is indeed the true state of being a Christian puts migrants and immigrants on the inside, as it were, rather than consigning them to the outside.

Reconciliation

The theological theme of reconciliation is of great interest in the world today. This comes about partially no doubt because of the large number of intrastate conflicts which have been experienced over the last two decades, as well as the end of oppressive social orders (Communism in Europe, apartheid in South Africa).[3]

---

[3]For more on this *see* Robert Schreiter, *Reconciliation: Mission and Ministry in a Changing Social Order* (Maryknoll, NY: Orbis Books, 1991).

A theme within the theology of reconciliation is the healing of memories and the coming to terms with the past. Many migrants carry with them the traumas of their past, either traumas which drove them from their home countries, or the trauma of the transition and the lack of acceptance in the new country. The ministry of reconciliation, in its concern with the reconstruction of societies and the lives of those who experienced the trauma and disruption which now must be healed, can be an important resource for those ministering with migrants and immigrants.

Catholicity

In a world living through the turbulence of globalization, with its paradoxical heightening of a sense of both the global and the local, Christian theology seeks an overarching vision which can serve as an alternative to the economic and social globalizing process. One place to find this is in a renewed concept of catholicity.[4] Catholicity is concerned about the embrace of the whole, especially in a fragmented world. It is concerned as well with the fullness of faith and, by extension, the fullness of life. Catholicity today, in a world of globalized communication, must also be concerned with communication, because developments in communications technology have democratized communication in much of the world.

Catholicity provides a theological framework for a theology which combats xenophobia, and situates the stranger in the midst of the new society (or in the old society, as viewed through the eyes of the long-time or life resident). It expands the generosity of spirit which marks Christian hospitality into a larger framework of anthropology and of human community.

CONTERVAILING NARRATIVES

In the previous two sections, we have looked at how biblical narratives and theological themes might serve to support a theology of migration and immigration, either in the articulating of a theology itself, or as a means of supporting a ministry among migrants and immigrants. In this final section, some suggestions are proposed for how the resources of theology can help to cri-

---

[4]I have explored this in *The New Catholicity: Theology between the Global and the Local* (Maryknoll, NY: Orbis Books, 1997).

tique the narratives about migration and immigration today, especially in light of globalization.[5] These critiques can represent countervailing narratives to those presented under the contemporary experience of globalization. I would suggest four of them.

Christ as the Way; Not Globalization as the Way

Globalization, in the comprehensiveness with which it girds the planet in communications and especially in economics, presents itself as the only way – there is no alternative. This is especially the message in economics. Even given the widespread antiglobalization sentiment, there is at this time still no alternative economic vision emerging. It has become more and more a matter of *how* we shall negotiate market capitalism, and not whether we can choose not to do so.

Faced with this situation, Christian faith reminds us that it is Christ who is the Way, the Truth, and the Life, not the trajectories of global capitalism. This is to be highlighted especially in those situations where human beings are moved around to meet the supply-and-demand exigencies of labor, just as capital and goods are moved around. Human beings are not simply another raw resource for the production of goods. The delicate social networks which surround each of us as human beings are not to be torn apart simply for the sake of capitalist need. That Christ is the Truth reminds us that globalization in itself has no goal or *telos* other than the reproduction of itself in ever faster, more technolgically sophisticated forms.

Gratuity, Not Indebtedness

A theology of graciousness and hospitality has already been alluded to above. As is well known, much of the poor world is burdened with heavy external debt, the servicing of which consumes much of those nations' resources. The depressing effect of external debt on national economies is one of the factors which contributes to the "push" of migration, as people leave their homes to seek new and better possibilities. Rather than exacting the payment of debts, the theme of forgiveness preached by Jesus – including the forgiveness of

---

[5]Much of this has been drawn from Paulo Suess, "Migração, peregrinação e caminhada como desafios da missão no mundo globalizado," *Revista Eclesiástica Brasileira* fasc. 238 (Junho 2000) 294–311.

debts (*cf.* Matt 18:23–35) – has been advocated by many groups (including churches) as a way to respond to the plight of the poor in the world today.

Neighborliness Instead of Xenophobia

The presence of the migrant or the immigrant as the Other in societies today, especially heretofore largely homogeneous societies, has made the problem of xenophobia a major one in many countries. The fears of international terrorism have only fueled these fears. People fear for their jobs and for their personal safety, whether rightly or wrongly.

The place of the stranger in Christian theological thinking has already been referred to above. In the situation described here, it is a matter of more than one-off hospitality; it becomes a question of just how people will live together. The parable of the Good Samaritan (Luke 10:39–37) is addressed specifically to the question of who is the neighbor. Here the neighbor is the stranger.

Solidarity Instead of Exclusion

Although the prophets of market capitalism proclaim that one day everyone will be included in its bounty providing they follow its rules, the immediate experience, however, is one of exclusion: first, the interruption of one's own way of life and making a living, and then exclusion from the patterns of exchange and growth. In reflections on the phenomenon of the oppression of the powerful and the rich today, theologians in Latin America have focused upon the phenomenon of exclusion.

Pope John Paul II has taken up this theme in his treatment of globalization today, especially as seen in light of Catholic Social Teaching. "No globalization without solidarity" has become a refrain of his, meaning that globalization is only proper and just in situations where individuals are not excluded or left behind in the process. It is a theme which has now been woven directly into his teaching. Again, it points to theological concepts of the human person and of society which must prevail even in the face of the apparent inevitabilities of globalization.

While this aspect of inclusion has been addressed particularly to societies being left behind by the juggernaut of globalization, it has special significance for the migrant and the immigrant, who are often left without social protection in the societies in which they arrive. Moreover, they are often excluded socially in the societies in which they settle. The theme of solidarity is one which theology can contribute to the development of policy regarding migrants and immigrants in society today.

CONCLUSION

Three approaches have been suggested here whereby theology might contribute to both the understanding of migration and immigration, and support a ministry to people on the move. As noted at the beginning, the narratives, themes, and countervailing approaches are little more than mentioned; each could be the subject of considerable elaboration. But a common denominator which runs through all of them is how close the idea of migration and immigration is to the Christian story itself. This should give theologians and those who minister among people on the move the encouragement to work toward a more comprehensive theology of and for migration and immigration.

Hacer teología desde el migrante: diario de un camino

Flor Maria Rigoni, c.s.

Gioacchino Campese, c.s.

Red Casas del Migrante Scalabrini

PREMISAS

"Lo que hemos oído, lo que hemos visto con nuestros ojos, lo que contemplamos y tocaron nuestras manos...eso les anunciamos para que también ustedes estén en comunión con nosotros" (1 Juan 1, 1–3).

El punto de partida de estas reflexiones teológicas se puede expresar con las palabras de los primeros versículos de la Primera Carta de Juan: lo que se va a compartir en estas páginas es lo que hemos visto, oído y tocado con mano en las veredas, en los cruceros, en los terminales de autobuses y trenes, en los desiertos, y especialmente en los albergues de los Misioneros Scalabrinianos de la frontera de México con Estados Unidos (frontera norte) y de Guatemala con México (frontera sur). En otras palabras, nuestra teología empieza con la experiencia de la migración, y sobre todo con el compromiso por los/as migrantes en las fronteras del continente norte y centroamericano. Consideramos que la geografía es un elemento importante de esta reflexión ya que creemos que las fronteras son unos de los lugares privilegiados para una lectura certera de la realidad migratoria, y de la vida de los/as que arriesgan sus vidas para realizar sus sueños. En este caso estamos hablando de países como Estados Unidos, México y naciones centroamericanas como Guatemala, El Salvador, Honduras y Nicaragua que no solamente están involucrados en un flujo migratorio masivo sino comparten también fronteras que se transforman en lugares de encuentro y todavía más frecuentemente de choque entre los pueblos y las leyes de estos países. Por eso sostenemos que estas fronteras son el contexto vital en el cual ubicamos nuestra reflexión teológica.

Otra premisa fundamental de este ensayo es que no se trata simplemente de una reflexión individual, del trabajo y experiencia de una persona, sino que más bien es una reflexión de conjunto, fruto de experiencias e ideas que un grupo de Misioneros Scalabrinianos trabajando en la frontera, en las Casas del Migrante para ser más específicos, ha ido compartiendo en diferentes conversaciones y encuentros durante los últimos tres años. No es la primera vez que este grupo comunica sus pensamientos: en ocasión del año 2000 se publicó un Mensaje Jubilar con el título de *El Clamor de los Indocumentados* en el cual se aprovechaba la celebración del Jubileo para compartir con el Pueblo de Dios la situación en la cual viven los/as migrantes más vulnerables que son los/as indocumentados/as, y el compromiso que como Iglesias y como seres humanos estamos llamados/as a tomar para responder a su clamor.[1] En estas páginas vamos de hecho a retomar mucho de lo que se afirmó en esta primera reflexión, pero el punto que queremos subrayar es que en estas reflexiones el "nosotros" va a predominar sobre el tradicional "yo" del teólogo o de la teóloga que individualmente se dedica a desarrollar sus ideas.

Insistimos en el hecho que estas reflexiones nacen de una experiencia con los/as migrantes, pero no representan la voz de los mismos/as migrantes. Gustavo Gutierrez y otros grandes teólogos de nuestro tiempo nos han recordado con frecuencia que no es apropiado decir que nuestra teología quiere ser la voz de los pobres, o que queremos ser voz de los/as que no tienen voz. Los/as pobres, los/as migrantes tienen su propia voz y parte de nuestra opción por ellos/as es crear el espacio para que la puedan expresar con libertad. Entonces esta reflexión teológica se alimenta de las voces de los/as migrantes, y al mismo tiempo espera crear la oportunidad y el espacio para que estas voces se escuchen con claridad en nuestras sociedades e iglesias. En este sentido podemos decir que este es un intento de hacer teología desde el migrante. Al mismo tiempo creemos también que de alguna manera estas voces representan la voz del Dios que nos llama al compromiso y el seguimiento de su Hijo Jesús en los caminos de la historia y de la humanidad. Queremos también aclarar desde el principio que de ninguna manera consideramos estas reflexiones como algo definitivo o intocable. El subtítulo de este ensayo quiere comunicar la naturaleza provisoria de este esfuerzo teológico. Este es el "diario de un camino", es decir, son notas que se han tomado y reflexionado a lo largo de nuestra experiencia de ministerio con los/as migrantes. Si tenemos en este momento el atrevimiento y la confianza de compartirlas es precisamente porque queremos entablar una conversación, un

---

[1]Red Casas del Migrante Scalabrini. *El Clamor de los Indocumentados.* www.sedos.org/spanish/scalabrini_1.htm

dialogo con nuestros hermanos y hermanas en la fe.   Estas notas incluyen todavía muchas preguntas y dudas: son un principio de reflexión teológica que seguramente se va a enriquecer con las preguntas, dudas, y comentarios de todas las personas que se han comprometido y se quieren comprometer en la misión con los migrantes.

El objetivo de este ensayo es sencillo: queremos, a partir de nuestra experiencia con los migrantes y de la migración, subrayar unas temáticas que, en nuestra opinión, pueden enriquecer la vida (praxis y teoría) de la Iglesia y la de los/as mismos migrantes. Empezaremos con unas notas metodológicas que consideramos cruciales porque nos dan las pautas para leer adecuadamente la realidad en la que vivimos. No tenemos aquí el espacio, ni la pericia necesaria para profundizar y usar esta metodología en un análisis comprensivo de la compleja realidad migratoria, pero nos interesa por lo menos empezar a crear este marco metodológico. En un segundo momento pasaremos a presentar los temas que a nuestro parecer contribuyen a una teología más atenta y sensible al fenómeno migratorio porque quiere escuchar el clamor de los/as migrantes.

NOTAS METODOLOGICAS

En la primera parte de este ensayo queremos presentar tres elementos que consideramos esenciales en nuestra metodología teológica. Lo hacemos con la conciencia que el método que sugerimos aquí necesita una reflexión adicional para profundizar y aclarar sus fundamentos y un dialogo serio con otras ciencias humanas que se ocupan del fenómeno migratorio, como la sociología, la psicología y la antropología cultural. Los elementos que vamos a considerar en este ensayo son los siguientes:

1   Nuestro punto de partida es la realidad migratoria, pero al hacer esta afirmación nos damos cuenta que hay diferentes "realidades migratorias" o, en otras palabras, podemos decir que existe en nuestra sociedad un conflicto de interpretaciones de la realidad migratoria. Para aclarar nuestra lectura de la realidad recurrimos a los escritos de los teólogos centroamericanos Ignacio Ellacuría y Jon Sobrino quienes han destacado clara y abundantemente la importancia de la realidad en el quehacer teológico: una teología valida, significativa y cristiana tiene que elevar la

realidad a concepto teológico, tiene que enfrentarse con la realidad, cargar con ella y encargarse de ella.[2] La "honradez con lo real" y "la fidelidad a lo real" son actitudes básicas para hacer teología.[3] A través de estas dos actitudes metodológicas, con las cuales nos queremos comprometer en nuestra reflexión teológica, queremos afirmar diferentes puntos. **Primero**, nos proponemos mirar a la realidad migratoria *desde abajo*, es decir, desde la perspectiva de los/as mismos migrantes, aunque tenemos que reconocer desde el principio que hay que ser verdaderamente migrante para ver la realidad como un migrante. Nuestro propósito es leer la realidad desde aquellos/as que lo arriesgan todo, hasta sus vidas, para realizar el sueño de la "tierra prometida", es decir desde la experiencia de los/as migrantes indocumentados/as. Este punto de vista particular nos permite ver dimensiones de la realidad migratoria que muchos de nosotros ignoran o se les hace cómodo ignorar, y aquí nos referimos sobretodo a los aspectos más trágicos y hasta mortíferos de la migración. En otro escrito hemos descrito esta situación como el "Calvario del Migrante", un verdadero Vía Crucis hecho de deshumanización, criminalización, violaciones, abusos, sufrimientos, y muerte.[4] Nos referimos aquí a la muerte de miles de migrantes, muchos de ellos/as todavía no identificados, en el camino y en las fronteras Norte y Sur de México.[5] **Segundo**, queremos tomar una actitud crítica frente a "la realidad no-real" que se nos ofrece en los discursos de la gran mayoría de los líderes políticos y económicos y, muchas veces, en los medios de comunicación. A los migrantes en estos medios se les presenta "como un riesgo", una amenaza, para la sociedad.[6] Esta actitud la aprendemos

---

[2]Jon Sobrino, "De una Teología solo de la Liberación a una Teología del Martirio," en *Cambio Social y Pensamiento Cristiano en América Latina*. Editores José, Comblín y José I. González y Jon Sobrino. Madrid: Editorial Trotta, 1993, pp. 106–109; Juan Estrada, "La Influencia de Zubiri en la Teología de la Liberación," *Proyección* 45 (1998) 293–295. Reconocemos que esta parte de nuestra metodología necesita de una profundización que honre el excelente trabajo que Ignacio Ellacuría hizo para fundamentar filosóficamente el método teológico, y por lo cual pagó con su propia vida.

[3]Jon Sobrino, *Liberación con Espíritu. Apuntes para una nueva Espiritualidad*. Santander: Sal Terrae, 1985, 24–29; "Teología desde la Realidad," en *Panorama de la Teología Latinoamericana*. Eds. Juan-José Tamayo y Juan Bosch. Estella: Verbo Divino, 2001, pp. 611–628.

[4]Vea nota 1.

[5]Vea por ejemplo la información sobre la muerte de los migrantes en la frontera Norte de México en <www.stopgatekeeper.org> de California Legal Rural Assistance.

[6]Olivia Ruiz, "La Migración en la Globalización de la Sociedad de Riesgo," www.sedos.org/spanish/ruiz.htm

de los mismos migrantes, cuando se preguntan "¿Cómo nos ven los que están arriba?", porque se dan cuenta que no vienen tomados en consideración como personas humanas. El problema es que la realidad migratoria muchas veces no viene solamente ignorada u olvidada, sino viene encubierta intencionalmente. No se quiere mirar a la totalidad de la realidad en sus ojos, porque parte de esta realidad, "el Calvario del migrante", huele mal, sangra, se está pudriendo... y sobre todo porque como afirma Sobrino: "Y es que, cuando lo que es evidente 'en otros' – los pueblos crucificados – nos hace evidente lo que en verdad somos 'nosotros', tendemos a ignorarlo, encubrirlo o tergiversarlo, porque simplemente nos aterra."[7] En otras palabras, ignoramos las dimensiones negativas porque van a enseñar nuestra verdadera identidad con sus lados oscuros y despiadados, y esto va a proyectar una imagen de nosotros que no nos gusta mostrar, una imagen que es seguramente diferente a la que se quiere proyectar públicamente. Además, hay intereses muchos más importantes que la vida de unos/as pobres migrantes. **Tercero**, afirmamos que no podemos ser neutrales en nuestra relación con la realidad. La neutralidad con la realidad no es una actitud cristiana. Aquí mencionamos lo que sostenía Mons. Romero frente a la situación dramática de su país: "Ahí se le presenta a la Iglesia, como a todo hombre, la opción más fundamental para su fe: estar a favor de la vida o de la muerte. Con gran claridad vemos que en esto no hay posible neutralidad. O servimos a la vida de los salvadoreños o somos cómplices de su muerte... o creemos en un Dios de vida o servimos a los ídolos de la muerte."[8] O estamos al lado de los migrantes que sufren o estamos en favor del sistema que los oprime. **Cuarto**, parte de nuestro quehacer teológico es también nuestro compromiso a la lucha en la fe y la esperanza para transformar una realidad de muerte que aflige a los migrantes en una oportunidad de resurrección y vida. **Quinto**, nos comprometemos a mantener una actitud de dialogo constante y abierto con las otras ciencias humanas para poder comprender las diferentes dimensiones de una realidad migratoria compleja y cambiante.

[7]Jon Sobrino, *El Principio~Misericordia. Bajar de la Cruz a los Pueblos Crucificados.* Santander: Sal Terrae, 1992, p.84.
[8]Oscar Arnulfo Romero, "La Dimensión Política de la Fe desde la Opción por los Pobres," www.servicioskoinonia.org/relat/135.htm

2   Mirar a la realidad desde la perspectiva del migrante quiere decir tener
       una visión más verdadera y auténtica de la misma. Esta es una posibilidad
       fundamental que cualquier persona que quiere hacer teología desde el
       migrante tiene que tomar en seria consideración. El crítico cultural indio
       Homi Baba sostiene que "ahora es posible que la percepción más ver-
       dadera ("the truest eye") pertenezca a la doble visión del migrante".[9] Este
       es un elemento de reflexión que diferentes teólogos/as hispanoameri-
       canos/as y asiático-americanos, que han tomado como su punto de parti-
       da su propia experiencia de inmigración o se identifican de alguna man-
       era con la experiencia del inmigrante, han destacado en sus escritos.[10] El
       migrante no es ni de aquí y ni de allá, como él/ella mismo/a afirma, pero
       al mismo tiempo es de aquí y de allá. En otras palabras, el migrante siente
       el peso y la dificultad de vivir en medio de dos o más culturas, vive "in-
       between", pero esta su condición, esta "in-betweenness", es también su
       fuerza, porque a partir de su cultura de origen, del camino que ha hecho,
       y de la cultura que va adoptando, tiene una visión privilegiada de la total-
       idad de la realidad, y sabe cómo desenvolverse en las diferentes situa-
       ciones en las cuales se encuentra. Analizando la experiencia de muchos
       migrantes, que han pasado por y vivido en diferentes países antes de lle-
       gar a su destino, podemos hablar no solamente de doble, sino de triple o
       cuádruple visión, lo que talvez se puede interpretar como estado de
       esquizofrenia psicológica y cultural. Al contrario, nosotros creemos que
       escuchar al migrante nos da la posibilidad de tener una visión más autén-
       tica y verdadera de la totalidad de la realidad, nos da la oportunidad de
       ser honestos y fieles con la realidad como nos sugiere Jon Sobrino.

3   Nos proponemos hacer teología con una actitud de apertura total al mis-
       terio del Dios cercano y más allá, del Dios que rompe con cualquier ima-
       gen que podemos hacernos de Dios. A veces tenemos que admitir que
       absolutizamos a tal punto estas imágenes que ya no nos permiten una
       relación sana y abierta con el Misterio de Dios, con el misterio del ser

---

[9]Homi K. Bhabha. *The Location of Culture*. London: Routledge, 1994, p. 5.

[10]Roberto Goizueta, *Caminemos con Jesús. Toward a Hispanic/Latino Theology of Accompaniment*.
Maryknoll: Orbis Books, 1995. Pp. 1–17; Peter Phan, "Betwixt and Between: Doing Theology with
Memory and Imagination," in *Journeys at the Margin. Toward an Autobiographical Theology in Amer-
ican-Asian Perspective*. Edited by Peter C. Phan and Jung Young Lee. Collegeville: Liturgical Press,
1999. Pp. 113–133; Fernando Segovia, "Two Places and No Place on Which to Stand: Mixture and
Otherness in Hispanic American Theology," *Listening* 27 (winter 1992) 26–40.

humano, y el misterio de la creación. En otras palabras, tenemos que empezar a cuestionar y evaluar nuestras imágenes de Dios, y crear maneras mas dinámicas y significativas para expresar hoy el Misterio. Una parte importante de este cuestionamiento, que hay que tomar con mucha atención y seriedad particularmente en nuestro periodo histórico, viene de personas que, con cierta o mucha razón, critican nuestra imagen de Dios, o el "factor Dios"[11] como lo define el escritor portugués José Saramago, en nombre de quien se han cometido y todavía se cometen los hechos más absurdos, crueles, sin sentido y horrendos de la historia de la humanidad.[11] Hemos dicho intencionalmente que todavía se cometen barbaridades en nombre de Dios, y no nos referimos solamente a los que en nombre de Dios se estrellan contra las Torres Gemelas o el Pentágono, sino también a los, entre los cuales líderes reconocidos de nuestras Iglesias, que hablan de "guerra justa" en respuesta a los trágicos atentados del 11 de septiembre.[12] Y las guerras no provocan solamente miles de muertes inocentes, sino también el desplazamiento masivo de la población civil que tiene que dejar su tierra para tener una oportunidad de sobrevivir a la violencia.

TEMAS

A partir de estas consideraciones metodológicas queremos proponer unos temas que nos parecen importantes para el desarrollo de una teología desde la experiencia del migrante. Hay muchos otros temas que pueden ser considerados para el desarrollo de esta teología, pero los siguientes han sido muy útiles en nuestra lectura teológica de la experiencia migratoria.

El Misterio de Dios y su Ambigüedad

"Nadie puede darle un nombre a Dios porque Dios es demasiado grande para expresarlo con palabras; si alguien se atreviera a decir que esto es posible quiere decir que está sufriendo de una locura incurable." Justino Mártir[13]

[11]José Saramago, "El Factor Dios," *El Pais* 18 septiembre de 2001.
[12]Robert Schreiter en su ponencia al Capitulo General de los Dominicos en Providence, Rhode Island, el 11 de Julio de 2001 con el titulo "Preaching the Gospel in the Twenty First Century," <www.dominicains.ca/providence/english/documents/schreiter.htm>, afirma que uno de los mayores retos para la misión de la iglesia en el siglo XXI es lo de la relación entre religión y violencia.
[13]Encontré esta frase de Justino Mártir en Chrys McVey, "Outside the Camp,"<www.sedos.org/english/chrys.htm>

El migrante rompiendo con sus fronteras geográficas y culturales y abriéndose
a otras nos ofrece una ventana nueva hacia el misterio de Dios: se trata de un
Dios que habla muchos idiomas, que tiene perfiles y semblantes diferentes,
que es hombre y mujer, que es Dios del pasado, del presente y del futuro. De
esta manera la migración rompe con la tentación de apoderarnos de Dios
haciendo de Dios un títere a nuestra imagen y semejanza, enjaulando a Dios
en nuestras teologías, filosofías, teorías políticas, económicas y culturales.
Nuestro Dios es el Dios de la tienda, el Dios que quiere ser libre para estar con
su pueblo, que no cae en las trampas de los monumentos que nosotros queremos crear para que se transforme en nuestra propiedad. Nos parece fundamental subrayar la dimensión del misterio en Dios, una dimensión que nos
hace comprender la "incurable locura" y "arrogancia" de afirmar un
conocimiento perfecto y verdadero de Dios, una actitud que nos lleva al
fanatismo que crea ídolos, en nombre y con el nombre de Dios, por los cuales
hasta las acciones más absurdas se pueden justificar.[14]

Jon Sobrino nos recuerda, usando las palabras de Karl Rahner, que "Dios
es el misterio santo, totalmente cercano y absolutamente inmanipulable" y
que "la teología católica, a pesar de sus numerosos dogmas y prescripciones
morales, sólo dice una cosa: el misterio permanece misterio eternamente."[15]
La experiencia del migrante es una invitación continua a abrirse al Misterio
que revela un Dios que va siempre más allá de lo que nosotros seres humanos
podamos imaginar, y se revela en lugares inesperados, como a los márgenes
de la sociedad o en la "tierra de nadie", y en personas desconocidas, como los
migrantes.

El Dios de la Tienda

*"Yo no he habitado en una casa desde el día en que saqué a los Israelitas de Egipto, sino
que he estado peregrinando de un sitio a otro en una tienda."* 1 Crónicas 17, 5

La experiencia caminante del migrante nos sugiere una imagen más dinámica
de Dios, una imagen que no encontramos en la Biblia por pura casualidad. De
hecho, el Dios de Israel se caracteriza por ser un Dios caminante, un Dios pere-
grino, un Dios que no está atado a un templo, a una montaña, o a un río como

---

[14] Chrys McVey OP, "Outside the Camp,"
[15] Jon Sobrino, "Teologia desde la Realidad,", 614.

muchos de los dioses que se adoraban en aquel tiempo en el Oriente Antiguo.[16] Siguiendo la narrativa del Éxodo podemos afirmar que el Dios de Israel no es un Dios sedentario y estático, sino un Dios que libera a su pueblo de la esclavitud de Egipto y lo acompaña y guía en el camino hacia la Tierra Prometida. Cuando el rey David quiere construir un templo en su honor, Dios responde que no necesita un templo, porque la tienda, esta casa móvil, es la morada de quien ha tomado la opción de estar con su pueblo (2 Samuel 7, 1–7). En el camino Dios habita en la "tienda del encuentro", porque es ahí que se hace presente y disponible a su pueblo y a su siervo Moisés (Éxodo 33, 7–11). Esta imagen de la tienda es tan importante en la Torá que aparece 40 veces en el libro del Éxodo y 44 veces en el Levítico.

La tradición del Dios de la tienda continúa también en el Nuevo Testamento. Hay un texto en particular que consideramos fundamental en la trasmisión de esta representación de Dios, pero desafortunadamente todas las modernas traducciones del texto griego esconden su sentido original. Nos estamos refiriendo al famoso Prólogo del Evangelio de Juan que en el versículo 14 dice que "la Palabra se hizo carne y habitó entre nosotros" afirmando así el concepto de la Encarnación de Dios en Jesús. Es muy interesante notar que el término griego traducido usualmente con el verbo "habitó" es *eskenosen* que proviene de la palabra *skene* que quiere decir "tienda". Entonces, la traducción literal de Juan 1, 14 es "la Palabra de hizo carne y plantó su tienda entre nosotros". En otras palabras este texto nos dice que Jesús, como en una carrera de relevos con el Dios de Israel, planta su tienda entre nosotros escogiendo una vez más esta presencia móvil con la humanidad en camino precisamente para orientarla hacia el Reino de Dios.

La perspectiva que nos propone esta tradición tan antigua de la tienda es muy lejana de nuestra mentalidad porque ahora la tienda es algo que se usa para el deporte, para el camping o para ir de excursión en montaña, o sea, evoca imágenes de vacaciones y tiempo libre. Los textos bíblicos nos representan aquí una manera de vivir en camino, un estilo de vida que es la manera de vivir de los migrantes que buscan la Tierra Prometida. Lo interesante es que Dios escoge este mismo estilo, esta manera totalmente diferente de ser Dios, para quedarse con su pueblo caminante. De esta manera la metáfora del

---

[16]Brother John of Taize, *The Pilgrim God. A Biblical Journey.* Washington D.C.: Pastoral Press, 1985, 13.

Dios de la tienda se transforma en uno de los modelos teológicos más significativos de nuestra época caracterizada por las migraciones masivas de personas en todo el planeta. Esta es seguramente una metáfora que necesita más reflexión y atención por parte de los teólogos/as también porque desempeña un papel crítico con relación a ciertas imágenes estáticas de Dios que tratan de encerrar lo divino en edificios, monumentos, templos, y tabernáculos. Esta es la tentación del cemento, de la morada cercada y estable donde se quiere manipular a Dios en lugar de darle la libertad de continuar su camino de esperanza con la humanidad. Para los cristianos esta metáfora representa precisamente la invitación a la itinerancia, a la movilidad, a salir más seguido del templo para seguir al Dios de la tienda por los caminos de este mundo.

El Cristo Extranjero

"Por eso también Jesús, para santificar al pueblo con su propia sangre, padeció fuera de la ciudad. Salgamos, pues, a su encuentro fuera del campamento y carguemos también nosotros con su humillación." Hebreos 13, 12–13

Los evangelios presentan a Jesús como un hombre de su pueblo, hijo y descendiente de Israelitas, pero no esconden en él una dimensión de extranjería que muchas veces no se toma en consideración. A partir de la genealogía de Jesús en Mateo 1, 1–17 encontramos esta dimensión en la presencia de mujeres extranjeras, Tamar, Rajab, la mujer de Urías, y Rut, que vienen sorprendentemente incluidas en la lista de los antepasados, casi todos varones, de Jesús. En el mismo evangelio de Mateo nos encontramos con Jesús que se tiene que hacer extranjero, refugiado, en Egipto, para huir de la furia del rey Herodes (2, 13–23). Jesús como extranjero se revela en el hecho que regresando de Egipto María, José y el Niño se establecen en la región de Galilea (Mateo 2, 23) conocida también como "Galilea de los paganos" (Mateo 4, 15) en cuanto en este territorio las poblaciones Gentiles y los Judíos se habían mezclado produciendo un mestizaje que los Judíos de Jerusalén consideraban impuro.[17] Por eso Natanael cuando escucha que Jesús viene de Nazaret, en Galilea, contesta "¿De Nazaret puede venir algo bueno?" (Juan 1, 47).

Hay otro evento fundamental de la vida de Jesús y de la historia de la salvación en el cual se manifiesta su ser extranjero. Nos estamos refiriendo a

[17]See Chrys McVey OP, "Outside the Camp"; Virgilio Elizondo, *Galilean Journey. The Mexican-American Promise.* Maryknoll: Orbis Books, 1983, 49–66.

dos aspectos de la muerte de Jesús: a) su muerte en la cruz, que es la muerte de los esclavos, de los criminales, y de los que no son ciudadanos del Imperio de Roma. De alguna manera la crucifixión nos presenta a Jesús como extranjero es su propia tierra colonizada en aquel tiempo por el poderío de Roma; b) el segundo aspecto se describe en el texto de la Carta a los Hebreos que encontramos al principio de esta sección, un texto que sostiene que también en el lugar de su crucifixión Jesús es extranjero. Jesús de hecho muere afuera de la ciudad, de los muros de Jerusalén que era la ciudad santa de todos los Judíos. En nuestra interpretación aquí Jesús sufre el rechazo y la humillación por las cuales muchos extranjeros, muchos migrantes, pasan. Lo interesante del texto es que continúa con la exhortación a los Cristianos a salir de la ciudad, a hacernos extranjeros para encontrar al Extranjero que ha sido rechazado por una civilización que desprecia y mata a los/as que vienen de afuera.

El Cristo extranjero, el Cristo que se identifica con el forastero en Mateo 25, 35, se transforma para nosotros en un símbolo de la humanidad peregrina que no encuentra un lugar que puede llamar "patria" y una comunidad que puede llamar "familia". Este mismo Cristo representa para los Cristianos un reto a la solidaridad con los migrantes, un reto a salir de la ciudad para encontrar a estas personas a los márgenes o hasta afuera de nuestra sociedad para incluirlos/as en una comunidad que no excluye al que viene de lejos, sino lo incluye como hermano y hermana en el Cristo extranjero.

La Fe del Migrante

"La fe es el fundamento de lo que se espera y la prueba de lo que no se ve."
Hebreos 1,11

La fe del migrante es seguramente otro tema crucial en el desarrollo de una teología desde su experiencia. No estamos hablando aquí de una fe cualquiera, sino de una fe que sorprende y desconcierta a quienes se encuentran con ella. Cuando miramos a la fe el migrante se nos hace casi natural relacionarlas con la fe de algunos personajes de los evangelios como el centurión Romano en Mateo 8, 5–13, la mujer Cananea en Mateo 15, 21–28, el leproso Samaritano en Lucas 17, 11–19, el mismo Buen Samaritano en Lucas 10, 25–37. Lo que asombra en estos pasajes es que son extranjeras, y no judías, las personas que destacan por su gran fe, por su gratitud, por su ejemplo de servicio y amor al prójimo. A veces los evangelistas a través de estos personajes ponen en vergüenza la conducta de los mismos discípulos de Jesús cuya fe y compasión falla frecuentemente.

Es precisamente esta fe asombrante, esta capacidad de abandonarse en las manos de Dios, esta esperanza que nunca muere la que hemos encontrado en los migrantes en su camino hacia la realización de sus sueños. Esto no quiere decir que no existe la desesperación entre los migrantes, que se debe a toda la serie de obstáculos que encuentran en el camino, empezando con las barreras geográficas y terminando con la crueldad de gente que los despoja, golpea y llega hasta a matarlos. Al mismo tiempo frente a estas adversidades se revela la fe del migrante en frases como "¡Gracias a Dios estamos vivos!" que es la expresión típica de la persona que ha sobrevivido a la guerra cotidiana de los acosos del camino y de los riesgos mortales de las fronteras. El migrante ha sobrevivido porque, como él/ella mismo lo afirma, nunca ha dudado en la presencia de Dios, porque este Dios de la tienda se ha revelado como compañero/a de camino.

La Catolicidad

"Les aseguro que jamás he encontrado en Israel una fe tan grande. Por eso les digo que vendrán muchos de Oriente y Occidente y se sentarán con Abrahán, Isaac, y Jacob en el banquete del reino de los cielos." Mateo 8, 10b-11

"La década de los 90 ha estremecido nuestro mundo con cambios profundos, rápidos y sorprendentes. La caída del Muro de Berlín puede ser el símbolo del final de una época. La construcción de otro muro, mucho más largo y mortífero en la frontera entre Estados Unidos y México, puede ser el símbolo del comienzo de otra época de grandes desafíos."[18]

Aquí no vamos a discutir la etimología, la historia y la teología del termino "católico" en la tradición cristiana, no porque no sea importante, sino porque este no es el objetivo de este ensayo.[19] La cuestión de la Catolicidad

---

[18]Benjamín González Buelta, "Rasgos de la Experiencia Cristiana en una Iglesia que Busca Justicia," *Christus* 65 (Julio-Agosto 2000) 2000, 7.

[19]Para una discusión más detallada de la catolicidad desde diferentes perspectivas véase: Eloy Bueno de la Fuente, *Eclesiología.* Madrid: Biblioteca de Autores Cristianos, 1998, pp. 251–308; Robert Schreiter, "The Theological Meaning of a Truly Catholic Church," *New Theology Review* 7 (1994) 5–17; *The New Catholicity. Theology Between the Global and the Local.* Maryknoll: Orbis Books, 1997; Jon Sobrino, *Resurrección de la Verdadera Iglesia. Los Pobres, Lugar teológico de la Eclesiología.* Santander: Sal Terrae, 1981, pp.127–132.

surge para nosotros frente a la realidad de un muro que representa no solamente la frontera que separa dos países, sino también, como lo aclara la cita
de Benjamín González, el símbolo de la época en la cual vivimos, una época
que había empezado con la esperanza del derrumbe de un muro que carac-
terizaba las divisiones que existían en el mundo. Pero la construcción de
muros no se ha acabado, sino que precisamente los que más se indignaban a
la presencia del muro de Berlín, ahora son los que están construyendo muros
para proteger su estilo de vida, "la libertad y la democracia". Lo que queremos hacer aquí es sencillamente proponer que la Catolicidad representa uno
de los mayores desafíos para los cristianos y las iglesias en este planeta en
movimiento, en el mundo globalizado y dividido al mismo tiempo, un mundo
en donde la economía no tiene fronteras, y los seres humanos, especialmente
los que la globalización económica ha excluido, tienen que enfrentar más y
más fronteras. Uno de los problemas que encontramos en este contexto es que
la globalización neoliberal está encubriendo de alguna manera la trágica
dimensión humana que se encuentra en esta frontera adonde muchas veces
los sueños y las esperanzas de muchos seres humanos se estrellan contra los
muros que se están construyendo. La imagen que se ofrece a la opinión pub-
lica es la de una "frontera que está desvaneciendo enfrente de nuestros ojos
creando un nuevo mundo para todos nosotros" como recitaba la portada de
un reciente cuaderno especial del Time.[20] Lo que no se puede entender es
como desaparece una frontera mientras se construyen más vallas para hacer
su presencia todavía más visible y aterradora. O si hay la intención de construir un mundo nuevo sobre los miles de cadáveres de migrantes que están
muriendo para cruzar esta frontera que supuestamente está desapareciendo.

Es importante entender que el problema no es la frontera en sí misma,
sino las actitudes y las opciones que esta simboliza y que mucha gente y
muchos gobiernos comparten. En otras palabras, queremos decir que en este
tercer milenio las migraciones, la diversidad que ellas conllevan, las actitudes
de rechazo y los choques que ellas provocan, van a ser el banco de prueba de
nuestra Catolicidad, y que sin una comprensión de esta dimensión fundamental de nuestra fe y sobretodo sin una pastoral apropiada no podremos ser
auténticos testigos de Dios en el mundo de hoy.

La palabra "católico" no se encuentra ni en el Antiguo ni en el Nuevo
Testamento, pero es una de las definiciones más antiguas de la iglesia. Desde

[20]"Welcome to Amexica," *Time* Special Issue, June 11, 2001.

el Concilio de Constantinopla en el año 381 profesamos nuestra fe en una Iglesia que es "una, santa, católica y apostólica". De hecho desde entonces la catolicidad ha sido considerada una de las cuatro notas fundamentales de la iglesia. La ausencia de esta dimensión en los dos Testamentos, no quiere decir que no tenga nada a que ver con la tradición bíblica. No hay duda para nosotros que la raíz de la catolicidad de nuestra fe y de la iglesia está en el Dios de nuestros antepasados/as y de los profetas que es el Dios de toda la creación y todas las naciones; en el Dios Espíritu Santo del Pentecostés que se comunica a todas las personas, creyentes, paganas, y no creyentes, en su propio idioma; en el Dios de Jesús que reconoce la diversidad, la aprecia, y proclama que en el banquete del Reino las puertas están abiertas para todos y todas. Desde un punto de vista más teológico Eloy Bueno sostiene: "La raíz ultima de la catolicidad es el misterio trinitario que, como hemos visto, pretende ofrecer la plenitud de la comunión divina al conjunto de la realidad creada, tanto humana como cósmica, respetándola en sus peculiaridades y diferencias".[21]

La afirmación de los fundamentos bíblicos y teológicos de la catolicidad es crucial porque es muy común explicar el sentido de esta dimensión con la palabra "universal", y con este término nos referimos frecuentemente al hecho que la Iglesia está presente en todo el mundo, es decir, vinculamos la catolicidad a un universalismo geográfico muy genérico, y a veces triunfalista en cuanto nos sentimos orgullosos que nuestra Iglesia esté presente en todo el mundo. Pero no es esto el verdadero sentido de la catolicidad. El teólogo Orlando Espín nos orienta en esta búsqueda afirmando que: "La catolicidad no es cuestión de presencia geográfica o territorial sino es una calidad de la Iglesia... la Iglesia es católica porque sus puertas están abiertas a cada ser humano, y a cada grupo humano, sin distinciones ni barreras. La Iglesia es católica porque rechaza la idea de que una cultura humana es superior a las demás... En verdad, es parte de la definición de catolicidad que las barreras nacionales, culturales raciales, políticas, de genero y económicas tienen que caer como directa consecuencia de la revelación de Dios en Cristo."[22] Especialmente en esta última parte de la definición de Espín podemos escuchar el eco de las palabras de la Carta a los Efesios: "Porque Cristo es nuestra paz. El ha hecho de los dos pueblos uno solo, destruyendo el muro de enemistad que

---

[21]Eloy Bueno de la Fuente, *Eclesiología*, 254.
[22]Orlando Espín, "Immigration, Territory, and Globalization: Theological Reflections," *Journal Of Hispanic/Latino Theology* 7 (2000:3) 55.

los separaba... El ha creado en si mismo de los dos pueblos una nueva humanidad, restableciendo la paz" (Efesios 2, 14–15).

Si ser católicos quiere decir apertura radical en nombre de un Dios que derrumba los muros de la enemistad, dialogo y convivencia con todos/as, romper barreras que nos dividen y en su lugar construir espacios que nos permitan comunicar, entonces, nos parece que la catolicidad que profesamos en nuestras iglesias no está en buena salud. No hay duda que en este momento histórico, que se define con la expresión del "choque de las civilizaciones",[23] necesitamos alimentar y vivir la catolicidad más que nunca.

Muchas preguntas, que necesitan de respuestas urgentes, surgen a partir de esta situación. ¿Qué quiere decir ser católicos/as en un mundo en donde estamos multiplicando las barreras que nos separan para proteger nuestro estilo de vida de los extranjeros, de los migrantes? ¿Qué quiere decir ser católicos/as en un ambiente en cual aumenta la sospecha y la discriminación contra el extranjero, especialmente si tiene un perfil "terrorista" o "criminal"? ¿Por qué nos acostumbramos tan fácilmente a las barreras, al rechazo, a los prejuicios raciales y culturales? ¿No es verdad que nosotros católicos/as estamos usando las mismas estrategias de los gobiernos: ellos construyen fronteras físicas, y nosotros empezamos a poner fronteras a la compasión, a la solidaridad, a la justicia, a la paz, a la santidad de la vida y de la dignidad humana? ¿Por qué nosotros que tenemos que ser testigos del Reino, cerramos sus puertas a los que consideramos extranjeros y sospechosos? Entonces al final: ¿qué tan católicos/as somos en verdad? Nos damos cuenta que "estamos todavía muy lejos de una comunidad eclesial que sea reconocida como 'casa de todos los pueblos y todas las culturas'".[24]

Para concluir nuestra reflexión sobre este tema tan significativo queremos afirmar que la catolicidad está presente y viva no solamente en los sínodos y otros encuentros multitudinarios, sino en cada cristiano y en cada comunidad cristiana, no importa que tan grande o pequeña, que tan importante o insignificante, que se comprometen a tener abiertas las puertas del Reino de Dios. Nuestra iglesia se ha distinguido desde su principio por esta apertura

[23]Esta frase tiene su origen en el libro de Samuel Huntington, *The Clash of Civilizations and the Remaking of World Order*. New York: Simon and Schuster, 1996.
[24]Commissione Teologica USG, *Nella Globalizzazione: Verso una Comunione Pluricentrica e Interculturale. Implicazioni Ecclesiologiche per il Governo dei nostri Istituti*. Roma: Editrice il Calamo, 2001. En esta cita el documento está mencionando palabras del teólogo Johann Baptist Metz.

radical. Los mismos "enemigos" de la iglesia, como Juliano el Apóstata, uno de los emperadores romanos que persiguió a los cristianos, lo reconocían: "Vemos que lo que más ha contribuido a desarrollar ese ateismo (el cristianismo) es su humanidad para con los extranjeros, su acogida para con toda clase de seres humanos...".[25] La fidelidad a la catolicidad de nuestra fe va a tener un banco de prueba decisivo en la actitud con la cual nos relacionamos con los migrantes quienes de hecho nos enseñan a vivir "católicamente" porque ellos/as han cruzado con valor y fe las fronteras que nosotros hemos construido y por eso tenemos que considerarlos como verdaderos "profetas de la catolicidad".[26]

Migración como Lugar de Encuentro y Revelación de Dios

"No olviden la hospitalidad, pues gracias a ella algunos hospedaron, sin saberlo, a ángeles" Hebreos 13, 2

Hemos empezado estas reflexiones con el objetivo de empezar a desarrollar una teología a partir de la experiencia del migrante con la convicción que la migración es hoy uno de los "signos de los tiempos" que la Iglesia tiene el deber de escrutar, e interpretar a la luz del Evangelio si quiere cumplir su misión.[27] Ahora queremos afirmar también que la migración es hoy, en nuestra opinión, uno de los lugares privilegiados que Dios ha escogido para revelar su Misterio a la humanidad. Al mismo tiempo sostenemos que es en el contexto de la migración, en el encuentro con los migrantes, los extranjeros y desconocidos, que podemos encontrar de manera especial el Dios Desconocido que nos invita a participar a la peregrinación hacia su Reino.

Queremos explicar este último tema del ensayo con cuatros historias que nos señalan cuatro actitudes vitales con relación a la misión con los migrantes, de las cuales los mismos migrantes son protagonistas y ejemplos.

1   **La hospitalidad.** Recientemente se han escrito trabajos muy interesantes en el campo de la teología cristiana sobre la hospitalidad y su importancia para la fe y la visión cristiana de la vida, de Dios y de la

---

[25]Vives, Josep, "Pobres y Ricos en la Iglesia Primitiva," www.servicioskoinonia.org/relat/274.htm
[26]Tassello, Giovanni Graziano. "Los Migrantes: Profetas de la Catolicidad," *Spiritus*, 42:2 (2001) 113–124.
[27]*Gaudium et Spes* 4.

creación.[28] La experiencia de las Casas del Migrante confirma este esfuerzo que algunos teólogos/as cristianos están haciendo para poner el tema de la hospitalidad al centro de la reflexión teológica hoy. En un contexto de hospitalidad ocurren eventos extraordinarios, como la amistad entre George, el gitano búlgaro, y Jimmy, el migrante guatemalteco. No había nada lingüísticamente y culturalmente que permitía esta relación. De hecho todavía no nos podemos explicar como estas dos personas tan diferentes se comunicaban, ya que George tenía un conocimiento muy limitado del inglés, el único idioma en común entre él y Jimmy. Después de un tiempo en la Casa del Migrante Jimmy encontró un trabajo y un lugar donde quedarse, pero venía a visitar regularmente a su amigo George que estaba todavía en la Casa tramitando sus papeles para el asilo político en los EE.UU. Lo que recordamos más es la sonrisa enorme de George quien cuando veía Jimmy decía con orgullo una de las pocas frases que conocía en inglés: "This is my friend", "Este es mi amigo". Lo que queremos subrayar a través de esta amistad es que la hospitalidad es algo más que una actitud ética que nos permite ayudar a personas que no tienen casa. La hospitalidad, en nuestra experiencia, es uno de los contextos privilegiados en el cual Dios se revela, entra en nuestras vidas, nos sorprende, y hace acontecer el perdón, la reconciliación, la conversión. La hospitalidad es un evento teológico, un *locus theologicus*, porque crea y ofrece el espacio para relaciones de amistad que parecen imposibles, relaciones que nos revelan el rostro de Dios. Esta visión de la hospitalidad que proponemos tiene profundas raíces bíblicas. En el contexto de la hospitalidad Dios sorprende Abrahán con la revelación del nacimiento de un hijo que nadie ya esperaba (Génesis 18, 1–15); en el contexto de la hospitalidad, casi escandalosa, porque Jesús no tiene miedo de entrar en la casa de un "pecador", se da la conversión de Zaqueo que se declara listo a devolver lo que ha robado; y finalmente la Carta a los Hebreos, retomando el pasaje de Génesis 18 nos deja una frase que es una invitación para todos los creyentes de todas las generaciones: "No olviden la hospitalidad,

---

[28]Lucien Richard, *Living the Hospitality of God*. New York: Paulist Press, 2000; Christine D. Pohl, *Making Room. Recovering Hospitality as a Christian Tradition*. Grand Rapids: W.B. Eerdmans, 1999; Brendan Byrne, *The Hospitality of God. A Reading of Luke's Gospel*. Collegeville: Liturgical Press, 2000.

pues gracias a ella algunos hospedaron, sin saberlo, a ángeles"(13, 2). El teólogo alemán Johann Baptist Metz comentando este pasaje afirma que: "es posible extraer de esta frase bíblica una indicación decisiva: los extranjeros no son enemigos, sino ángeles; no son solo mano de obra barata, sino – y en ello semejan a los ángeles – mensajeros, consejeros. Deberíamos, por tanto, prestar atención a la profecía extranjera de hombres venidos de otros mundos culturales."[29] En un contexto de hospitalidad cristiana se da una percepción diferente del migrante, en oposición a una percepción común que considera el migrante como un riesgo y una amenaza para la sociedad.

2   **La solidaridad.** Este es un término que se ha usado y se usa con facilidad y superficialmente, sin considerar lo que verdaderamente quiere decir y lo que comporta en la vida de la persona que toma un compromiso serio de solidaridad. Para mucha gente esta es una expresión retórica que quiere dar la impresión de un interés por la vida de los/as pobres y excluidos de este mundo. Jon Sobrino define la solidaridad como "una concepción y práctica de la vida cristiana a la que le es esencial la referencia al 'otro', tanto para dar como para recibir".[30] Con este episodio queremos ofrecer un ejemplo dramático de cómo ocurre la práctica de la solidaridad entre los migrantes. Pasó en Chiapas, en un tramo que recorre el tren carguero, el tren de la muerte o de la esperanza, dependiendo de las perspectivas y consecuencias. La locomotora del tren acababa de arrancar, y dos indocumentados se avientan al mismo tiempo para subirse al tren en movimiento. El primero está ya sentado arriba cuando se da cuenta que su compañero se ha quedado entrampado en los resortes de un vagón hasta que se le pierde a la vista arrastrado y machucado por las ruedas de acero. Este migrante nos confesaba que por un momento estuvo tentado de decirse a sí mismo, y al compañero desconocido: "ni modo, cuate, uno la hace y otro se chinga". Pero pensó a la madre de aquel desventurado: se tiró del tren en movimiento, y fue a entregarse a la Migra mexicana, pidiendo a los oficiales de regresarse unos kilómetros atrás y recoger el cuerpo martirizado de su compañero. Una crucecita recuerda hoy en el panteón del pueblo a este migrante y a su compañero que prefirió quemar

---

[29]Johann Baptist Metz, "Perspectivas de un Cristianismo Multicultural," en *Cristianismo y Liberación. Homenaje a Casiano Floristán.* Ed. Juan-José Tamayo. Madrid: Editorial Trotta, 1996, p. 35.
[30]Sobrino, *El Principio~Misericordia*, 215.

una oportunidad para ser gesto de solidaridad hacia un muerto.

3   **El ecumenismo.** Lo hemos definido el "ecumenismo de la compasión y de la solidaridad", un ecumenismo que va en dirección opuesta a una historia manchada por guerras religiosas, cruzadas e intolerancia dogmática.[31] Es el ecumenismo del Buen Samaritano quien frente al ser humano golpeado y abandonado no se pregunta si este es su compatriota o miembro de su iglesia o religión, sino piensa con la compasión. Es también el ecumenismo de la oración. Tres jóvenes migrantes musulmanes de Bangladesh que estuvieron en nuestras Casas del Migrante mientras arreglaban para el asilo político en los EE.UU., eran un ejemplo para todos nosotros de dedicación a Dios en la oración cinco veces al día, en la celebración del Ramadan, en su participación silenciosa pero significativa en la Eucaristía. Todo en un contexto histórico, el post 11 de Septiembre de 2001, en el cual todo lo que habla del Islam se mira con sospecha y hasta miedo.

4   **La reconciliación.** Recientemente también el tema de la reconciliación se ha destacado especialmente en el campo de la teología de la misión, al punto que algunos teólogos proponen la reconciliación como el modelo de la misión.[32] Este es seguramente un tema fundamental en un mundo en el cual la búsqueda de la paz es muchas veces una apariencia, porque las guerras, entre ellas las "justas" y las "santas", y los conflictos armados son más convenientes, desde un punto de vista político, y lucrativos, desde un punto de vista económico. No olvidemos también las tensiones continuas y, a veces, los conflictos abiertos entre diferentes grupos étnicos en el mismo país. La verdadera reconciliación tiene sus fundamentos en la justicia, en el reconocimiento de la dignidad de cada ser humano y de cada cultura, en el esfuerzo humano de decir la verdad y vivir en harmonía, y sobretodo en la fe en un Dios que es reconcil-

---

[31]Vea Mensaje Jubilar de la Red Casas del Migrante-Scalabrini en la nota 1.
[32]Robert Schreiter, *Reconciliation. Mission and Ministry in a Changing Social Order.* Maryknoll: Orbis Books, 1992; *The Ministry of Reconciliation. Spirituality and Strategies.* Maryknoll: Orbis Books, 1998; "Globalization and Reconciliation. Challenges to Mission," in *Mission in the Third Millennium.* Edited by Robert Schreiter. Estos dos libros han sido traducidos y publicados en español en la Colección Presencia Teológica de la Editorial Sal Terrae de Santander, España> Para mayor información consulte <www.salterrae.es>; Maryknoll: Orbis Books, 2001 pp.121–143; Donal Dorr, *Mission in Today's World.* Maryknoll: Orbis Books, 2000, pp. 128–143. Miroslav Volf, *Exclusion and Embrace. A Theological Exploration of Identity, Otherness, and Reconciliation.* Nashville: Abingdon Press, 1996.

iación, que nos quiere dar este don para que los diferentes pueblos de la tierra convivan y compartan juntos. La realidad nos dice que la reconciliación es muy difícil para lograr, al punto que unas personas que han estado involucradas en este proceso lo consideran casi imposible. Nuestra experiencia en un contexto de hospitalidad en las Casas del Migrante nos ha enseñado que la reconciliación se puede dar de maneras inimaginables. Es lo que ocurrió en una de las Casas cuando uno de los voluntarios, un ex-militar de los EE.UU., veterano de la guerra del Golfo, encontró a un grupo de migrantes cristianos caldeos de Irak que huían el régimen de Saddam Hussein, entre ellos ex-militares del Ejército, ellos también veteranos de la guerra del Golfo. Hace diez años estas personas, sin conocerse, eran enemigos mortales en una situación de guerra que los obligaba a matarse. Ahora aquí estaban en la Casa del Migrante, comunicándose, conociéndose y uno ayudando a los otros en el proceso de pedir asilo político en los EE.UU. Muchas veces nos hemos preguntado durante los días de permanencia de este grupo de migrantes de Irak: ¿Qué nos quiere decir Dios con esta situación impensable? La conclusión por el momento es que la reconciliación es otro de los muchos dones inesperados de Dios, dones que alimentan la esperanza en un mundo mejor.

CONCLUSION

En realidad se nos hace difícil terminar estas páginas con una conclusión ya que consideramos este ensayo como algo provisional, el "diario de un camino", como el principio de una reflexión sobre un fenómeno social tan complejo como es el de la migración que aún no ha recibido mucha atención en el campo teológico. Uno de mismos/as migrantes, dándole prioridad a la situación de los/as indocumentados/as porque son ellos quienes sufren más en el camino de la migración. Por esta razón hemos querido concluir estas reflexiones con algunas experiencias concretas de nuestros encuentros con los/as migrantes, encuentros que no podemos considerar casuales porque han representado para nosotros la revelación de Dios de la tienda que de maneras inesperadas e inimaginables nos reúne y nos hace entender que a sus ojos no hay extranjeros ni desconocidos. principales de este trabajo es precisamente empezar y promover un proceso de reflexión teológica de cara a los movimientos migratorios. El otro objetivo es desarrollar esta teología a partir de las experiencias de los mismos/sconocidos porque todos somos parte de la misma humanidad que Dios mismo ha creado. Esta es la esperanza que nos da la fe, el valor y la motivación para continuar este camino de reflexión y de solidaridad con los/as migrantes.

REFERENCES

Baba, K. H.
1994   *The Location of Culture*. London: Routledge.

Brother John of Taize
1985   *The Pilgrim God. A Biblical Journey*. Washington D.C.: Pastoral Press.

Bueno, E.
1998   *Eclesiología*. Madrid: Biblioteca de Autores Cristianos.

Byrne, B.
2000   *The Hospitality of God. A Reading of Luke's Gospel*. Collegeville: Liturgical Press. California Legal Rural Assistance <www.stopgatekeeper.org>

Commissione Teologica USG
2001   *Nella Globalizzazione: Verso una Comunione Pluricentrica e Interculturale. Implicazioni Ecclesiologiche per il Goberno dei Nostri Istituti*. Roma: Editrice Il Calamo.

Dorr, D.
2000   *Mission in Today's World*. Maryknoll: Orbis Books.

Elizondo, V.
1983   *Galilean Journey. The Mexican-American Promise*. Maryknoll:
        Orbis Books.

Espín, O.
2000   "Immigration, Territory, and Globalization: Theological Reflections," *JHLT* 7:3:46–59.

Estrada, J. A.
1998   "La Influencia de Zubiri en la teología de la Liberación," *Proyección*, 45:285–296.

Flannery, A., OP (ed.)
1975   *Vatican Council II. The Conciliar and Post Conciliar Documents*. Collegeville: Liturgical Press.

Goizueta, S. R.
1995   *Caminemos con Jesús. Toward a Hispanic/Latino Theology of Accompaniment*. Maryknoll: Orbis Books.

González Buelta, B.
2000   "Rasgos de la Experiencia Cristiana en una Iglesia que Busca Justicia," *Christus* 65. Julio-Agosto.

Huntington, S.
1996   *The Clash of Civilizations and the Remaking of World Order*. New York: Simon and Schuster.

Jonas, S. and S. D. Thomas, eds.
1999   *Immigration. A Civil Rights Issue for the Americas*. Wilmington: SR Books.

McVey, C., OP
"Outside the Camp," <www.sedos.org/english/chrys.htm>.

Metz, J. B.
1996   "Perspectivas de un Cristianismo Cultural." En *Cristianismo y Liberación. Homenaje a Casiano Floristan.* Ed. Juan-José Tamayo. Madrid: Editorial Trotta. Pp. 31–41.

Phan, C. P.
1999   "Betwixt and Between: Doing Theology with Memory and Imagination."
        In *Journeys at the Margin. Toward an Autobiographical Theology in American-Asian Perspective.* Ed. P. C. Phan and J. Y. Lee. Collegeville: Liturgical Press. Pp. 113–133.

Pohl, D. C.
1999   *Making Room. Recovering Hospitality as a Christian Tradition.* Grand Rapids: W.B. Eerdmans.

Red Casas del Migrante Scalabrini. *El Clamor de los Indocumentados.*
        <www.sedos.org/spanish/scalabrini. 1.htm>.

Richard, L.
2000   *Living the Hospitality of God.* New York: Paulist Press.

Romero, O. A.
"La Dimensión Política de la Fe desde la Opción por los Pobres," <www.servicioskoinonia.org/relat/135/htm>

Ruiz, O.
"La Migración en la Globalización de la Sociedad de Riesgo," <www.sedos.org/spanish/ruiz.htm>

Saramago, J.
2001   "El Factor Dios," *El País* 18 de septiembre de 2001.

Schreiter, J. R.
"Preaching the Gospel in the Twenty First Century," <www.dominicains.ca/providence/english/documents/schreiter.htm>

_____
2001   "Globalization and Reconciliation. Challenges to Mission." In *Mission in the Third Millennium.* Edited by Robert J. Schreiter. Maryknoll: Orbis Books. Pp. 121–143.

_____
1998   *The Ministry of Reconciliation. Spirituality and Strategies.* Maryknoll: Orbis Books.

_____
1997   *The New Catholicity. Theology Between the Global and the Local.* Maryknoll: Orbis Books.

_____
1994   "The Theological Meaning of a Truly Catholic Church," *New Theology Review* 7:5–17.

_____
1992   *Reconciliation. Mission and Ministry in a Changing Social Order.* Maryknoll: Orbis Books.

Segovia, F.
1992   "Two Places and No Place on which to Stand: Mixture and Otherness in Hispanic American Theology," *Listening,* 27:26–40.

Sobrino, J.

2001   "Teología desde la Realidad," en *Panorama de la Teología Latinoamericana.* Editores Juan-José Tamayo y Juan Bosch. Estella: Verbo Divino. Pp. 611–628.

1993   "De una Teología solo de la Liberación a una Teología del Martirio." En *Cambio Social y Pensamiento Cristiano en América Latina.* Editores José Comblin, José I. González Faus y Jon Sobrino. Madrid: Editorial Trotta. Pp. 101–121.

1992   *El Principio~Misericordia. Bajar de la Cruz a los Pueblos Crucificados.* Santander: Sal Terrae.

1985   *Liberación con Espíritu. Apuntes para una Nueva Espiritualidad.* Santander: Sal Terrae.

1981   *Resurrección de la Verdadera Iglesia. Los Pobres, Lugar Teológico de la Eclesiología.* Santander: Sal Terrae.

Time Special Issue
2001   "Welcome to Amexica." June 11.

Tassello, G. G.
2001   "Los Migrantes: Profetas de la Catolicidad," *Spiritus,* 42(2):113–124.

Vives, J.
"Pobres y Ricos en la Iglesia Primitiva," www.servicioskoinonia.org/relat/274.htm>

Volf, M.
1996   *Exclusion and Embrace. A Theological Exploration of Identity, Otherness, and Reconciliation.* Nashville: Abingdon Press.